STANFORD BOOKS IN

World Politics

STANFORD BOOKS IN WORLD POLITICS

GRAHAM H. STUART, *Editor*

British Labour's
Foreign Policy

British Labour's Foreign Policy

ELAINE WINDRICH

STANFORD UNIVERSITY PRESS
Stanford, California
GEOFFREY CUMBERLEGE   OXFORD UNIVERSITY PRESS
LONDON

STANFORD UNIVERSITY PRESS, STANFORD, CALIFORNIA
London: Geoffrey Cumberlege, Oxford University Press

THE BAKER AND TAYLOR COMPANY, HILLSIDE, NEW JERSEY
HENRY M. SNYDER & COMPANY, 440 FOURTH AVENUE, NEW YORK 16
W. S. HALL & COMPANY, 457 MADISON AVENUE, NEW YORK 22

Library of Congress Catalog Card Number: 52-8309

PREFACE

Although the Socialist experiment in Great Britain has attracted considerable attention in recent years, it has been in the domestic rather than in the international sphere that such interest has been manifested.

This book is neither a history of the Labour party nor a history of British foreign policy. It is an account of the socialist experiment in the international field: the Labour party's attitudes and policies regarding problems of international relations in the twentieth century. The international issues selected for consideration are those which illustrate the theoretical basis and the practical application of British Labour's foreign policy. However, issues arising within the British Empire or Commonwealth of Nations, such as India or Palestine or Eire, are beyond the scope of this inquiry, which does not deal with questions of imperial or colonial policy. The framework of this study is thereby limited to British foreign policy and the Labour party's reaction to that policy.

The theme of the book is the continuity of British Labour's international policy—a continuity unbroken from the formation of the party at the beginning of the century to the accession to power of the party at mid-century. Whether in opposition or in office, the Labour party has consistently adhered to and advocated certain principles regarding the conduct and control of international affairs. It is upon the basis of these principles that the concept of a Labour, or Socialist, as distinct from a Conservative or a Liberal, foreign policy is derived. The assertion of such a concept is the negation of the traditional British doctrine of continuity in foreign policy. In effect, it is the disavowal of the principle and the practice of a bipartisan foreign policy in Great Britain.

The preparation of the book was begun at Margate, England, during the forty-ninth annual conference of the Labour party in October 1950. Largely through the efforts of H. G. Reynolds, J. P. and party agent, interviews were obtained with many of the members of the Labour government and party, including the Prime Minister, Clement Attlee; Herbert Morrison, Lord President of the Council and Leader of the House of Commons; George Isaacs, Minister of Labour and National Service; Aneurin Bevan, Minister of Health; Edith Summerskill, Minister of National Insurance; George Lindgren, Parliamentary Secretary, Town and Country Planning; Alice Bacon, Party Chairman; Harry Earnshaw, Party Vice-Chairman; Lord Burden; John Corina of the Co-operative Union; Jennie Lee, Freda Corbet, John Cooper, Members of Parliament; Mr. Fienburgh, Mr. Carthy, Mr. Mennell, and Mr. Williams of Transport House. The co-operation of the entire staff at Transport House, Labour party headquarters in London, was invaluable in the process of collecting materials for the book. The manuscript was completed at the Hoover Library, Stanford University, where generous assistance was provided by the members of the staff. Appreciation is expressed to Professor Graham H. Stuart of Stanford University for reading the manuscript and to Dr. N. C. Hall for the valuable editorial assistance. For the errors and for the opinions expressed, the author assumes sole responsibility.

ELAINE WINDRICH

STANFORD UNIVERSITY
STANFORD, CALIFORNIA
May 1952

TABLE OF CONTENTS

British Labour's
Foreign Policy

I

THE OLD DIPLOMACY

In British politics the doctrine of "continuity" in foreign policy irrespective of electoral change was not seriously challenged until the appearance of the Labour party. At the turn of the twentieth century the generally accepted view was that international affairs were the concern of a small class of diplomats and ministers, beyond the arena of partisan politics and public discussion. Foreign-policy issues were not raised during electoral campaigns, nor were they properly considered in parliamentary debates; in the former case the principle of continuity precluded the discussion of international affairs and in the latter, the practice of "secret diplomacy." With the rise of the Labour party to a position of political effectiveness, the first real protest was made against this removal of foreign affairs from popular or party control.

In rejecting the traditional approach, British Labour was determined to establish "a well-thought-out and constructive foreign policy" of its own.[1] It denounced as "manifestly foolish and impossible" the suggestion that the socialist and trade-union movement should concern itself only with domestic questions and social problems and take little interest in imperial matters and foreign affairs. Every problem, domestic and foreign, was regarded as a Labour problem, touching the welfare of the people. Many of these problems could not be grappled with except by organized working-class action on international lines. British Labour was convinced that in each country working people were "beginning to think out these matters for themselves" and were no longer "content to be pawns in the game of diplomats and financiers." A movement that stood for social reconstruction could not "shut its eyes to the terrible waste of national resources involved in war." To maintain peace, to fight militarism, to arrest the growing burden of armaments was the first interest of the Labour movement. How otherwise could it secure the conditions necessary for social progress and industrial reform? A wise and pacific foreign policy meant a reduction in military and naval expenditure. But the burden would be constantly increased if foreign policy, "dark and

---

[1] Ramsay MacDonald, "Labour Party Conference on Disarmament and the Present International Situation, Leicester, January 31, 1911," *Labour Leader*, February 3, 1911, p. 74.

secret in its methods," were "to back up the aggression of one nation as against the aggression of another." Such a policy would bring about "fettering and entangling alliances" arousing suspicion and ill will among the nations. Hence, at many points, the socialist movement found its interests either helped or hindered by developments in foreign affairs.[2]

The principles of Labour's foreign policy were derived mainly from nineteenth-century "radicalism" and working-class internationalism. The radical tradition was pacifist and humanitarian. It suspected all entanglements with foreign powers and held that armed forces, potentially dangerous to popular liberties, should be kept at a minimum. At the same time, it looked upon Great Britain as the champion of liberty against tyranny and the supporter of all peoples rightly struggling to be free from domestic or foreign oppression. The discrepancy between holding strong pacifist views while claiming the right to denounce oppression all over the world and to call upon Britain to use her strong arm to protect the weak was primarily due to the strategic position of the British Isles. The conciousness of Britain's insularity and agelong immunity from invasion had tended to provide an exaggerated sense of security.

British Labour was also united with the international labor movement by a common rejection of the doctrines and ideals of militarism and imperialism. Socialists in all countries were convinced that the political and economic salvation of mankind was to be found in the broadest and most generous international co-operation and that social justice was the only basis of a peaceful world.[3] War was considered as "ruinous to the worker's cause": it stirred international bitterness and hate, arrested social reform and destroyed the rights, independence, and freedom of native populations. Modern wars, fought by European nations, were "without exception sordid and squalid." Armaments were closely bound up with foreign policy; and the European nations piled up armaments, not in self-defense, but in dread of losing the lands they had stolen or in hope of adding to them. The international labor and socialist movement "set its face against aggression"; and where right and wrong were concerned, its members were "fellows without a fatherland."[4]

Before the first World War, British Labour sought to apply its foreign-policy principles to the twofold problem of removing the

[2] William C. Anderson, chairman of Independent Labour party, "Socialism and Foreign Affairs," *Labour Leader*, December 8, 1911, p. 771.

[3] Clement Attlee, *The Labour Party in Perspective* (London: Gollancz, 1937), pp. 199–203.

[4] William C. Anderson, *loc. cit.*

causes of war and devising the means of preventing it by the united action of the working class. The question of war-resistance had been repeatedly debated at the international socialist congresses with which the British Labour party and the leading British socialist bodies—the Independent Labour party, the Fabian Society and the British Socialist party—were affiliated. For years Keir Hardie on behalf of the Independent Labour party had urged the adoption of a pledge that the socialists of all countries would "reply to the proposition of a war by an appeal to the people to declare a general strike." However, the Socialist International was unable to prescribe one set mode of action to the working classes to avoid the outbreak of war. At most, it was able to agree that in case of the threat of war, the working classes and their parliamentary representatives in the countries concerned should strive to take every step possible to avoid the outbreak of hostilities. If, nevertheless, war occurred, "it would be their first duty to intervene in order to bring it to a speedy termination and to employ all their power to utilise the economic and political crisis created by the war in order to rouse the masses of the people and thereby to hasten the downfall of capitalistic class domination."[5]

The British Labour movement itself was not in agreement on the international general strike as the most effective sanction for averting war. In accordance with a request from the International Socialist Bureau for the opinion of the organized working-class movement of the world on the utility of the strike as a means of preventing war, British Labour was obliged to take a stand on the war-resistance issue. The action taken by the British Labour Party Conference was in line with that of the International in that it approved of a proposal "to investigate and report on whether and how far a stoppage of work, either partial or general, in countries about to engage in war would be effective in preventing an outbreak of hostilities." However, Arthur Henderson made it clear that the Labour Party Executive accepted the resolution with the emphasis on the words "investigate and report" and as an indication of its support for the International Socialist Bureau.[6] The Independent Labour Party Conference, on the other hand, was willing to go much further in the direction of a commitment to antiwar action, declaring its belief in "the utility of the strike as an effective method of preventing war."[7] The views expressed at the two conferences were somewhat reconciled by a joint statement issued

[5] Resolution adopted at Stuttgart Congress, 1907, reaffirmed at Copenhagen (1910) and Basel (1912), *Report of the Thirteenth Annual Conference of the Labour Party*, 1913, p. 125.

[6] *Report of the Twelfth Annual Conference of the Labour Party*, 1912, p. 101.

[7] Resolution of Birmingham Conference, *Labour Leader*, April 28, 1911, p. 262.

under the signatures of Arthur Henderson and Keir Hardie. In this statement it was explained that those who supported an antiwar strike did not do so as an alternative to political action, but as supplemental to that action, and only to be used as a last resort where political action was not yet sufficiently developed to prevent it. British Labour agreed that

a tremendous backing would undoubtedly be given to this fierce struggle for peace by the parliamentary representatives were it known that in both cases the trade unions had a firmly grounded undertaking, mutually arranged, to cease work, if need be, rather than tamely to sit still and allow their masters and rulers . . . to force war upon them.[8]

At the same time, British Labour, not satisfied merely to reject war as a possibility and devise means for its resistance, was aware of the necessity for providing a more positive approach to international peace. It was convinced that a durable peace system could be constructed only by attacking the causes of war. In order that it might work effectively for the establishment of international peace, Labour insisted upon the democratization of foreign policy and the abolition of the old system of secret diplomacy. Wars in the past were alleged to have been caused by alliances, secret treaties, and a precariously balanced system of power politics. In place of secret diplomacy, Labour proposed to work in the open, placing foreign affairs under parliamentary control. It believed that secret diplomacy was contrary to the spirit of true international co-operation and that by giving full publicity to international negotiations suspicion, jealousy, and rivalry among the nations would be removed. The Labour party was unanimously resolved that "no treaty, agreement, understanding or entente be entered into with any foreign power by any person whatsoever on behalf of the British State" until such proposals had been brought before the House of Commons.[9] All international treaties and agreements were to be published *in toto* and subject to legislative approval and enactment. To facilitate the acquisition of information on international affairs, it was further proposed that a Foreign Relations Committee be established in the House of Commons for the purpose of devoting adequate time and attention to the discussion of questions of international policy on the basis of relevant material and data supplied by the government.[10] Labour would consider the democratization of foreign policy as finally achieved when the government,

[8] Text of Letter, *Report of the Thirteenth Annual Conference of the Labour Party*, 1913, p. 124.
[9] *Report of the Twelfth Annual Conference of the Labour Party*, 1912, p. 91.
[10] Noel Buxton, 53 *H.C.Deb.*, May 29, 1913, cols. 406–7.

"before concluding any treaty, and before sanctioning any acquisition, cession or exchange of territory, and before entering into any commitment" involving national responsibility, would consult the House of Commons and get a vote upon it.[11] Only then would Parliament exercise the real power and control over issues of war and peace.

The democratization of foreign policy was to provide the means whereby the Labour members of Parliament could offer their peace proposals in a national forum and bring them to the attention of public opinion. Until a change could be effected in the method of conducting foreign affairs, however, Labour would have to depend on means other than parliamentary to publicize its peace program. The Labour Opposition, to make known its views, took full advantage of the one or two days of each year set aside by the government of the day for parliamentary discussion of international affairs. Labour members and their "radical" allies repeatedly complained to the government of the neglect of Parliament, both as to information and opportunity for debate on international issues. On more than one occasion, Labour members attempted to secure from the government information regarding the nature and extent of Britain's alliances and commitments to foreign nations. Information was denied, however, and there was not sufficient opportunity either to obtain the facts or to offer a constructive alternative policy. As a result, Labour's activities in Parliament were limited to denouncing the practice of secret diplomacy and proposing a system which would introduce democracy into the realm of foreign policy. The party was, therefore, obliged to carry on its struggle for a new approach to international affairs throughout the country, in public forums, mass meetings, and demonstrations, at party conferences on the local and national level, in Labour journals of opinion, such as the *Socialist Review* and the *Labour Leader*, and even outside the national arena at international socialist and trade-union congresses.

Included in Labour's peace program and foreshadowing its fully developed postwar program was the goal of substituting law for force in the international field. In place of settling international disputes by force of arms, Labour proposed a system of arbitration which would provide for the application of the rule of law in international relations. If nations could be assured of a reasonable settlement of their grievances and their differences by disinterested third-party judgment, one of the chief reasons for a resort to arms would be eliminated. It was essential to provide means for peaceable change in the world and methods for reasonably altering injustices inherent in

[11] Arthur Ponsonby, 40 *H.C.Deb.*, July 10, 1912, col. 1947.

the preservation of the international status quo. To assure the constant availability of machinery for the application of the rule of law, Labour suggested the adoption by states of permanent treaties of arbitration and the establishment of tribunals of arbitration to which all disputes between nations would be submitted. With the creation of permanent—rather than *ad hoc*—and compulsory—rather than voluntary—machinery for the pacific settlement of international disputes, there would be no legal justification for a nation's resorting to force of arms to settle its grievances. A nation with aggressive intentions would be readily identified by its disregard of the provisions for arbitration or its flaunting of the judgment reached by the tribunal. In those cases where a government refused to accept the decision of the board of arbitration, the final decision on the question of war or peace would be vested directly in the people.[12]

Before the nations would consent to abide by the rule of law in their international relations, they would need some assurance of security. Labour felt that the balance-of-power policy was at the root of all international difficulties; and that Britain's constant interference in European politics was simply due to the fact that it had to be "adjusting those scales." As a sense of security had not been produced by the balance-of-power system, Labour's alternative was the policy of the "concert of Europe."[13] Labour would seek "friendly understandings" with all nations, but "crippling alliances" with none. International security could be firmly founded only upon the basis of good will, friendship, understanding, and solidarity among the nations of the world. In addition, it was essential to have an organized system of international co-operation which would provide "a guarantee of the independence of all nations and their protection from military attacks and violent suppression." A Labour foreign policy would "talk less of the balance of power and more of the federated States of Europe," would aim at the establishment of a United States of Europe and the ultimate creation of a United States of the world.[14]

The establishment of a system of international arbitration and security would pave the way for the realization of Labour's disarmament program. The menacing arms race preceding the war was regarded as a natural counterpart of the balance-of-power system and

[12] Cf. resolutions, *Report of Proceedings of International Workers Congress*, London, July–August 1896 (London: *Labour Leader*, 1896), pp. 36–37; *Report of the Thirty-ninth Annual Conference of the T.U.C.*, 1906, p. 147; *Report of the Twelfth Annual Conference of the Labour Party*, 1912, p. 99.

[13] Arthur Ponsonby, 32 *H.C.Deb.*, December 14, 1911, col. 2616.

[14] Fenner Brockway, "Failure of Liberalism, the Government and Foreign Policy," *Labour Leader*, January 29, 1914, p. 6.

the practice of secret diplomacy. Repeatedly protesting against the "constant increase in armaments," and the "insidious attempts" to introduce conscription, Labour demanded the "simultaneous abolition of standing armies."[15] Rather than increasing international security, armaments had contributed to the growing tension and suspicion among the nations. It was the duty of Labour, through its parliamentary representatives, to combat militarism by refusing the means for increased armaments.[16] Socialist opposition to the arms race was a two-fold one: not only did it endanger international good will and peace, but it also tended to arrest social progress and reform and to impose a needless tax on the lives and wages of the working class. If the manufacture of armaments could be taken out of private hands, the efforts of the "great war trusts" to engage in "scaremongering" in order to increase the expenditure on war preparations would be restrained.[17] A Labour foreign policy "would spend less money on the means of destroying life and more on the means of redeeming it. Above all, it would curb and make subservient to national well-being those world-wide financial interests which, unbridled and unchecked, work infinite havoc and drag nations into mean, inglorious and criminal wars." It would then be possible to undertake the progressive reduction and ultimate abolition of the machinery of war. The arms race was one more indication to Labour that foreign affairs could not be separated from home affairs and that the proper conduct of both was of vital concern to the workers.[18]

Thus, by 1914, the British Labour movement had devised a foreign policy which contained the fundamental principles of its future international program. In place of the old, traditional approach to foreign affairs with its emphasis on secret diplomacy, balance-of-power politics, militarism, and imperialism, Labour offered a new world order. Labour would strive for a policy of international co-operation based upon the practices of open diplomacy, pacific settlement of disputes, disarmament, and collective security against aggression. Labour's concern with foreign affairs became an immediate necessity with the occurrence of war and the breakdown of the pre-1914 world society.

[15] Resolutions, *Report of Proceedings of International Workers Congress*, 1896, pp. 36–37; *Report of the Thirty-ninth Annual Conference of the T.U.C.*, 1906, p. 147; Chairman's address, J. R. Clynes, *Report of the Ninth Annual Conference of the Labour Party*, 1909, p. 59.

[16] Copenhagen resolution, *Labour Leader*, February 3, 1911, p. 74.

[17] Resolution, *Report of the Fourteenth Annual Conference of the Labour Party*, 1914, p. 121.

[18] William C. Anderson, *loc. cit.*

2

WAR AND PEACE

The approach of war in 1914 was the occasion for great debate and soul searching within the British Labour movement. Heretofore, Labour had directed much of its activity in the field of international relations to the problem of how to prevent the outbreak of war, and if it occurred how to resist it effectively. At the same time, however, Labour had devised a system of securing peace which did not entirely rule out the use of war or force of arms. The dilemma facing the party was how to apply its previously conceived principles of foreign policy to the international situation of 1914. Was it possible simultaneously to adhere to a policy of resistance to "war" and resistance to "aggression"?

British Labour's immediate reaction to the crisis of July 1914 was to take all possible action to prevent what at first appeared to be a local incident between Austria and Serbia from spreading into an international conflagration involving the Great Powers bound by alliances to the two contestants. Although the Labour party had received no information from the government that Britain was committed to go to the aid of France or her ally Russia in case of their involvement in a war, the party's constant inquiries on this subject in the House of Commons indicated that it suspected as much. Consequently, following the Austrian ultimatum to Serbia and the mobilization of Russia, the British Labour delegates—Keir Hardie, Bruce Glasier, and Dan Irving—supported the International Socialist Bureau in the effort to avert a general war. By unanimous vote, the bureau declared it to be "an obligation for the workers of all nations concerned not only to continue but even to strengthen their demonstrations against war in favour of peace." The workers of Great Britain were to sustain the efforts of the French and German workers to deter their governments from war "with all the power in their command."[1] Accordingly, the British section of the International Socialist Bureau issued a manifesto, drafted by H. M. Hyndman of the Social Democratic Federation, calling upon the workers to protest "against the greed and intrigues of militarists and armament mongers," to "stand together for peace," and to "combine and conquer the military enemy and the self-seeking imperialist once and for all."[2] Following the German

[1] Declaration at Brussels, July 29, 1914, *Labour Leader*, August 6, 1914, p. 8.
[2] *Ibid.*, July 31, 1914, p. 3.

10

declaration of war upon Russia, huge "stop the war" meetings, under the auspices of the bureau and the Labour party, were held in London and many other cities throughout the country. At the Trafalgar Square demonstration, where 15,000 citizens of London were represented, a joint resolution was moved by Arthur Henderson, secretary of the British section, viewing "with serious alarm" the prospects of a European war into which every European power would be dragged owing to secret alliances and understandings which, in their origin, were never sanctioned by the peoples. The resolution pledged support for the efforts of the workers of the nations concerned to prevent their governments from entering upon war. In addition, the demonstration demanded that the British government "rigidly decline to engage in war" and "confine itself to efforts to bring about peace as speedily as possible."[3] Following the meeting, the demand was presented to the government in the House of Commons by Party Secretary Ramsay MacDonald.[4]

Even with the invasion of Belgium and the British ultimatum to Germany, the Labour party was not deterred from its efforts for peace. Notwithstanding the declaration of war, on August 5 the National Executive Committee of the party unanimously adopted a resolution reiterating the fact that it had opposed the policy which led to the war and that its duty now was to secure peace at the earliest possible moment on such conditions as would provide "the best opportunities for the re-establishment of amicable feelings between the workers of Europe."[5] The National Council of the Independent Labour party concurred by indicting the diplomatic policies pursued by the European powers as "underground, secret, deceitful, and deliberately aimed at dividing Europe into two armed, antagonistic camps."[6] However, a cleavage of opinion within the Labour movement appeared when the majority of Labour members of Parliament refused to agree to their chairman's proposal to present this resolution to the House of Commons. Upon losing the confidence of his followers, Ramsay MacDonald turned over the chairmanship of the parliamentary group to Arthur Henderson. After the initial rift, the breach was widened by the agreement of the Labour members of Parliament (with the exception of MacDonald and his I.L.P. supporters Hardie, Jowett, and Richardson) to co-operate with the other parties in promoting a joint recruiting campaign and by the decision of the National Executive to

[3] *Ibid.*, August 2, 1914.
[4] Cf. 65 *H.C.Deb.*, August 3, 1914, cols. 1830–31.
[5] *Socialist Review*, XII (October–December 1914), 315.
[6] "The War in Europe," *Labour Leader*, August 13, 1914, p. 1.

place the electoral machinery of the party at the disposal of the Joint Committee for recruiting purposes.

The support of the war effort by the overwhelming majority of the Labour movement was not, as its critics alleged, either a reversal of its resolution issued upon the outbreak of the war or a repudiation of its traditional foreign policy. As to the former charge, Labour did not cease to believe, as stated in its resolution of August 5, that a balance-of-power policy produced wars or that peace should be secured at the earliest possible moment on such conditions that would provide for "the re-establishment of amicable feelings between the workers of Europe." The agreement to support the war was not necessarily incompatible with either of the above propositions. As to the latter criticism, Labour held that it was on the basis of those traditional policies that a decision to support the war had been reached. Prior to 1914, one of the fundamental tenets of a Labour foreign policy had been resistance to the aggressor. Labour had arrived at its definition of aggression by the test of willingness to submit international disputes to arbitration. Since the Central Powers had rejected pacific settlement of the Sarajevo incident and Great Britain had "exhausted the resources of peaceful diplomacy" to no avail, the responsibility for the war did not rest upon the policy or conduct of Great Britain. In addition, Labour had consistently upheld the sanctity of treaties openly arrived at and the preservation of the territorial integrity and political independence of small nations. Regarding the violation of the neutrality of Belgium as a direct breach of the rule of law in international relations, the Labour party held that Britain "was bound in honour, as well as by treaty, to resist by arms the aggression of Germany." Finally, Labour had maintained that the best guaranty for the establishment of peace in the world was "the preservation and maintenance of free and unfettered democratic government." As the victory of Germany would mean "the death of democracy in Europe," the Labour party, "as representing the most democratic elements in the British nation," had given its support in Parliament, had joined in the task of raising an army and had pledged "to make any sacrifice necessary to bring the war to a definite and honourable conclusion."[7]

Throughout the duration of the conflict the Labour party regarded the successful termination of hostilities as essential to its long-term objective of establishing a durable and honorable peace. During this

[7] Declaration of Labour Party Leaders and Members of Parliament, Management Committee of General Federation of Trades Unions, Parliamentary Committee of the Trades Union Congress and British Socialist Party, quoted in William Walling, *The Socialists and the War* (New York: Holt, 1915), pp. 162–66.

period Labour was compelled to fight for the application of its principles on two fronts. On the one hand, it was determined that its pledge of support to the government should not be regarded as a blank check giving the government a free hand to conduct the war in any manner which it thought fit. Although Labour had acquiesced in what amounted to a political truce for the duration, it had not renounced its right of "loyal opposition" and criticism of the government's methods of prosecuting the war. Nor had it necessarily reversed its prewar opposition to militarism, secret diplomacy, and balance-of-power politics. It was determined, therefore, to impress upon the government the fact that its support was a conditional one, based upon the assumption that a war undertaken for the purpose of defense and liberation would not be transformed into a war of imperialism and conquest.[8]

The other serious problem facing Labour was the cleavage which had developed within the movement over the issue of supporting or resisting the war. Although the minority opposing the war was negligible in terms of size, it contained such highly respected and revered pioneers of the movement as Keir Hardie, founder of the Independent Labour party, Ramsay MacDonald, former chairman of the parliamentary group and secretary of the party, Bruce Glasier, editor of the *Socialist Review*, Fenner Brockway, editor of the *Labour Leader*, F. W. Jowett, chairman of the Independent Labour party, and George Lansbury of the Social Democratic Federation. Those who opposed the war did so on the basis of one of two premises: pacifism or class war. Adherents of the former doctrine abhorred the use of violence and force for any purpose whatsoever, made no distinction between just and unjust wars, and preached nonresistance as the only way to universal peace. In contrast with the pacifists, the advocates of class war did not reject the use of force in all cases. The working class was not to resort to force for the purpose of furthering imperialistic wars, but only for the purpose of combating the real evil, capitalism itself.

The dissenting minority claimed that the Independent Labour party "alone," of all the organizations affiliated with the Labour party and with the British section of the International, had "withstood the onrush of war passion" that had overswept the nation and "refused to identify itself and Socialist and Labour principles with the foreign policy that led the country into the war."[9] In its "Manifesto on the

[8] Declaration of Conference of Socialist and Labour Parties of Allied Nations, London, February 14, 1915, *Report of the Fifteenth Annual Conference of the Labour Party*, 1916, p. 32.

[9] *Socialist Review*, XII (October–December 1914), 316.

War in Europe," the I.L.P. had, in fact, condemned the diplomatic policies leading to the war. However, the I.L.P. had not been "alone" in this act, as the National Executive Committee of the Labour party, in its resolution issued after the declaration of war, had also unanimously opposed the foreign policy that led to the war. Nor was it entirely true to claim that the I.L.P. had "withstood the onrush of war passion" as far as its attitude toward supporting the war was concerned. In the manifesto itself, participation in the war was nowhere ruled out. While the supporters of the manifesto had declared that they could not "rejoice in the organised murder of tens of thousands of workers of other lands," they nevertheless added the significant admission, "Our nationality and independence, which are dear to us, we are ready to defend."[10] In addition, the I.L.P. delegates to the Conference of Socialist and Labour Parties of the Allied Nations, including Keir Hardie, Ramsay MacDonald, Bruce Glasier, and W. C. Anderson, had supported a compromise resolution declaring that socialists were "inflexibly resolved to fight" until victory was achieved.[11] The attempt to reconcile the obvious inconsistency between the Independent Labour party's support for "fighting the war to a finish" and "peace at the earliest possible moment" was made by Ramsay MacDonald, who was alleged to have been one of the authors of the compromise resolution. MacDonald explained that the phrase "fighting the war to a finish" had to be interpreted in "a Socialist sense and not in the popular sense." There was no use to talk about "stop the war," he said; "the war had got to finish." Surely, MacDonald insisted, no one could "point to clearer declarations than his that the war ought not to be carried further than the political point when the forces of democracy in Germany were liberated" and "when the forces of Europe were ready to take things into their own hands."[12]

Nor was the Independent Labour party's stand on recruitment a really consistent one. Although dissociating the I.L.P. from the decision of the Labour members of Parliament and the National Executive of the Labour party to take part in the recruiting campaign, the National Council had also held that enlistment and the urging of recruiting were "matters for the individual conscience." The I.L.P. Conference, although not explicitly declaring against recruitment, had registered its disapproval of I.L.P. members of Parliament "speaking on platforms on which attempts were made to justify the war and the foreign policy of the Liberal Government which led to the war." So

10 *Labour Leader*, August 13, 1914, p. 1.
11 *Report of the Fifteenth Annual Conference of the Labour Party*, 1916, p. 32.
12 I.L.P. Conference at Norwich, *Labour Leader*, April 8, 1915, p. 2.

far as the leading I.L.P spokesmen on the subject—MacDonald, Glasier, and Jowett—were concerned, they could not, as socialists, take part in recruiting. However, they could see how Socialists might "quite conscientiously disagree on this matter," and did not want "to drive those who differed from them on this question out of the Party."[13] MacDonald himself saw "nothing inconsistent in Socialists saying that their native land should be protected in its day of trial or that when it finds itself in a war it should be helped to get out of it without disgrace and dishonour."[14]

Although the differences of opinion within the Labour movement on the issue of supporting or opposing the war were to continue throughout the conflict, there were many other questions raised by the war on which the Labour movement was able to achieve agreement. On the most important of these problems, conscription, Labour closed its ranks to present a solid front of opposition to the government's proposal for the measure. Prior to the protest against conscription, the annual conferences of the Labour party and the Trades Union Congress had given unqualified support to the government's war effort in recording, by overwhelming majorities, their approval of the government's participation in the war as "fully justified" and their pledge to "assist the Government as far as possible in the successful prosecution of the War." In addition, both conferences had enthusiastically declared their support for the national recruiting campaign and for the participation of Labour party representatives in the Coalition government.[15] To conscription, however, the Labour party and the Trades Union Congress, joined by the I.L.P., refused to give their approval. The Labour party, at a special conference in London, reaffirmed the decision of the Bristol Conference of the Trades Union Congress, unanimously protesting against compulsory military service in the name of three million organized workers. The conference emphatically recorded its opinion that no case had been made for any measure of limited or temporary compulsion and declared that all men required for military and industrial purposes could be obtained by a continuation of the voluntary method. The protests of the London Conference were reinforced and its decisions ratified by the annual conference of the Labour party when it assembled at Bristol.[16] In ad-

[13] *Ibid.*, pp. 3, 8.
[14] "Socialism During War," *Socialist Review*, XII (October–December 1914), 348.
[15] Cf. Reports of the *Forty-seventh Annual Conference of the T.U.C.*, 1915, pp. 317, 331; *Fifteenth Annual Conference of the Labour Party*, 1916, pp. 100, 109, 125; *Sixteenth Annual Conference of the Labour Party*, 1917, pp. 126–28.
[16] Cf. *Report of the Fifteenth Annual Conference of the Labour Party*, 1916, pp. 117, 124.

dition, local Labour parties and trade-union councils throughout the country expressed their "emphatic condemnation" of the government's Military Service Bill (No. 2), demanding that it be withdrawn. In this struggle, the I.L.P. played an important role and its members were most active in establishing and operating a "National Council Against Conscription." The Labour movement as a whole felt that the unity and solidarity of the nation had been gravely imperiled and industrial and political liberty seriously menaced by the action of the "compulsionists."[17]

The Labour movement was also in agreement upon the necessity of striving for the establishment of a just and lasting peace at the conclusion of the war. As previously noted, the Labour movement, prior to the outbreak of the war, had directed its attention to the construction of a system to secure international peace. The fact that a world war had occurred was, to Labour, a confirmation of its condemnation of the government's foreign policy and an indication that, had its own policy been followed, peace might have been maintained. However, as war had occurred, it was now the task of the Labour movement to advocate the creation of a peace system which would prevent the recurrence of war in the future.

Immediately after the declaration of war, all sections of the Labour movement had accepted the duty to secure peace on such conditions as would provide "the best opportunities for the re-establishment of amicable feelings between the workers of Europe." In addition, British Labour had joined the Conference of Socialist and Labour Parties of the Allied Nations in declaring that the victory of the Allied Powers should be "a victory for popular liberty, for unity, independence and autonomy of the nations in the peaceful Federation of the United States of Europe and the World."[18] In spite of the differences between those who advocated "immediate peace" and those who supported "fighting the war to a finish," there was virtual agreement on the necessity of doing everything possible "to secure some good from the war."[19] It was on the basis of this agreement that the I.L.P. supported the conference declaration and took the initiative for British Labour in formulating a program of peace which anticipated later pronouncements of the Labour party and the Trades Union Congress. The terms of the "Peace Programme" adopted by the I.L.P. annual conference were in the traditional pattern of Labour's prewar

---

[17] *Labour Leader*, January 8, 1916, p. 3; January 20, 1916, p. 7.

[18] *Report of the Fifteenth Annual Conference of the Labour Party*, 1916, p. 32.

[19] Ramsay MacDonald, "Socialism During War," *Socialist Review*, XII (October–December 1914), 351.

foreign policy, including such demands as self-determination of nations, democratic control of foreign policy, reduction of armaments, arbitration, and a federation of nations. To reiterate those principles publicly, the I.L.P. felt, would be "the surest blow at German militarism." Thus far, no one had attempted to answer the question: "for what was Britain fighting?"[20]

The question raised by the I.L.P. was taken up by all sections of the Labour movement at the annual conferences, at local Labour party meetings, in the Labour press, in Parliament and at the international labor and socialist congresses. Labour was convinced that its vital role in supporting the war on both the industrial and military fronts gave it a justifiable claim to take an equally important part in the making of the peace. In view of the sacrifices made by the working class in the course of prosecuting the war, it was of great concern to all workers that a settlement be made which would, as far as possible, obviate the possibility of a future war. The Labour party conference therefore issued the demand that "the British delegation of plenipotentiaries to the conference to negotiate the terms of Peace should contain an adequate number of Parliamentary representatives of organised Labour." In addition, the conference asked that the British representatives work for the formation of an "International League to enforce the Maintenance of Peace" and to restrain by any means necessary any nation acting "in violation of the Laws and Judgments of the International Court."[21] It was Labour's hope that by gaining public support for its terms of settlement it could, if denied a place at the peace conference, at least influence the government in the direction of establishing a durable peace.[22]

The culmination of Labour's efforts for a lasting peace was the proclamation, by a special conference of the party and the Trades Union Congress at the end of 1917, of a *War Aims Memorandum*, which related the traditional principles of Labour's foreign policy to the problems and issues raised by the war and the approaching peace settlement. Of all the war aims, the *Memorandum* emphasized that none was so important to the peoples of the world as that there should be "henceforth on earth no more war." To achieve this end, Labour relied very largely upon the complete democratization of all countries,

[20] *Labour Leader*, April 8, 1915, p. 8.

[21] *Report of the Sixteenth Annual Conference of the Labour Party*, 1917, p. 134.

[22] For Labour's peace plans, cf. "Towards a Permanent Peace," *Labour Leader*, September 24, 1915, p. 1; March 26, 1915, p. 3; April 1, 1915, p. 5; April 8, 1915, p. 1; April 15, 1915, p. 3; April 22, 1915, p. 1; April 29, 1915, p. 5; May 20, 1915, p. 5; "Towards a Federated World," *Socialist Review*, XII (November–December 1915), 745; "Peace Guarantees," *ibid.*, XIV (January–March 1917), 30.

the suppression of secret diplomacy, the placing of foreign policy under the control of popularly elected legislatures, the universal abolition of compulsory military service, the general limitation of armaments and abolition of profit-making armament firms, the abandonment of every form of imperialism, the assertion of self-determination, and the development of the resources of every country for the benefit of the peoples of the world. In addition, Labour demanded that as an essential part of the treaty of peace there should be established a "super-national authority" or "league of nations" adhered to by every independent state. Such a league should provide an international court for the settlement of justiciable disputes; appropriate machinery for prompt and effective mediation between states; an international legislature representative of all sovereign states; the gradual development of international legislation binding upon the several states and agreement by all states to make common cause against any state failing to resort to peaceful settlement. The moral support of the members would thus be supplemented by a joint organized power—military and economic—capable of enforcing the decisions of the league.[23]

The *Memorandum* on war aims actually anticipated the Fourteen Points and included many of the proposals of the declaration issued by President Wilson and adhered to by the Allied Powers as a basis for the negotiation of the peace settlement. Therefore, when the British government, shortly before the Armistice, endorsed the Fourteen Points, Labour was convinced that the government had, in fact, accepted Labour's own war aims as well. With the adherence of the Allied Labour and Socialist parties to the *Memorandum*,[24] international agreement among the allied peoples on the peace terms appeared to be complete. The governments as well as the labor movements had approved what in effect was an identical program of peace. However, British Labour did not realize at the time that the government, although pledged to a peace based upon the Fourteen Points, was also committed to a peace of annexation and conquest provided by the secret treaties concluded by the Allied Powers.

British Labour's struggle for the adoption of the *Memorandum* was carried directly to the people during the General Election which followed immediately after the Armistice. The party's electoral program—*Labour and the New Social Order*—based its foreign policy pronouncements upon the principles of international co-operation pro-

[23] *Labour Leader*, December 20, 1917, p. 2.

[24] Third Inter-Allied Labour and Socialist Conference, London, February 20, 1918, *Report of the Eighteenth Annual Conference of the Labour Party*, 1919, p. 7.

vided in the *Memorandum*. In this program, the party reaffirmed its support for a "universal League or Society of Nations, a Supernational Authority" with an international high court, an international legislature, and an international council of mediation. In addition, the party promised the electors that Labour would seek "an ever-increasing intercourse, a constantly developing exchange of commodities, a steadily growing mutual understanding and a continually expanding friendly co-operation among all the peoples of the world."[25] Unfortunately for Labour, its "Call to the People" was made in an atmosphere of war passion and revenge. Consequently, a majority of the voters refused to register approval for "a peace of reconciliation and international co-operation." Nevertheless, the tremendous increase in the party's popular vote was, at the least, some indication that its appeal had not fallen on completely barren ground.

After the General Election it soon became obvious that the government was not prepared to honor its pledge to Labour of a part in the negotiation of the peace settlement. It had been on the basis of this pledge that Labour, in spite of the war weariness, the industrial unrest, the drastic measures of industrial and military conscription, the loss of trade-union safeguards, and the mounting desire for a negotiated peace, had stayed in line until victory was assured. With the Armistice, Labour had received the further assurance that the peace terms would be based upon the principles of Wilson's Fourteen Points. However, during the preparation for the peace conference, Labour was excluded from active participation. Denied an official part in the settlement, Labour continued to work through such channels as the League of Nations Society and the Union of Democratic Control, hoping to influence the peacemakers and gain mass support for its own program of peace. Throughout the proceedings of the peace conference Labour carried on a fight for a reasonable peace without victors or vanquished. At the conclusion, it was compelled to admit that its unofficial role had been largely an ineffective one. Given its full share in winning the war, it claimed that it was denied its part in making the peace.

[25] *Labour and the New Social Order* (London: Labour Party, 1918).

3

HIS MAJESTY'S LOYAL OPPOSITION

Toward the end of the war a gradual transformation of the
Labour party had been taking place which was to have a considerable
effect upon the development of the party's foreign policy. In the first
place, the Labour party had achieved national status by opening its
ranks for the first time to individual members conforming to the
definition of "workers by hand or by brain." It was thus made possible for anyone who accepted the party's principles to become a
regular member without necessarily being affiliated with either a
trade-union or a socialist society. Secondly, the party had adopted a
comprehensive postwar program—*Labour and the New Social Order*
—which provided a socialist solution to both national and international problems. The program represented a victory for the socialist
elements within the movement, particularly of the Fabian Society,
which had repeatedly advocated the adoption by the party of a specifically socialist policy. Finally, as a result of the first postwar General Election the party had increased its popular vote to the extent of
achieving the status of His Majesty's Opposition.[1] This position was
assured by the rapid disintegration of the Liberal party and strengthened by the steady flow of "radicals" into the ranks of Labour. The
prospect of attaining power was no longer a remote one; the Labour
party was an alternative government. Foreign policy had now to be
regarded from the point of view of power and responsibility.

In spite of these gains, the Labour party had suffered a temporary
setback in the loss of most of its leading spokesmen on foreign affairs
as a result of the General Election. Those members, "radicals" as
well as Labour, who had been the prewar pioneers in the advance of
popular interest in foreign policy—MacDonald, Snowden, Henderson, Robertson, Ponsonby, Trevelyan, Dilke, King, Outhwaite, and
many others—were gone from the Parliament which assembled at the
beginning of 1919. As a result, the Labour party's leadership in foreign affairs in the House of Commons remained weak and ineffective
throughout the session of that Parliament. As one Labour member la-
mented the situation, "in foreign affairs Parliament has now no voice

[1] The 1918 Labour party vote increased from the prewar peak of 505,690 to
2,244,945.

20

and no ears."[2] Nevertheless, the party was not deterred from its interest or activity in the international field merely by its parliamentary impotence. Instead, it sought other means—the press, the party conferences, meetings, demonstrations, and the international labor and socialist congresses—for the expression of its views on foreign policy while preparing to regain its parliamentary losses at the next General Election.

In contrast with the postwar parliamentary situation, circumstances throughout the country were favorable to the reception of Labour's views on foreign policy. The chief asset of Labour was the widespread interest in problems of foreign policy manifested by the general public at the conclusion of the war. Public apathy before 1914 had been shaken by the outbreak of a world-wide conflagration. After the war came the belated realization that foreign affairs "did matter" and that "the War was the outcome of them."[3] Although Labour had, before 1914, repeatedly advocated the democratization of foreign policy, there had been little popular support for the achievement of such a reform. Participation in a total war, however, had made a difference. The people were now vitally concerned with foreign affairs, and particularly determined that the conduct of international policy should not again lead the country into war. The most important goal of foreign policy was now generally regarded as the creation of a peace system which would put an end to the possibility of the recurrence of war. It was upon the basis of this desire that the nation anxiously followed the proceedings at Versailles and awaited the results of the peace settlement.

The demand for a just and durable peace had been in the forefront of the Labour party's aims. Having no direct part in deciding the terms of the settlement, Labour could only hope for a peace that would conform to the principles accepted with the adoption of the Fourteen Points. When the Versailles Conference concluded its sessions and revealed the product of the peacemakers' efforts, the reaction of the Labour movement was one of universal condemnation. The Trades Union Congress and the Labour Party Conference declared that the peace treaties "grossly" violated not only the professed objects for which the Allied nations had entered the war, but also the terms of the Armistice to which the Allied governments had solemnly pledged their faith. The treaties were denounced as a destructive rather than a constructive settlement, and their immediate revision in accordance

[2] Colonel Wedgwood, "The Constitution and Foreign Affairs," *Foreign Affairs*, II (September 1920), 33.

[3] J. W. Kneeshaw, "Do Foreign Affairs Matter?" *ibid.*, I (July 1919), 10.

with the terms agreed to under the Armistice was demanded. British Labour, in conjunction with the international labor and socialist movement, was to undertake a "vigorous campaign" for the revision of the "harsher" provisions of the treaty, including the violations of self-determination, the reparations settlement, the disposition of the Saar, the occupation of the Rhineland, the exclusion of Germany and Russia from membership in the new international organization, and the inadequate provision for a genuine "league of peoples."[4]

Along with its struggle against the injustices of Versailles, Labour carried on an active campaign against the government's policy of intervention in the internal affairs of the new Russian republic. Although Labour had enthusiastically welcomed the Russian Revolution and the destruction of the Czarist autocracy, it had been reluctant to protest against Allied intervention, believing at first that it was a necessary part of the strategy of German defeat and, later, that it was for the purpose of restoring law and order in that country to ensure the meeting of a constituent assembly. However, when intervention was continued with increased fervor after the European war had been concluded, Labour vigorously opposed the participation of the British government in this policy. In response to the government's action, the Transport Workers, the Railwaymen and the Miners Federation issued a demand for the removal of British troops from Russia and the raising of the blockade. The Labour Party Conference endorsed the demand of the leading trade-unions and advocated co-operation for effective action to enforce these demands by the "unreserved use" of political and industrial power.[5] The trade-unions, impatient with parliamentary impotence, proposed the resort to industrial power by holding a strike demonstration to halt British intervention. As a result, when the government attempted to supply arms to the Poles who had joined the attack on Russia, the British trade-unions refused to participate in the loading of munitions for use against the Russian peoples.

The threat of a general war against Russia became imminent after the defeat of the Polish armies and the advance of the Russians on Warsaw. Fearing British participation in such a war, British Labour

[4] Cf. Reports of the *Nineteenth Annual Conference of the Labour Party*, 1919, pp. 23–25, 139–42, 197, 210, 216–17; *Twentieth Annual Conference of the Labour Party*, 1920, p. 132; *Twenty-first Annual Conference of the Labour Party*, 1921, pp. 200–223; *Twenty-second Annual Conference of the Labour Party*, 1922, p. 193; *The International at Lucerne* (London: Labour Party, 1919), pp. 3–5; *Labour and Socialist International Congress*, 1920 (Geneva: I.L.O. Studies and Reports, A.6), p. 23; *International Socialist Conference*, 1921 (London: I.L.P., 1921), p. 10.

[5] *Report of the Nineteenth Annual Conference of the Labour Party*, 1919, pp. 156–57.

took immediate action. At a joint meeting, the Parliamentary Committee of the Trades Union Congress, the Executive Committee of the Labour party and the Labour members of Parliament unanimously decided to form from the three bodies a "Council of Action" for the purpose of preventing the British government from joining Poland in a war against the Soviet Union. The Council of Action was instructed to prevent the giving by Britain of any armed assistance to Poland and to obtain the lifting of the British blockade of Russia, the recognition of the Soviet government, and the establishment of trading relations between Britain and Soviet Russia. In addition, the council was authorized "to call for any and every form of withdrawal of labour" which circumstances might require for the enforcement of such a policy.[6] Actually, it did not prove necessary for the council to resort to industrial action, because the danger of a general war was averted when the Russians and the Poles agreed to conclude hostilities.

The withdrawal of British troops from Russia was regarded by Labour as a victory for its policy of refusing to take part in a general war against the Soviet Union. Not all of the aims of the Council of Action had been realized, however. It was now the task of Labour to work for a policy of co-operation with the new Soviet government. The party's most persistent demand was that diplomatic recognition be accorded by the British government.[7] The government, however, was unwilling to grant this request, and limited its policy of co-operation with the Bolsheviks to the negotiation of a trade agreement with the Soviet government at the end of 1921. The government's general feeling of hostility toward the Bolsheviks for quitting the war, confiscating property, and repudiating debts was not a condition favorable to the resumption of "friendly co-operation." Consequently, the resumption of diplomatic relations with Soviet Russia was to await the arrival of a Labour government in Great Britain.

The Versailles peace treaties and Allied intervention in Russia were viewed by Labour as indications that imperialism and militarism had not, in fact, been destroyed as a result of the Great War. The reaction to these two developments was one of despair and disillusionment, a feeling that the war had been of no avail so far as the establishment of a better world was concerned. The Labour party took

[6] Cf. "British Labour Council of Action," *Foreign Affairs*, II (October 1920), 53; (November 1920), 82.

[7] Cf. Reports of the *Twentieth Annual Conference of the Labour Party*, 1920, p. 132; *Twenty-second Annual Conference of the Labour Party*, 1922, p. 193; *Twenty-third Annual Conference of the Labour Party*, 1923, p. 221; *Twenty-fourth Annual Conference of the Labour Party*, 1924, p. 192; *New Leader*, February 16, 1923, p. 7.

the view that the "disastrous" economic, social, and political conditions prevailing throughout Europe after the war were very largely
the result of the unwise policies pursued by the Supreme Council and
Allied governments since the conclusion of the Armistice. The British
government had its share of responsibility for the existing international situation since it had concurred in the peace treaties, which had
"crushed and impoverished" the peoples of Central Europe, and the
blockade and intervention which had been "ruinous" to the peoples of
Russia.[8] In addition, the revelation of the British government's part
in the secret treaties to despoil the Central Powers had further convinced Labour that it had somehow been tricked into supporting a
war of imperialism under the pretense of a war to make the world safe
for democracy.[9] This anxiety and fear of being dragged into another
such war prompted the Labour Party Conference to endorse an Independent Labour party resolution providing that socialist and labor
parties of all nations agree to oppose "any war entered into by any
Government, whatever the ostensible object of the war."[10] The acceptance of this resolution represented a victory for that section of
the movement which, having opposed the first World War, now hoped
to justify that position on the basis of the circumstances prevailing
throughout Europe as a consequence of the war.

The only legacy of the war which Labour regarded with any
optimism was the League of Nations. Labour had played an important part in stimulating discussion and support for the idea of a league
following the conclusion of the war. The *War Aims Memorandum* as
well as *Labour and the New Social Order* clearly envisaged a "society
of nations, a super-national authority" as an essential factor in the
maintenance of world peace. Many of the final provisions of the
Covenant owed their origin to the efforts of the Labour members who
participated in the Union of Democratic Control, the League of Nations Society, and the Fabian Research Department. Throughout the
war the Union of Democratic Control carried on an active campaign
to formulate a program and organize support for a policy that would
lead to an enduring peace.[11] The work of the Union of Democratic
Control was particularly significant as its membership included such
leading Labour spokesmen on foreign policy as MacDonald, Pon-

[8] *Report of the Twenty-second Annual Conference of the Labour Party*, 1922,
p. 193.

[9] Cf. E. D. Morel, *Diplomacy Revealed* (London: National Labour Press, 1921).

[10] *Report of the Twenty-second Annual Conference of the Labour Party*, 1922,
p. 200.

[11] The U.D.C. was founded in November 1914, and in 1919 it began the publication of *Foreign Affairs*, edited by E. D. Morel, M.P.

sonby, Thomas, Snowden, Trevelyan, Morel, Buxton, Brailsford, Pethick-Lawrence, Attlee, and Morrison. By operating through such unofficial organizations these members were able to continue their efforts to gain support for an international organization in spite of the fact that the postwar parliamentary election had deprived most of them of a national forum for the expression of their ideas. However, as Labour's influence remained an unofficial one during the proceedings of the peace conference, many of its ideals were never realized in the final draft of the League of Nations Covenant.

After the ratification of the Covenant the Labour party proclaimed its conviction that in the League of Nations, "strengthened and democratised," existed the "most hopeful official machinery for the preservation of international peace."[12] Although the party was willing to pledge its support to the League in its existent form, it retained the hope of bringing the Covenant into harmony with its own conception of an ideal international organization. Such an organization, it believed, should be established on a democratic basis, providing for a "true association of peoples," not merely a "league of governments." It should be universal, including within its membership all nations organized on the principle of self-determination; Germany and Russia should be granted full membership at once. It should provide for the adjustment of world disputes and the alteration of national boundaries; the provisions for reparations and territorial limits should be subject to modification and revision. It should abolish the right to make war, arbitration should be compulsory, sanctions should be provided against aggression, and disarmament should be promoted. In addition, it should attack the causes of war by hastening the disappearance of the "old economic antagonisms." It should provide the organization for the international payment of debts, foreign exchanges, the international supply of raw materials, food products, commercial tonnage, and transport. If such ideals had been realized in the Covenant, the League would have conformed with Labour's view of a "genuine organisation of international co-operation and democratic representation."[13] Nevertheless, Labour hoped that the

[12] Report of the Twenty-second Annual Conference of the Labour Party, 1922, p. 193; Report of the Fifty-fourth Annual Conference of the T.U.C., 1922, p. 89.

[13] For Labour's criticisms of the League, cf. Report of the Nineteenth Annual Conference of the Labour Party, 1919, pp. 139, 197, 210; "I.L.P. Conference," 1919, Labour Leader, April 24, 1919, p. 3; "The Covenant of the League," Foreign Affairs, I (September 1919), 1; Report of the Twentieth Annual Conference of the Labour Party, 1920, p. 132; J. R. MacDonald, A Policy for the Labour Party (London: Parsons, 1920), pp. 133–34; J. H. Thomas, When Labour Rules (New York: Harcourt, Brace, 1921), pp. 192–97; Report of the Twenty-second Annual Conference of the Labour Party, 1922, p. 193; H. N. Brailsford, After the Peace (New York: Seltzer,

new organization would provide some means for the re-establishment of international conciliation.

The Labour party had interpreted the ratification of the League Covenant as a solemn undertaking to consider all international issues in the light of the principles embodied in the Covenant. Consequently, its own policy was to ensure that the government made use of the machinery of the League whenever possible in the sphere of international relations.[14] The party was in a better position to implement this policy following the General Election of 1922, which had resulted in an increase in the size and quality of its parliamentary membership.[15] In the field of foreign affairs, the party was considerably strengthened in the House of Commons by the return of its leading spokesmen on that subject. Ramsay MacDonald resumed the position of parliamentary leader and Thomas, Snowden, Jowett, Ponsonby, Trevelyan, Wedgwood, Lees-Smith, Lansbury, Morel, Buxton, Attlee, Greenwood, Alexander, and Shinwell were returned as members of the Opposition. In contrast to its parliamentary inactivity during the sessions immediately following the war, the party now was prepared to accept the role of an effective parliamentary Opposition. As such, on matters of foreign policy it was determined to see that the government adhered to the pledges undertaken with regard to the League Covenant.

The Labour party hoped that by working through the League of Nations it would be possible to deal with the defects of the peace treaties and restore a general atmosphere of international good will and co-operation. It therefore opposed such attempts by the government to conduct its foreign policy outside the realm of the Covenant as the conclusion of special pacts or partial alliances contrary to the spirit of the League. In particular, Labour feared that the government's postwar treaty negotiations with France would result in perpetuating the system of alliances which had culminated in the last war.[16] Labour believed that if the League were strengthened to provide security and enlarged to embrace the victorious as well as the vanquished nations, partial alliances would be rendered wholly un-

1922), pp. 152–54; *Report of the Fifty-fourth Annual Conference of the T.U.C.*, 1922, p. 89; "Manifesto of I.L.P.," *New Leader*, February 16, 1923, p. 7; "I.L.P. Conference," *ibid.*, April 6, 1923, p. 16; *Report of the Twenty-third Annual Conference of the Labour Party*, 1923, pp. 221, 241, 263.

[14] *Report of the Twenty-second Annual Conference of the Labour Party*, 1922, p. 193; *Report of the Fifty-fourth Annual Conference of the T.U.C.*, 1922, p. 89.

[15] The 1922 Labour vote increased to 4,337,000, and Parliamentary representation to 142 seats.

[16] *Report of the Twenty-first Annual Conference of the Labour Party*, 1921, p. 201.

necessary. Labour could not agree that Germany should be "isolated, ostracised," kept in "economic subjection" and in "financial embarrassment" because the French government was "obsessed by fears" which, in Labour's opinion, were "largely the result of its own reactionary policy."[17] For the British government to support France was to condone a policy of revenge and prolong the existence of the antagonisms inherited from the war. Although the British government concurred with Labour in the view that peace was dependent upon the reconciliation of all of the peoples of Europe and the political and economic recovery of Germany, it was hesitant to endanger what was left of the Entente, realizing that concessions to Germany would provoke the hostility of France. Consequently, the government found itself in the incongruous position of being considered by the French as pro-German and by the Opposition as pro-French. To the Opposition it appeared that the government had devised no policy at all which would "check the progressive economic ruin of Europe," and it registered that complaint by a vote of censure against the government in the House of Commons.[18]

The Labour party did not oppose friendship with France but feared rather that the British government would demonstrate that friendship by allowing France to be "let loose upon the Ruhr" for the purpose of enforcing the provisions of the peace treaties. From the very outset, Labour had considered reparations as one of the most serious blemishes of the peace treaties. It had expected that reparations, like the other defects of Versailles, would be subject to revision through the efforts of the members of the League of Nations. Until this could be realized, however, it was not willing to allow France alone to insist forcibly upon "fulfillment." While opposing French policy on reparations, the Labour party denied that it was necessarily anti-French. Labour refused to consider France as "synonymous with Poincaré," and pointed out the fact that the working class of France, represented in the Labour and Socialist International, had already agreed upon the inclusion of reparations among the essential modifications of the Treaty of Versailles.[19]

Labour's criticism of the reparations settlement was a twofold one. In the first place, the provision operated as a deterrent to the recovery of Germany; economically it held her in bondage, and politically it estranged her from her creditors. Secondly, Labour was con-

[17] Arthur Henderson, 160 *H.C.Deb.*, February 19, 1923, col. 714.

[18] The Labour amendment to the Address was supported by the Liberals and defeated by the government, 277–180. *Ibid.*, February 15, 1923, col. 363.

[19] Charles Trevelyan, *ibid.*, col. 460.

vinced that the financial arrangement had destroyed British trade in Europe as well as the whole economic life of that continent. So long as reparations were insisted upon in their present form it would be impossible either to reconstruct Europe or reopen British markets. At the same time, however, the Labour party denied that it had ever been prepared to release Germany from her obligations under the treaties. Rejecting the doctrine that Germany should be prevented from becoming strong enough to pay her way, Labour demanded an economic and industrial policy which would enable Germany to restore her trade in order to meet her obligations. Labour proposed that the amount of reparations be definitely settled and fixed at a level deemed satisfactory by experts, that an international loan be negotiated to facilitate the process of German recovery, and that a moratorium be agreed to by all of the powers to ensure sufficient time for German recovery. Above all, Labour felt that it was essential to have an agreement which Germany would accept and which would be carried out by means of good will rather than by the power "to step in and take control."[20]

On the basis of such reasoning the Labour party was convinced that the French policy of occupying the Ruhr after the Reparations Commission had voted German "default" would not achieve the end for which it was "professedly conceived." If it had been so essential to obtain reparations, France had been given the opportunity of examining and discussing the repeated offers from Germany, at Spa and also at Paris, to repair the devastated regions of France. Was the collection of reparations the motivating force which had inspired France to resort to invasion? Labour asked. Or rather, was it "a desire to tear away from Germany the whole of her territory on the left bank of the Rhine"? The Labour party, claiming that the British government as a signatory to the peace treaties had both the right and the duty to make its position clear with regard to the fulfillment of the obligations, reproached the government for its "do-nothing" policy. If the government's inaction was due to its hesitation to interfere with the French quest for security, its efforts should have been directed to devising a policy which would provide France with some hope of a different kind of security guaranteed by all of the nations of Europe. However, for the British government to send a note merely protesting against the French occupation of the Ruhr was no policy at all. The alternative was for the British and French governments, acting in co-operation with the other members of the League, to

[20] Ramsay MacDonald, E. D. Morel, 159 *H.C. Deb.*, November 24, 1922, cols. 222–23, December 14, 1922, cols. 3239–45.

consider the issues of reparations and the Ruhr in conjunction with the whole problem of European security.[21]

As the Labour party had predicted, the French invasion of the Ruhr did not achieve the end for which it was "professedly conceived." However, the failure of the French method to ensure the payment of reparations was not to be attributed to the active resistance of the British government but rather to the passive resistance of the Germans themselves. Although Labour had failed to convince the government of the necessity for League action in the Franco-German dispute, it was able to see many of its other suggestions eventually advanced by the British government to the French. As a result, by the end of 1923 the French government had accepted the British proposal to investigate Germany's capacity to pay, and consented to the creation by the Reparations Commission of a "Committee of Experts" for this purpose. An adjustment of British and French views upon Germany and the reparations question appeared to be in sight before the end of the Baldwin Conservative administration. However, other difficulties—the Separatist movement in the Palatinate and the Cologne railways dispute—were to postpone a genuine reconciliation until the advent of a Labour government in Great Britain.

Since the conclusion of the war the Labour party had directed its efforts in the international field to the achievement of a peace of reconciliation and co-operation. It had opposed the harsh provisions of the peace settlement, the intervention of the Allied Powers against the Soviet Republic and the efforts of the Entente to prevent Germany's recovery. As a means of achieving a just and durable peace, Labour had supported the League of Nations. During the General Election of 1923 the Labour party appealed to the people with the vision of an "ordered world," embracing the nations then "torn with enmity and strife." Labour stood for a policy of international co-operation through a strengthened and enlarged League of Nations and the settlement of disputes by conciliation and arbitration. Labour would deal with the revision of the Versailles treaties, especially the problems of reparations and debts. It would treat Germany on terms of equality and would resume "free economic and diplomatic relations" with the Soviet Union. Such a policy, Labour promised, would pave the way for disarmament, "the only security for the nations." A universal league embracing victors and vanquished alike and providing

[21] 160 *H.C.Deb.*, February 15, 1923, cols. 363, 393, 460–61. The Labour party supported a Liberal party amendment to the Address, proposing that reparations and the Ruhr problems be referred to the League of Nations, which was defeated by the government, 305 to 196. *Ibid.*, February 19, 1923, cols. 709–13. Also cf. 161 *H.C.Deb.*, March 6, 1923, col. 324; 162 *H.C.Deb.*, March 28, 1923, col. 610.

for the adjustment of international grievances, the economic recovery of the impoverished peoples and the security of all nations, large and small, was Labour's policy for the postwar world.[22] The response of the electorate to Labour's appeal was significant in terms of the increase in Labour's parliamentary representation.[23] However, the "true" significance of the election, according to the party, was that its views on foreign policy were no longer confined to members of the Union of Democratic Control or the parliamentary Labour party and its supporters in the country. These views had been endorsed by an overwhelming majority of the electorate, which had repudiated the foreign policy of the Baldwin administration.[24]

[22] "Labour's Appeal to the Nation," December 6, 1923, *Report of the Twenty-fourth Annual Conference of the Labour Party*, 1924, p. 192.

[23] Labour gained almost fifty seats, increasing its parliamentary representation to 191.

[24] F. W. Pethick-Lawrence, "The True Significance of the Election," *Foreign Affairs*, V (January 1924), 134.

4

THE NEW DIPLOMACY

The General Election of 1923 conferred upon the Labour party the responsibility of office and the opportunity of implementing its principles of foreign policy. However, the opportunity was a limited one, dependent upon the approval of the Liberal members of Parliament. The Liberal party, temporarily reunited in opposition to Baldwin's electoral appeal for a "protectionist" program, had secured sufficient representation to prevent either of the other parties from forming a government without its support. Although the number of Labour members of Parliament had been increased to 191, the party was not able to command a parliamentary majority from its own members alone. As a result of this parliamentary alignment, the Liberals held the balance and the decision rested with them. The Labour members were given the chance to constitute a government as soon as the Liberals joined with them in voting out Baldwin's Conservative administration. The first Labour government was to be a minority one, owing its origin, its continuance, and its demise to the Liberal party.

The decision to form a government was made by the Labour party in spite of the fact that it would not be able to rely upon a parliamentary majority to support a specifically socialist program. In domestic affairs, the party was aware that the application of socialist principles would be decidedly limited by the necessity for Liberal approval. Social reform rather than socialism would be the accepted point of departure for Labour's internal policy. In the realm of international affairs, however, Labour was more optimistic regarding the possibilities of effecting its foreign-policy program. The basis for this conviction was the fact that the Liberal party had on many occasions sided with Labour in opposition to the foreign policy carried out by the postwar Conservative administrations. Since the breakup of the Lloyd George Coalition government the Liberals had become increasingly critical of the peace settlement and had lined up with Labour members of Parliament to advocate a revision of the treaties. Even Lloyd George, one of the architects of the peace treaties, had since assumed the role of the "innocent victim of M. Clemenceau."[1] Liberal members of Parliament had endorsed the proposals of Labour

[1] Robert Dell, "Our Relations with France," *Foreign Affairs*, IV (July 1922), 3.

that the League of Nations be made representative of all peoples and employed for conciliation and arbitration in pressing matters, such as reparations and the occupied territories.[2] In addition, both of the parties had challenged the tariff policy proposed by Baldwin's Conservative government. If the Liberals continued to adhere to such concepts, Labour believed that it would be possible to achieve Liberal support for the application of its international policy.

The chief asset with which the Labour party approached the conduct of British foreign policy was that it had no past to be ashamed of and no heritage to live down. It had played no part in the secret diplomacy preceding the war or in the peace settlement concluding the war. It had no responsibility for the blockade or the armed intervention against Soviet Russia. It had, in opposition, denounced these policies and proclaimed that it would never be bound, as a government, by secret treaties or arrangements with foreign nations which it might find in existence when it assumed power. Its advocacy of a just peace and its insistence upon the reconciliation of the victors and the vanquished had an immense appeal to a world divided by hostility and suspicion. It was on such a basis that Labour was prepared to inaugurate a new era of international good will and co-operation.

During the nine months in which the Labour government was in office it was able to effect, or at least to initiate, most of the international policies to which it was pledged. Much of the success of Labour's program in the international field was due to the personal efforts of the Labour Prime Minister, Ramsay MacDonald, who acted as his own Foreign Secretary. MacDonald succeeded in winning the friendship of the French government where his predecessors since the war had failed. It was MacDonald's conviction that the only way to reach a general European settlement was through Anglo-French understanding. The co-operation of France was essential to any scheme for the revision of the peace treaties, and so long as the status quo of Versailles existed, the recovery of Germany would be prevented. MacDonald's strategy was to convince the French that their search for security was to be found not in an impoverished Germany but in a strengthened League of Nations. An all-inclusive league which would embrace Germany as well as Soviet Russia would provide the best opportunity for the reconciliation of the nations then divided by hatred and strife. No one was better qualified to undertake such a task than Ramsay MacDonald, whose pacifist leanings were a welcome

---

[2] Cf. 160 *H.C.Deb.*, February 15, 1923, col. 363. Labour M.P.'s also supported a Liberal amendment demanding League action on reparations and the Ruhr. *Ibid.*, February 19, 1923, col. 709.

relief to a Europe demoralized by enmity and war. It was said that when MacDonald assumed office, "the War Office was totally eliminated as an element in diplomacy." The party and the Prime Minister were pledged to a policy of "open, straightforward and honest" diplomacy.[3]

The Labour government had inherited from its Conservative predecessors the problem of reaching a general settlement with France on the outstanding issues arising from the war and the peace treaties. Actually, some progress in this direction was evidenced during the concluding stages of the Baldwin administration, but it was forestalled by the appearance of further difficulties and disputes. For the Labour government, the solution of the general problem was aided by the removal of two sources of contention between the governments which had thus far evaded settlement. After MacDonald assumed the office of Foreign Secretary, the proposals of his predecessor, Lord Curzon, were at last accepted by M. Poincaré; and the French government agreed to renounce its ambitions for control of the Cologne railways and its support of the Separatist movement in the Palatinate. MacDonald had brought the negotiations with Poincaré to a successful conclusion, thus paving the way for the achievement of agreement on the remaining problems of reparations, the Ruhr and security. The latter task would be facilitated for the Labour government by the conciliatory policies of M. Poincaré's successor, M. Herriot.

Although the Labour party was committed to a policy of revising reparations, it could not carry out this pledge until it had first received the consent of the other signatories of the peace treaties. The prospect of achieving consent had been somewhat improved by the French agreement to the creation of a committee of experts to consider the problem of reparations. However, there remained the task of converting the French to the view that reparations should be regarded as an economic possibility, dependent upon Germany's capacity to pay. As long as the collection of reparations could be exploited by France as a means to ensure "fulfillment," it would be impossible to achieve either economic recovery or political equality for Germany. The Labour government hoped for a compromise proposal which would take account of the legitimate French claims to restitution as well as the economic ability of the Germans to comply. It therefore welcomed the report submitted to the members of the Reparations Commission by the Committee of Experts. The report of the First Committee, presided over by the American delegate General Dawes, unlike previous

[3] George Glasgow, *MacDonald as Diplomatist* (London: Jonathan Cape, 1924), p. 33.

expert plans, not only provided for a schedule of annual payments, but indicated the sources from which the money should be raised and the methods by which it should be handed over. After the report had been presented, the British Prime Minister took the initiative of announcing that the plan would be the basis of the Labour government's reparations policy.[4]

The British government was determined that the plan be accepted and applied as an indivisible whole by the other members of the Reparations Commission. Acceptance by the French government was assured by the June elections which had brought M. Herriot, pledged to support the Dawes plan, to the premiership and to the Foreign Office. MacDonald lost no time in conferring with the new Radical Foreign Minister, and one of the results of their meeting at Chequers was an agreement to hold a conference in London to deal with the economic problems of putting the Dawes plan into operation. The military problem of the Ruhr occupation was to be reserved for consideration at a subsequent conference devoted to the problem of European security. Accordingly, the Reparations Conference assembled in London and after a month of deliberation the Allied Powers and Germany reached agreement upon the adoption of the provisions of the Dawes plan.

The success of the London Conference was largely due to the personal efforts of the British Prime Minister. He succeeded in obtaining French acquiescence to a fundamental revision of one of the defects of the Versailles settlement. The adoption of the Dawes plan was, in fact, a vindication of British Labour's reparations policy. The two major alterations in reparations policy introduced by the plan had been repeatedly advocated by the Labour party since the conclusion of the peace treaties. In the first place, reparations were in the future to be regarded on a business basis, necessarily contingent upon Germany's economic recovery. The burden of payments was to be graduated and accompanied by international monetary aid to foster financial and commercial recovery. Secondly, arbitration was to replace force as a method of ensuring "fulfillment." German default was no longer to be the concern of France alone, but of the Allied Reparations Commission, on which an American was to have representation, and, if necessary, an arbitral commission. Sanctions were to be applied only in cases of "flagrant default" and then only after agreement among the Allied Powers.[5]

[4] *Towards a European Settlement—Reparations* (London: Labour Party, Can Labour Rule Series, No. 7, 1924), p. 3.

[5] Cf. Proceedings of the London Reparations Conference, July and August, 1924, *British State Papers*, Cmd. 2270 (1924).

As significant as the change in reparations policy was the new spirit of compromise and co-operation manifested at the London Conference. France had been conciliatory and willing to make concessions to other points of view. Germany had taken part in the concluding stages of the conference and, as a negotiating member, had accepted the provisions of the plan. Remaining as a deterrent to reconciliation was the prolongation of the military occupation of the Ruhr. However, MacDonald was confident that this difficulty could also be overcome given French willingness to continue co-operation. He had already received M. Herriot's consent to consider a solution to the problem in conjunction with the general question of European security. MacDonald epitomized the mood of the conference when he concluded that "this Agreement may be regarded as the first Peace Treaty because we sign it with a feeling that we have turned our backs on the terrible years of war and war mentality."[6]

After the reparations conference, the Labour government was hopeful that the practice of co-operation inaugurated at London would lead to a solution of the problem of security to be considered by the Foreign Ministers at the Assembly of the League of Nations. Although the Labour party sympathized with the French search for security, it did not approve of the methods pursued. In particular, it objected to the French policy of keeping Germany militarily powerless while France continued to maintain strong armed forces. It held that France's resort to special alliances and military pacts with the smaller nations of Europe fostered a feeling of suspicion and rivalry which was contrary to the spirit of the League of Nations Covenant. The Labour party consistently opposed any attempts to conclude a defensive alliance with France, although it emphasized that this did not preclude friendship with France. Labour's conception of security was not a qualified one, limited to security for France or security against Germany. Security was a universal aim to be realized only within the framework of an all-inclusive and strengthened League of Nations.

Although it was convinced that security could be achieved only through the League, the Labour party was aware of the shortcomings of that organization. The fact that France had chosen to search for security outside the League was a further indication that the League had not, in fact, succeeded in providing the necessary guaranty. The Labour party never abandoned its initial hope of reforming the Covenant for the purpose of strengthening the security provisions. It regarded as one of the most serious weaknesses of the Covenant the provision conceding to nations failing to settle their disputes by pacific

[6] *Towards a European Settlement—Reparations*, p. 4.

means the right to engage in war. Labour's aim was to close the "gaps" in the Covenant by outlawing the use of war in any circumstances. Arbitration, not force, would be the accepted method of settling international disputes; the nation resorting to war in violation of an arbitral award would be deemed an aggressor and subject to sanctions. If the Covenant were so amended, the security of all nations would be guaranteed, and the creation of special alliances rendered unnecessary. It was on the basis of this concept of security that the Labour government hoped to gain the co-operation of the French at the Geneva meeting.

Before the Labour government was able to propose its own security scheme, it was presented with a plan which had been drafted by the League's Temporary Mixed Commission for the Reduction of Armaments. The Commission, consisting of a combined membership of experts and laymen, had been set up by the First Assembly of the League for the purpose of preparing a plan for the reduction of armaments in accordance with Article VIII of the League Covenant. During the course of the Commission's deliberations, it had become evident that the achievement of a reduction of armaments was dependent upon the provision of security for the member nations. As a result, the Commission proceeded on the basis of this assumption, and the result of its efforts was the Draft Treaty of Mutual Assistance, presented to the League Assembly in 1923. The Assembly subsequently called upon the Council to submit the treaty to the governments with a request for their consideration of the plan. Thus the British Labour government was required to make a decision on a security plan which had been devised by the representatives of its predecessors, and in the creation of which it had played no part.

After a careful consideration of the treaty, the Labour government concluded that it did not provide a sufficient guaranty of security to justify a state's reducing its armaments. In comparing the treaty with its own policy for achieving security, Labour found the former to be wanting in several respects, and even contrary to many of the Labour party's principles of foreign policy. The most serious omission of the treaty was its failure to provide an all-inclusive arbitration system as an alternative to war. Although the effectiveness of the plan was to a considerable extent dependent upon the ability of the Council of the League to determine which nation was the aggressor, the proposers of the treaty neglected to produce a definition of aggression. The draft considered only the two principles of security and disarmament, and the latter was of an "inadequate and rather problematical kind." There was no guaranty that there would be any really effective diminution of armaments. The only obligation included was that the powers "inform" the Council of the reduction or limitation of armaments which they considered "proportionate to the security furnished." The emphasis of the whole plan was upon sanctions or military assistance, and even here the provisions were defective. A system which involved prolonged delay before the first step in bringing military pressure to bear on an aggressor nation could be taken did not reach that standard of effectiveness essential to the successful imposition of sanctions. To the Labour party, the key to the draft treaty was that security was to be obtained by separate treaties of defensive military alliance between two or more of the states subscribing to the general treaty. This arrangement it considered most inconsistent with its own views upon foreign policy, and emphatically rejected it as a perpetuation of the prewar alliance system and as a defeat of the whole spirit and purpose of the League of Nations. Under such special treaties it would be possible for the signatory states, without obtaining the consent of the League Council, to decide whether the action in a particular case was "aggressive" or not, and accordingly, undertake the prearranged plan of military assistance. In his letter of reply to the secretary general of the League of Nations, the Labour Prime Minister stated the opinion that it was owing to the defects inherent in the general treaty that the proposal was made to superimpose a system of partial treaties between groups of countries. According to MacDonald, the draft treaty, far from being an effective system of disarmament based upon security, did not provide security for the present, nor was it likely to lead to disarmament in the near future.[7]

At the same time, however, the Prime Minister made it clear that rejection of the draft treaty did not mean that Great Britain was unconcerned with the problems of security and disarmament. There was no question to which the British government attached greater importance than the reduction and limitation of armaments. For that reason, it felt that as soon as a favorable opportunity presented itself, all of the governments should meet in conference with the object of devising a scheme for the reduction of armaments. The years of patient investigation which had been devoted to this subject by the various organs of the League, and the sentiment expressed in practically all of the replies of the governments to the League, were themselves a "proof" of the desire of the members to find a solution to the

[7]Reply from the British government, July 5, 1924, League of Nations, *Documents*, A.35, 1924, ix. Also cf. Lord Parmoor, 58 *H.L. Deb.*, July 24, 1924, cols. 964-82.

difficult question of the reduction and limitation of armaments. If these efforts had not so far resulted in the submission of a draft treaty of mutual assistance in an acceptable form, the reports which had been under consideration nevertheless contained some "encouraging and suggestive" passages as to other lines of inquiry which might be followed with useful results. However, it was the policy of the British government to keep itself free to consider any and every practicable proposal, and to commit itself at present only to a general undertaking in favor of the reduction of armaments.[8] The Prime Minister's concern was that the French government, which was favorably inclined toward the adoption of the draft treaty, would interpret the British government's rejection as a repudiation of its interest in the European security problem. Since the two governments were, at that time, in the midst of negotiating the reparations settlement, it was essential to the success of the London Conference that no doubts be cast upon the intentions of the British government. MacDonald's method of reaching an agreement with France was to settle the reparations question first and then proceed to a consideration of the security problem. Consequently, in his communication to the League he hesitated to include a counterproposal for the achievement of security while the reparations issue remained outstanding. The Prime Minister hoped to solve the European security problem at the League of Nations Assembly in Geneva.

The Labour government's support of the League was indicated by the appearance of the Prime Minister himself at the Fifth Assembly. In opening the discussion on the "Reduction of Armaments," MacDonald reiterated his government's objections to the draft treaty, stressing the belief that military alliances would not bring the desired security. Pointing out that the draft treaty covered only security and disarmament, he introduced a third element—arbitration—which was to make the whole system effective by the provision of a complete organization for the peaceful settlement of disputes between nations. It was MacDonald's conviction that arbitration would promote security, and that "ample provision" for initiating arbitration, and for the sanctions that were necessary, was already contained in the Covenant. What was required at this point was that the Covenant be "elaborated."[9] While the British Prime Minister stressed arbitration and the French Premier security, the difference in emphasis did not prevent their concurrence upon a resolution presented to the Assembly by

[8] Reply from the British government to the League, League of Nations, *Documents*, A.35, 1924, p. 17.

[9] *Verbatim Record* of the Fifth Assembly of the League of Nations, Sixth Plenary Meeting, September 4, 1924, pp. 2–4.

MacDonald and seconded and supported by Herriot. According to the terms of the resolution, an "International Conference on Armaments" was to be summoned by the League of Nations at the earliest possible moment. In preparation for that conference, the Third Committee of the Assembly (Reduction of Armaments) was requested to examine all of the material dealing with security and the reduction of armaments, particularly the observations of the governments on the draft treaty and the other plans presented to the League since the publication of the treaty. In addition, the Third Committee was to review the obligations contained in the Covenant in relation to the guaranties of security that a resort to arbitration and a reduction of armaments might require. The First Committee of the Assembly (Legal and Constitutional) was called upon to consider, in view of possible amendments, the articles of the Covenant relating to the settlement of disputes and the clause (Article 36, paragraph 2) in the statute of the Permanent Court of International Justice providing for the use of arbitration. The aim of the joint resolution was to strengthen the "solidarity and the security" of the nations of the world through settling by pacific means all disputes which might arise between states.[10]

The result of the work of the Committees of the Assembly was the proposal of a "Protocol on the Pacific Settlement of International Disputes" which was accepted in the Assembly by unanimous vote. The device of the "protocol" was only "supplementary" to the Covenant; it was not a new and independent instrument. The most significant contribution to the already existing peace machinery was the definition and the prohibition of aggressive war. The Protocol embodied a system of arbitration which no international dispute, whether judicial or political, could escape. It laid down as a fundamental condition of international intercourse that all disputes should be settled by pacific means, and it provided alternative machinery—the League Council, the Arbitral Committees, and the Permanent Court of International Justice—for every type of dispute to be settled. It cited the criteria for deciding which was a covenant-breaking state by defining as aggression the refusal to submit to pacific settlement and the rejection of a judicial or arbitral award. The system of compulsory arbitration was coupled with a collective understanding to apply the prescribed sanctions, under Article XVI of the Covenant, against any state which failed to observe its obligations. The Protocol thus closed the gaps through which one nation could resort to aggressive war

---

[10] *Ibid.*, Eleventh Plenary Meeting, September 6, 1924, p. 7.

against another nation without incurring the moral condemnation of the whole community of nations and encountering their combined material resistance.

The Protocol conformed to the Labour government's view that there could be no security without disarmament. Within the limits of the scheme it would be possible to reduce armaments in all countries within the League to the point at which they would be sufficient to serve as an international police force and no more. As disarmament was an integral part of the plan, it was provided that an international conference for the reduction of armaments would be convened the following year if the Protocol had then been ratified by at least a majority of the permanent members of the Council and ten other members of the League Assembly. In preparation for the convening of the conference, the Council of the League was to draw up a general program for the reduction and limitation of armaments which would be communicated to the governments and then laid before the conference. The Protocol would come into force as soon as the plan for the reduction of armaments had been adopted by the International Conference. Thus the tripod—arbitration, security, and disarmament—were linked, to stand or fall as a whole. Before the close of the Fifth Assembly, ten members of the League, including France, had already signed the Protocol. The future of the Protocol, and of the International Conference for the Reduction of Armaments, was now dependent upon the action of the British government.

In Great Britain the decisive debate upon the Protocol actually took place after the resignation of the Labour government. The text of the plan had not been brought out of the committees until October 1, and by the end of that week the Labour government had been voted out of office. However, during this brief interval there was already some indication of the nature of the opposition which was to result in the eventual scrapping of the Geneva Protocol by the succeeding Conservative government. The Labour party believed that most of the criticism of the Protocol revealed a complete lack of understanding of the obligations imposed by acceptance of the League of Nations Covenant. It, therefore, stressed the fact that the Protocol created no new obligations to use armed force which were not specifically or by implication already contained in the Covenant. The plan would enlarge the commitments of the signatories only with regard to the submission of disputes to pacific settlement. Commitments to the use of force would be restricted rather than enlarged, and there would be actually less probability of the use of force than under the Covenant, as unamended, or under the Draft Treaty of Mutual Assistance. To oppose the use of force by the League in any circumstances was not only a rejection of the Protocol but a repudiation of Articles X and XVI of the Covenant, which provided for the application of sanctions by the members of the League. These articles had been made "more precise" and "readily applicable" for the purpose of meeting the French demand for security, not to impose new obligations upon the signatories to maintain by force the status quo of the peace treaties. Under the League Covenant, as amended by the Protocol, there would be not only machinery for enforcing the law on the basis of existing conditions, but also "legal, peaceful and constitutional means" for altering those conditions whenever necessary.[11] "Give us ten years of the working of the Protocol," the Labour Prime Minister pleaded, "and we will have Europe with a new habit of mind."[12] MacDonald's request, however, was not to be granted by his Conservative successors. The survival of the Geneva Protocol had now become inseparably linked with that of the British Labour government.

In the midst of its struggle for the adoption of the Protocol, the Labour government was confronted with the loss of its parliamentary majority by the defection of the Liberal members. The decision of the Liberal party to sever its relations with the Labour party was the culmination of a rising hostility between the two political groups regarding the government's policy toward Soviet Russia. The opening of negotiations with the Soviet Union had been one of the first acts of the Labour government; the conclusion of those negotiations was to be the last.

The Labour party was committed, according to its Election Manifesto, to a policy of resuming "free economic and diplomatic relations" with Soviet Russia. Consequently, shortly after assuming office, the Labour government took the first step in this direction by granting *de jure* recognition to the Soviet government. It was the Prime Minister's contention that diplomatic recognition would create the "friendly atmosphere" which he considered the "essential preliminary" to successful negotiations. MacDonald thus reversed the policy of his predecessors, who concluded the Anglo-Soviet trade agreement, by making recognition the first, rather than the last, step in reaching a general agreement. However, the continuation of the "friendly atmosphere" resulting from the act of recognition was dependent upon the ability of the two governments to adjust the differences

[11] Arthur Henderson, *Verbatim Record* of the Fifth Assembly of the League of Nations, Twenty-seventh Plenary Meeting, October 1, 1924, p. 6; *Labour and the Geneva Protocol* (London: Labour Party, 1925), p. 13.

[12] 182 *H.C.Deb.*, March 24, 1925, col. 342.

remaining from the conclusion of the 1921 Trade Agreement. For the latter purpose the Prime Minister sent to Moscow a complete statement of the disputed issues and, in return, received from the Soviet government its agreement to refer to an Anglo-Russian commission all of the details regarding such problems as debts and other subsidiary claims. Before proceeding to a settlement, the Prime Minister assured Parliament that so far as government credit was concerned, he had no intention of going any further than overseas credit, trade-facilities credit, and such things as had already, in principle, been approved by Parliament with regard to other countries.[13]

The second step in the Labour government's policy of achieving friendly relations was undertaken with the opening of treaty negotiations with the Soviet delegation in London. The task for the Labor government was a particularly difficult one as it had inherited from its postwar predecessors a number of political and economic issues which had continued to prevent a reconciliation with the Soviet government. As a result, the British negotiators had not only to clear away the disputes remaining from the civil war and intervention, but also to consider the current questions of Russian loans and credits. In view of the magnitude of the agenda, it was agreed that the proceedings of the conference would be facilitated by dividing the work among various committees which in turn would present their recommendations to the plenary conference. Accordingly, four committees were designated to deal respectively with: (1) debts, claims, and Russian credit in Britain, (2) commerce and navigation, (3) territorial waters, and (4) treaties contracted between Russia and Britain. It soon became evident that the most difficult problem for the committees would be that of reconciling the divergent views of the two delegations upon the questions of debts, claims, and credits. As a result, the consideration of these issues was removed from the first committee to the plenary conference itself.[14]

The British negotiators were determined that the Russians acknowledge and honor their prewar debts owed to the British government, since a repudiation on the part of the Russian government would create a precedent for Britain's other creditors. In addition, the British delegation was convinced that a satisfactory settlement of the "legitimate" claims of British citizens for property confiscated or loans repudiated by the Soviet government was an essential condition for the granting of a guaranty for a Russian loan. The Russian

---

[13] 169 H.C.Deb., February 12, 1924, cols. 768–69.
[14] Cf. the Prime Minister's account to Parliament, 175 H.C.Deb., June 30, 1924, cols. 911–12.

delegation, on the other hand, took a different view; and its objections to the conditions attached to the guaranty of a loan resulted in a complete deadlock in the negotiations. Since no agreement seemed possible, the head of the British delegation, Arthur Ponsonby, announced that the treaties would not be signed. However, the breakdown of the negotiations prompted a group of back-bench Labour members of Parliament to attempt a reconciliation between the views of the two delegations. In this process of informal diplomacy, they approached Ponsonby—and in turn the members of the Soviet delegation—with the object of arriving at a compromise formula acceptable to the two groups. As a result of their intervention, agreement was reached, negotiations were resumed, and the Anglo-Soviet treaties were successfully concluded.[15]

Immediately following the conclusion of the agreements, the Undersecretary of the Foreign Office, Arthur Ponsonby, informed Parliament that a general treaty and a separate commercial treaty had been agreed upon by the British and Soviet delegations.[16] According to the terms of the commercial treaty, the British government received "unconditional most-favored-nation treatment" for British commerce and coastal trade in return for admitting Russia to the Export Credits Scheme. Under the general treaty, Great Britain obtained Russia's promise to pay three important classes of British claimants. The Soviet government admitted liability for the claims of British bondholders and provided the assurance of negotiation. "Miscellaneous claims" were to be investigated and a "lump sum" agreed upon. With regard to property claims, both sides were to appoint members to a committee which would investigate the claims and reach a decision as to compensation. Both the questions of government debts and interventionist claims were set aside by mutual agreement. The Undersecretary emphasized the fact that the general treaty was in the nature of an agreement "in principle," and was to be followed by a second treaty which would embody the decisions reached on Russia's liability for all of the different categories of debts and claims. With the satisfactory conclusion of this second treaty, the British government would submit to Parliament a financial reso-

[15] The Labour M.P.'s who played an important part in this episode included E. D. Morel, R. C. Wallhead, Jack Mills, W. Mackinder, Susan Lawrence, George Lansbury, A. A. Purcell. Cf. "How the Anglo-Soviet Treaty Was Saved," *Foreign Affairs*, V (September 1924), 51–52.

[16] Cf. General Treaty Between Great Britain and the U.S.S.R., signed at London, August 8, 1924; Treaty of Commerce and Navigation Between Great Britain and the U.S.S.R., signed at London, August 8, 1924, *British State Papers*, Cmd. 2260, 2261 (1924).

lution and a bill guaranteeing the interest and the sinking fund of a loan to the Soviet government. The amount, the conditions, and the employment of this loan would be determined by parliamentary authority. In the meantime, the present treaties, signed by the British government, would remain for twenty-one parliamentary days subject to the necessary sanction of the House of Commons.[17]

As soon as the Anglo-Soviet treaties were presented to the House of Commons it became evident that upon this issue the Labour government would meet a parliamentary defeat. Until this time, the Liberal party had not challenged the Labour government's policies in the field of international affairs. However, on the very day that the treaties were announced, it appeared that the Liberals would join forces with the Conservatives in order to prevent the ratification of the agreements. At the outset, it had not been certain that the Liberal party as a whole would endorse such a plan, as the initial attack from the Liberals in the House of Commons had been primarily the work of Lloyd George.[18] But no doubt remained after Liberal party headquarters issued a pamphlet denouncing "The Sham Treaty," and former Prime Minister Asquith added his condemnation to that of Lloyd George, thus uniting the two main wings of the party in opposition to the treaties.[19] The culmination of the Liberal party's campaign against the government's Russian policy was reached with the decision of Asquith to submit to Parliament a motion rejecting the adoption of the treaties.[20]

In spite of the combined disapproval of the Liberals and the Conservatives, the Labour party was united in its determination to support the treaties. Most of the criticism directed against the treaties was based upon an objection to either negotiating with the Russians or promising to guarantee them a British loan.[21] In reply to these attacks of the Opposition, the Labour party insisted that its plan for reaching an agreement with the Russians was, in fact, a continuation of the policy initiated by the Lloyd George Coalition government with the negotiation of the Anglo-Soviet Trade Agreement. This agreement, according to its preamble, had been regarded by that government as a preliminary to a general peace treaty regulating the economic and political relations between Great Britain and the Soviet Union. This

[17] 176 *H.C.Deb.*, August 6, 1924, cols. 2012–18.

[18] Cf. *ibid.*, cols. 3031–36; August 7, 1924, cols. 3175–83.

[19] Birch Crisp, "The Russian Treaty and the Liberals," *Foreign Affairs*, VI (October 1924), 78–79.

[20] Text, *Daily Herald*, October 2, 1924, p. 1.

[21] Cf. Asquith letter to *The Times*, September 22, 1924, p. 12.

objective of a general peace treaty with the Russians had been further pursued, but to no avail, by Prime Minister Lloyd George at The
Hague and again at Genoa. The precedent for negotiating with a Bol-
shevik government which had not paid its foreign debts had thus been
set by the leader of the Liberal party with the approval of the Conservatives supporting the Coalition government.[22] Therefore, to
attack the Anglo-Soviet treaties as a "sham, settling nothing and leading to nothing"[23] was to repudiate the objective of the 1921 treaty
and to disregard the advance made upon the achievement of that
agreement. The present treaties were to be considered merely as a
step toward the next stage of Anglo-Soviet negotiations, which would
come when the amounts due to the various British claimants were
settled by the Soviet government. Then, and only contingent upon a
satisfactory settlement, would the proposed loan guaranteed by the
British government be submitted for parliamentary approval.[24] If
the Opposition parties refused to allow the continuation of the Soviet
negotiations, as provided in the present treaties, the Labour government would accept the challenge in Parliament and appeal to the
country.

The Labour government was not to have the opportunity of defending the Soviet treaties against the motion of rejection submitted
by the Liberal party. Before the motion could be considered in Parliament, the government was defeated on an issue of domestic politics—
the "Campbell case"—by a vote of censure carried by the Liberal and
Conservative parties.[25] The Prime Minister, therefore, decided not
to wait for the forthcoming debate on the ratification of the Soviet
treaties, as the outcome had already been determined by the withdrawal
of the Liberal party's support from the government. MacDonald
accepted the defeat on the vote of censure and dissolved Parliament
in preparation for a General Election. He hoped that an appeal to
the country would result in the return of a sufficient number of Labour
members to constitute a parliamentary majority independent of Liberal

[22] J. R. Clynes at Manchester, *Daily Herald*, September 18, 1924, p. 5.
[23] "The Sham Treaty," *The Times*, September 16, 1924, p. 10.
[24] Arthur Ponsonby, *The Anglo-Soviet Treaties* (London: Labour Party, Can
Labour Rule Series, No. 6, 1924), p. 1.
[25] Cf. 172 *H.C.Deb.*, October 8, 1924, cols. 581–619. The government was cen-
sured for the withdrawal of criminal proceedings instituted by the Director of Public
Prosecution against the editor of *Worker's Weekly*. The charge against Campbell—
circulating subversive propaganda for the purpose of inciting the armed forces—was
investigated by the government and later withdrawn. The Liberal motion called for
a select committee "to investigate and report upon the circumstances leading up to
the withdrawal of the proceedings." The government took the view that the case
was closed with the withdrawal of proceedings.

support. It would then be possible to secure the necessary sanction of the House of Commons for the Anglo-Soviet treaties.

In its "Appeal to the People," the Labour party pointed out that in the field of international affairs it had continually worked for "peace among the nations" and "the restoration of industry and commerce." On that basis, it had refused to exclude from its policy of "general pacification" the Russian people. Labour believed it essential, in the interests of the unemployed and of the country as a whole, that trade be resumed with Soviet Russia. It was now for the people to decide whether this work for peace and prosperity would be allowed to continue.[26] The attention of the electorate, however, was soon distracted from the program presented by the Labour party. Toward the conclusion of the electoral campaign, all other issues were suddenly overshadowed by the publication of the so-called "Zinoviev letter." The letter, containing detailed instructions for inciting revolution in Britain, was alleged to have been written to the British Communist party by Zinoviev, the president of the Communist International and a leading member of the Russian Communist party. The revelation of an international Communist conspiracy in Great Britain at the height of the Labour party's campaign for closer relations with Soviet Russia was to ensure the defeat of the Labour government and with it the Anglo-Soviet agreements. Although defeat had come, in Parliament on the "Campbell case," and in the General Election on the "Zinoviev letter," the real issue in both instances had been the opposition of the Liberals and the Conservatives to the Labour government's relations with the Soviet Union.

When the Labour government resigned from office at the end of 1924, it had already achieved much of the foreign-policy program to which it had been committed. In the international field it had engaged in a "new" diplomacy which resulted in the substitution of good will and co-operation for the hostility and antagonism of the postwar world. The embittered relations between France and Germany had been greatly improved and cordial relations with France firmly established. Germany's economic recovery had been initiated by the provision for an international loan under the Dawes plan and its political equality given recognition at the London Conference. Important steps had been taken toward enlarging and strengthening the League of Nations: the admission of Germany and Russia had been proposed, and a plan for achieving arbitration and security had been adopted. The call for a general disarmament conference had been initiated at

[26] "Labour's Appeal to the People," October 29, 1924, *Report of the Twenty-fourth Annual Conference of the Labour Party*, 1924, p. 194.

Geneva; and as proof of its own willingness to disarm, the Labour government had halted the construction of the Singapore naval base. Diplomatic relations had been resumed with Russia, and progress had been made toward the achievement of a general settlement with that country. The democratization of foreign policy had been implemented by the practice of "open diplomacy" and by the undertaking to reveal to the House of Commons all treaties involving national obligations.[27] The complete realization of Labour's foreign-policy program, by the necessary sanction for the ratification of the Geneva Protocol and the Anglo-Soviet treaties, was precluded by the results of the General Election.

[27] Foreign-policy resolution, *Report of the Twenty-fifth Annual Conference of the Labour Party*, 1925, p. 252.

5

MISSED OPPORTUNITIES

After the General Election the Labour party returned once more to the ranks of the Opposition. This time, however, the party reverted to its former position with a new approach and attitude. The party had behind it the experience and the prestige of governmental responsibility. The period in office, brief though it was, had given Labour the opportunity of implementing the foreign policy which it had formulated and consistently advocated while in the Opposition. The achievements of the government in the international field were sufficiently notable for Labour to dispel, with some basis, the charge of its opponents that in foreign affairs it had no constructive alternative program. From its administrative experience, the Labour party had gained a working knowledge of the governmental machinery for conducting foreign affairs and an acquaintance with the international conditions which necessarily limit the application of a government's foreign policy. With this background, the Labour party felt more competent to judge the efforts of its successors in the sphere of international relations. In addition, the Labour party could derive some satisfaction from the results of the recent General Election. Although it had failed to obtain a parliamentary majority and had, in fact, lost a considerable number of seats in the House of Commons, its popular support in the country had been increased by over a million votes. The Liberal party, having precipitated the election by withdrawing its support from the government, had suffered the most serious defeat and its losses had been turned into Conservative gains in terms of parliamentary seats. As a result of this new alignment of parties, Labour, in the Opposition, could not hope to defeat the foreign policy of a government based upon an overwhelming Conservative majority in the House of Commons. At the most, it could attempt, by proposing an alternative program, to influence the conduct of the government's foreign policy and the decision of the country in the next General Election.

Of immediate concern to the Labour party, after relinquishing office, was the disposition of its security plan by the Baldwin administration. The Geneva Protocol was to have been under the consideration of the members of the League Council during the session scheduled for December of 1924. On the basis of its recent accession to office, however, the British Conservative government pleaded that the question should not be raised at the Rome session of the Council in order that the new cabinet might be allowed additional time to consider the terms of the Protocol before arriving at a conclusion on the matter. Regarding the request as a valid one, the Labour party continued to hope that the Conservative government, committed to a pledge of support for the League of Nations, would consent to the final ratification. However, its apprehension steadily increased as months passed without any decision on the part of the government. During this interval, Labour renewed its campaign for the adoption of the Protocol. All sections of the Labour movement urged the country to do everything in its power to obtain the acceptance of the principles of the Protocol on the ground that it furnished "the only practical plan for obtaining disarmament and substituting arbitration for war as the method of settling disputes."[1] British Labour joined the international labor and socialist movement in a warning that if the Protocol were not ratified and the disarmament conference were not held, the nations would be driven to seek security in special treaties which would increase the danger of war.[2]

The Labour party also viewed with serious alarm the rapid deterioration of the Allied reconciliation with Germany, which was taking place while the British government was holding up the adoption of the Protocol. It recalled the good feelings between the Allies and Germany which had been fostered at the London Conference, with the reparations settlement, and at the Fifth Assembly of the League, with the decision to admit Germany to full membership and the agreement to consider German disarmament as a part of the whole problem of world disarmament. This reconciliation with Germany had been made possible by the simultaneous provision for a security system, under the Protocol, to meet the demands of France. Now, however, if the British government were to reject the obligations of the Protocol, the French government would be deprived of a sense of security and would be reluctant, therefore, to encourage the recovery of Germany. In addition, without the British ratification of the Protocol, the necessary condition for the proposed disarmament conference would not be fulfilled. The Allies would have failed to meet their own commitments to disarm in accordance with the Covenant and the Versailles Treaty, and Germany would be convinced that her arma-

[1] Resolution of the National Committees of the Labour Party and the T.U.C., January 25, 1925, *Report of the Twenty-fifth Annual Conference of the Labour Party*, 1925, p. 61.

[2] Resolution of the Bureaux of the L.S.I. and I.F.T.U., Brussels, January 3–4, 1925, *ibid.*, p. 342.

ments were the only ones to be restricted. The doubts and fears caused by the British government's hesitations had already resulted in a crisis between the Allied Powers and Germany over the fulfillment of Germany's disarmament obligations under the peace treaties. The Allied Powers, through the Commission of Control, had recommended the prolongation of the occupation of the First Rhineland Zone, which was to have been evacuated after five years, on the basis of the charge that Germany had not faithfully carried out the conditions of the treaties with regard to disarmament.[3] The Allied decision to postpone the evacuation of the Rhineland was condemned by British Labour as a "breach of faith" hindering the "consolidation of peace." The party demanded a "return to legality" by the immediate evacuation of the First Zone and the inclusion of Germany in the League of Nations.[4]

The Labour party was aware that if the British government decided not to accept the Protocol, it would have to agree to another method of meeting the French demand for security in order to maintain the friendship of France and her co-operation in the recovery of Germany. Even before announcing its decision on the Protocol, the government had already begun to consider an alternative plan, suggested by the German government, for a Western security pact expressly guaranteeing the present territorial status on the Rhine. The Foreign Secretary conferred with the French government on the new proposals, and then proceeded to Geneva to inform the League Council that the British government could not accept the "excessive obligations" of the Protocol. Mr. Chamberlain was careful to add, however, that the British government was deeply concerned with the problems of arbitration and disarmament.[5] As the British government was obviously unwilling to shoulder the responsibilities involved in the Protocol, the only alternative for those powers concerned with their own security was to accept the British view that the best way of dealing with the security problem was to make "special arrangements" to meet "special needs." On this basis, Franco-British negotiations on the German proposal were resumed and a decision was reached

[3] Cf. Correspondence between the Ambassadors' Conference and the German Ambassador at Paris Respecting German Disarmament, Evacuation of the Cologne Zone and Modification in the Rhineland Regime, *British State Papers,* Cmd. 2527 (1925).

[4] Resolution of the Executive of the L.S.I., Brussels, January 4–6, 1925, *Report of the Twenty-fifth Annual Conference of the Labour Party,* 1925, p. 341.

[5] Statement by the Rt. Hon. Austen Chamberlain on behalf of His Majesty's Government to the Council of the League of Nations respecting the Protocol for the Pacific Settlement of International Disputes, Geneva, March 12, 1925, *British State Papers,* Cmd. 2368 (1925).

to meet with the other interested powers at Locarno for the purpose of concluding a security agreement with Germany.[6] The result of the deliberations at Locarno was the Treaty of Mutual Guarantee (Rhineland Pact) in which the signatory powers (Britain, France, Germany, Belgium, and Italy) guaranteed the inviolability of the existing Western frontiers and the demilitarized zone provided by the Treaty of Versailles. France and Germany were pledged to renounce war against each other and to settle their differences by pacific means, and Great Britain was designated (with Italy) as the guarantor of these provisions.[7] The successful conclusion of the Pact represented a victory for the traditional British view of security and for Mr. Chamberlain's efforts in converting the other signatory powers to that view.

The British government's rejection of the Protocol for "special arrangements" was attacked by the Labour party as a "retrograde step" encouraging a return to the "discredited and dangerous policy of limited alliances" which had led to the last war. The party declared that it was resolutely opposed to any separate pact of a military and permanent character which would result in dividing the world into armed camps. Throughout the entire period of the Locarno negotiations, from the receipt of the German proposal to the initialing of the Pact, Labour insisted that the Treaties of Locarno were "no compensation for the universal and more effective system of the Geneva Protocol."[8] In spite of these protests, the government was not deterred from the completion of its plans. Therefore, when the concluded Treaties were presented for parliamentary approval, the Labour party was confronted with a *fait accompli*. The Protocol had been scrapped by the British government, and the only remaining shred of hope for pacification in Europe while the Conservative government was in power was the Pact. The attitude of the Opposition toward

[6] For an account of the negotiations leading to the conference cf. Papers Respecting the Proposals for a Pact of Security Made by the German Government on 9th February 1925, *ibid.*, Cmd. 2435.

[7] The Locarno Pact contained a Final Protocol; Five Annexes including a Treaty of Mutual Guarantee, arbitration treaties between Germany and Belgium, Germany and France, Germany and Poland, Germany and Czechoslovakia; a Collective Note from the signatory powers to Germany on the League Covenant; treaties between France and Poland and between France and Czechoslovakia. Cf. Final Protocol of the Locarno Conference; Treaty of Mutual Guarantee between the United Kingdom, Belgium, France, Germany, and Italy, Locarno, October 16, 1925, *ibid.*, Cmd. 2525 (1925), 2764 (1926).

[8] Cf. 182 *H.C.Deb.*, March 24, 1925, cols. 293–305, 341–42, 398–401; 185 *H.C.Deb.*, June 24, 1925, cols. 1602–7, 1669; resolution of Bureau of L.S.I., London, July 4, 1925, *Report of the Twenty-fifth Annual Conference of the Labour Party*, 1925, p. 345; *L.S.I. Conference*, Marseilles, August 27, 1925 (London: Labour Party, 1925), p. 286; Ramsay MacDonald, *Protocol or Pact* (London: Labour Party, 1925), pp. 2, 6.

the concluded Pact was "there it is," and what can we, as a minority, do about it?[9] The fact that the government commanded a sufficiently large Conservative majority in the House of Commons ensured the approval of the Treaty regardless of the action of the Opposition. Nevertheless, the Labour party insisted upon expressing its doubts and anxieties by moving an amendment to the government's motion supporting the ratification of the Pact. While approving the various provisions for arbitration in the Treaties, the impending entry of Germany into the League of Nations, and the improvement of Franco-German relations evidenced at Locarno, the Labour Opposition saw little prospect of enduring peace on the basis of the Locarno Treaties.[10] For one reason, the agreements were "partial" and "sectional," thus contributing to the division of powers into groups potentially hostile. Russia was to remain outside; and the further isolation of Russia from the West would result in her being "thrown into the Asiatic orbit." The Treaty did not deal with the underlying causes of conflict beyond the Rhine frontier, and its methods could not be applied in Middle and Eastern Europe where such conflicts were likely to "burst out into war." The only security provided by the Pact was for the participating powers themselves, and the guarantor of that security was not the League of Nations but the British government, a signatory of the Treaty. The British government, which had repeatedly expressed its objections to accepting for its own part the principle of compulsory arbitration was committed to enforce this principle upon the other parties to the agreement. Even German security was questionable, with no safeguard against renewed attack by the Allied Powers under cover of enforcing the provisions of the Treaty of Versailles, and with the other European powers heavily armed. The real test of security was disarmament, and under the present Pact there was no provision for a general disarmament conference in which the Allies would fulfill their obligations in accordance with the Covenant and the peace treaties. At most, Labour regarded the Locarno Pact as a "first step" toward the ultimate aims of the Geneva Protocol—universal arbitration, disarmament, and security. However, as an alternative, the Locarno Treaty would be of no value whatsoever unless accompanied by a modification in the occupation policies of the Allied Powers and a "speedy" evacuation of the Rhineland and the Saar; the participation of Russia in European agreements and its

[9] H. M. Swanwick, "There It Is," *Foreign Affairs*, VII (December 1925), 158–59.

[10] The amendment moved by Ponsonby was defeated, 332–130. 188 *H.C.Deb.*, November 18, 1925, col. 465.

inclusion in the League of Nations; the conclusion of compulsory arbitration treaties between all states; and the establishment of a general conference to deal with the question of universal disarmament.[11]

With the ratification of the Locarno Pact the Labour party was forced to concede that, for the present at least, the Geneva Protocol was dead. As far as Labour was concerned, the Protocol remained the ultimate objective of its foreign policy, and it refused to accept as a satisfactory substitute a limited or partial arrangement. However, the party realized the futility of attempting to convert the government to the virtues of the Protocol as against the Pact. The only hope, while the Conservative government remained in power, was that the Locarno Pact would be only a "first step," followed by other measures to complete the security of Europe. Although the government had rejected the Protocol, it had, at the same time, pronounced approval for the aims of arbitration and disarmament. There was some basis, therefore, for the Labour party's belief that it might yet be possible to convince the government of the necessity for going beyond the limits of Locarno. Supplemented by the changes suggested by the Labour party, the Locarno Pact would achieve the objectives of the Protocol.

The Labour party's desire to supplement the Locarno Treaty was apparently shared by the French government, which also was aware of the inadequacies of a system of partial security. The British government, however, showed no intention of progressing beyond the limited guaranties undertaken in the Pact, and from all indications, regarded the security problem as settled at Locarno. The Labour party continued to urge the government to abandon "sectional understandings" and to take a "bold initiative" toward the establishment of a scheme of international security guaranteed by the League of Nations.[12] While the British government remained opposed to the assumption of "extended and dangerous obligations,"[13] the French government resumed its search for security in other directions. In the attempt to find additional guarantors for her security, France turned to the United States with the proposal for a treaty "outlawing war." The United States responded favorably, on the condition that the pact be a multilateral one, and a draft of the proposed treaty was submitted to the British

[11] *Ibid.*, cols. 435–47, 530–34; resolution of Executive Committee of L.S.I., London, November 6, 1925, *Report of the Twenty-sixth Annual Conference of the Labour Party*, 1926, p. 321; resolution of the U.D.C., November 2, 1925, *Foreign Affairs*, VII (December 1925), 182.

[12] Motion of censure, 208 *H.C.Deb.*, July 11, 1927, cols. 1761–62.

[13] Government amendment moved by Duff Cooper against Labour motion of censure, 210 *H.C.Deb.*, November 24, 1927, col. 2173.

government for consideration. The Labour party welcomed the note on the "elimination of war from national policy," dispatched by the American Secretary of State, and urged the British government to accept it "in principle" without delay.[14] Labour felt that such a declaration, as contained in the note, would make it impossible for the nations to threaten war. The Kellogg Proposal was a "new gesture," capable of pulling the League of Nations out of "the old militarist rut of criticising negatively every proposal for peace."[15] Believing a gesture to be insufficient, however, the Labour party pointed out that the note contained no provision for its own application. It suggested, therefore, that the Pact should be made a "really effective instrument for the maintenance of world peace" through the acceptance by all powers of a procedure for the pacific settlement of international disputes, and that the sincerity of the "outlawry of war" by the powers should be demonstrated by their acceptance of measures for "drastic disarmament."[16]

It was evident from the British government's reply to the Kellogg Proposal that it had no intention of accepting "without reservations."[17] Instead of making the Pact a "really effective instrument," the government attached a series of "declarations regarding signature," which had the effect of greatly weakening the original proposals. In the first place, the government insisted that the Treaties of Locarno, the League Covenant and "certain regions of the world" remain unaffected by the new agreement. As Britain had given "ungrudging support" to the League of Nations and had undertaken the "burden" of the guaranty embodied in the Locarno Treaty, it would not agree to any treaty which would undermine these engagements. In addition, as the welfare and integrity of certain regions of the world constituted a "special and vital interest" for the peace and safety of the British Empire, interference with these regions would not be "suffered"; and their protection against attack would be regarded as a measure of "self-defence." The British government would accept the proposed pact upon the explicit understanding that it did not restrict or impair in any way the right of self-defense, and that "each State alone" would be competent to decide when circumstances necessitated recourse to war for that purpose. Before consenting to ratification, the government

[14] Resolution of National Executive Committee, *Report of the Twenty-eighth Annual Conference of the Labour Party,* 1928, p. 43.

[15] Ramsay MacDonald's address to British Commonwealth Labour Conference, July 2, 1928, *ibid.,* p. 305.

[16] Resolution of General Council of T.U.C. and National Executive of Labour Party, June 26, 1928, *ibid.,* p. 43.

[17] As suggested by Ramsay MacDonald, 217 *H.C.Deb.,* May 10, 1928, col. 446.

added the final observation that with regard to participation in the Pact, "universality" would be difficult of attainment, and might even be "inconvenient," because there were some states whose governments had not yet been universally recognized. Although the reference was obviously made with the intention of excluding the Soviet Union from the declaration renouncing war, the government did not press the matter and concluded that it was, after all, a "minor question as compared with the attainment of the more important purpose in view."[18] The British government therefore joined the other original signatory powers at Paris, and the Pact for the "outlawry of war" was signed and opened for further ratifications.[19]

The government's conditional acceptance of the Kellogg Pact was condemned by the Labour party as an "international disaster." It accused the government of paying "lip-service" to the cause of international peace while placing every possible obstacle in the way of attaining it. In the light of the British reservations, the original proposal for the "unqualified renunciation of war" had lost much of the "purity" and "simplicity" insisted upon in the Kellogg note. The British "Monroe Doctrine," claiming freedom of action in certain regions of the world, was held to be not only inconsistent with a pact outlawing war but contrary to Article XI of the League Covenant. Self-defense, although undefined, had been recognized as a legitimate excuse for war. If the government intended to give to the expression self-defense a very wide and elastic interpretation, it would be able to construe any interference with certain unspecified regions as a threat to the British Empire. The government had thus set the example of proclaiming a "Monroe Doctrine," and as a result, would bear a heavy responsibiilty for the expression of similar claims of special and vital interests by the other signatory powers. The Labour party hoped that, in spite of the many reservations, the declaration to renounce war and to settle disputes by pacific means might still have "some moral value." However, if there was any real intention behind the declaration, it would have to be supplemented by a definition of "war," of "aggression," and of "self-defense." The test of the effectiveness of the Pact would be whether it was followed by the adoption of a system of all-inclusive arbitration and a policy of general disarmament.[20]

Within a few days of the signing of the Kellogg Pact, a spokesman of the British government announced that the "renunciation of war"

[18] Correspondence with U.S. Ambassador Respecting the U.S. Proposal for the Renunciation of War, *British State Papers,* Cmd. 3109, 3153 (1928).

[19] Cf. text of International Treaty for the Renunciation of War as an Instrument of National Policy, Paris, August 27, 1928, *ibid.,* Cmd. 3410 (1929).

[20] 220 *H.C.Deb.,* July 30, 1928, cols. 1816–18, 1860.

would make no difference in the government's building program and defense measures.[21] Apparently, the "outlawry of war" had not affected the government's attitude toward the question of disarmament. The Labour party noted, with "profound disappointment," that the government had been pursuing an armaments policy based upon the assumption that the Covenant of the League of Nations, the Locarno Treaty and the Kellogg Pact had contributed nothing to the security of the world. Labour recalled the eloquent defense by members of the Baldwin government of the plea that there could be "no disarmament without security."[22] However, it also recalled that after the adoption of the Locarno Treaty the government had announced that security had been achieved. On this basis, therefore, the government was pledged to a policy of promoting disarmament. To repudiate such an obligation was to acknowledge the inadequacy of its own conception of security. In addition, if the government was sincere in its assertion that there also could be "no security without disarmament," then it was committed to supplement the Locarno and Paris pacts by supporting a general disarmament convention. The Labour party emphasized the "very serious responsibility" of the Conservative government in pursuing in a "pre-War spirit" a policy which had prevented any progress toward disarmament since the end of 1924.[23]

Since its resignation from office, the Labour party had repeatedly urged the government "to do everything in its power to promote the holding of a World Disarmament Conference."[24] One of the main provisions included in the Geneva Protocol had been the preparation for an international conference on disarmament. However, the Conservative government, in discarding the Protocol, had also prevented the meeting of the conference, as specified by the Protocol, in June of 1925. As soon as it had become evident that the government was determined to substitute "special arrangements" for a universal security system, the Labour party had demanded that such special pacts should not be used to hinder any measures of disarmament established under the control of the League of Nations.[25] While the Locarno Pact did

[21] Quoted by Norman Angell, "Behind These Failures," *Foreign Affairs*, XI (October 1928), 2.

[22] Cf. Report of the British Delegates on the Sixth Assembly of the League of Nations, *British State Papers*, Cmd. 2576 (1926).

[23] *Report of the Twenty-fifth Annual Conference of the Labour Party*, 1925, p. 252; I.L.P. Conference, April 12, 1925, *New Leader*, April 17, 1925, pp. 14–15.

[24] Ramsay MacDonald, *Report of the Twenty-eighth Annual Conference of the Labour Party*, 1928, p. 183.

[25] Arthur Henderson, *Second Labour and Socialist International*, Marseilles, August 22–27, 1925 (London: Labour Party, 1925), p. 286.

not actually hinder disarmament, it did not in any way further its realization. The most that the signatories had conceded was their "firm conviction" that the Pact would "hasten on effectively" the disarmament provided for in the Covenant and their "sincere co-operation" to the work relating to disarmament already undertaken by the League of Nations.[26] Even this commitment, however, was not being carried out by the British government. While negotiating the Pact, the government had, at the same time, submitted to Parliament an enlarged program of naval shipbuilding. Instead of "hastening" the reduction of armaments, the British government, by increasing its naval construction, had "flagrantly violated" the Covenant of the League and the preamble to Part 5 of the Versailles Treaty.[27] Under Article VIII of the Covenant, the League members had also undertaken "to interchange full and frank information as to the scale of their armaments." However, at the Geneva Conference on Traffic in Arms and Munitions, the British government had "whittled away" the original Draft Convention.[28] The British delegation, the only one which consisted almost entirely of military experts, had insisted upon inserting a crippling amendment excluding from the scope of the convention "ships of all kinds designed exclusively for war, with their armaments" (including submarines and submersibles) and also airships and airplanes.[29] Having succeeded in weakening the final Draft Convention, the British government nevertheless refused to consent to its ratification.[30] When the League Assembly attempted to implement Article VIII of the Covenant by requesting the Council to make "preparatory arrangements" for a conference on the reduction of armaments, the British representatives on the Third Committee, instead of giving the League the "sincere co-operation" promised at Locarno, opposed the convening of a disarmament conference as "premature." The British delegation, deprecating raising hopes of actual

[26] Cf. Final Protocol of the Locarno Conference, *British State Papers,* Cmd. 2525 (1925).

[27] Lt. Cmdr. J. M. Kenworthy, M.P., "The Naval Policy of the British Government," *Foreign Affairs,* VII (September 1925), 64.

[28] For conference proceedings cf. International Conference on the Control of the International Trade in Arms, Munitions, and Implements of War, Geneva, May 4–June 7, 1925, League of Nations, *Documents,* A.13, 1925, ix.

[29] The amendment was carried as regards vessels of war and their armaments, and a new article was inserted providing for certain information to be published—more limited, however, than in the case of other armaments. C. R. Buxton, "Arms Traffic, Arms Manufacture and Arms Abolition," *Foreign Affairs,* VII (July 1925), 18–19.

[30] Labour demanded that the government "ratify the Convention on Traffic in Arms and Munitions and take steps with a view to the projected Convention on the Manufacture of Arms being completed and ratified without delay." *Report of the Twenty-seventh Annual Conference of the Labour Party,* 1927, p. 236.

disarmament before "moral" disarmament was attained, insisted that the Council make a "preparatory study" rather than the "arrangements" for such a conference.[31] In accordance with the resolution of the Assembly, as amended to meet the British objections, a "Preparatory Commission" began its "study" the following year, "with a view to a Conference on the Reduction and Limitation of Armaments."[32]

The Labour party soon became impatient with the "slow progress" made by the Preparatory Commission. It urged the British government to bring before the commission "precise plans for the drastic reduction of its own armaments" with the object of inducing the other governments to make corresponding offers, and thus facilitate the holding of a world disarmament conference "without delay."[33] The government, however, showed no inclination to "take the lead" suggested by the Labour Opposition.[34] Instead, the British representatives on the Preparatory Commission even opposed the fixing of a date for the projected disarmament conference. The British government finally responded to the Assembly's warning to the Preparatory Commission to "hasten" the completion of the technical work so that the disarmament conference might be convened before the Eighth Assembly[35] by submitting to the commission its own draft convention as a basis for discussion. When the French government followed the British with a counterproposal, it proved impossible for the commission to reconcile the views contained in the two drafts. Not only were the participating powers at odds with each other, but the British delegation itself was sharply divided. According to the chief delegate, Viscount Cecil, there was a "fundamental difference" between his view and that of the cabinet as a whole as to the "importance" of the effort to reach an international agreement on the reduction and limitation of arms. The members of the cabinet were not opposed to it, Cecil claimed, "but they did not think it mattered much." The representatives of the Admiralty "scarcely concealed their indifference, if not their hostility," and Cecil was unable to convince the cabinet of the advisability of "taking a stronger line" with the technical advisers.[36] As a result of the deadlock

[31] League of Nations, *Official Journal*, Special Supplement 36, Records of the Sixth Assembly, Minutes of the Third Committee, September 1925.

[32] For proceedings of first session cf. Report to the Council of the League of Nations on the Work of the First Session of the Preparatory Commission for the Disarmament Conference, *British State Papers*, Cmd. 2681 (1926).

[33] Executive Committee resolution, *Report of the Twenty-sixth Annual Conference of the Labour Party*, 1926, p. 254.

[34] Motion of censure, 208 *H.C.Deb.*, July 11, 1927, col. 1873.

[35] Resolution adopted by the Seventh Assembly on the proposal of the Third Committee, September 24, 1926, League of Nations, *Documents*, A.40, 1927, ix.

[36] Cecil also differed with the cabinet on the proposals contained in the British convention, 69 *H.L.Deb.*, November 16, 1927, col. 88.

reached in the proceedings, the Preparatory Commission was compelled to adjourn for an indefinite period.[37]

The Labour party blamed British policy for creating the existing deadlock in the preparatory negotiations and for diminishing the chances of the success of a disarmament conference. It held that the opposition of the British government to any limitation of the expenditure on armaments or of the equipment of modern armies, and to any effective international supervision of the observance of limitation was a "serious drawback" to the conclusion of an adequate treaty of disarmament.[38] The government's "general reactionary attitude" had hindered any progress by the League of Nations: the Preparatory Commission was "no nearer to changing anything than when it had first started its deliberations."[39] The Labour party demanded that the Preparatory Commission continue its meetings in public session until a draft convention was completed for presentation to the General Disarmament Conference, and it laid down the necessary provisions for an "effective" disarmament treaty. Such a treaty would limit the personnel of all armed forces, including trained reserves; the number of conscripts to be called up year by year and the period of instruction; the store of arms and munitions which individual states might hold in readiness for war; the number of heavy guns, tanks, and fighting aircraft; navies both in respect of their aggregate strength and of the various categories of ships; and the expenditure of each state on its armed forces. It would provide for the international supervision of the enforcement of these limitations, for the national and international supervision of the manufacture, trade, and transport of war matériel, and for the international control of civil aviation. Labour called upon the members of the government to "abandon their opposition" by announcing their readiness to effect an "immediate all-round drastic reduction of armaments, as part of a plan of total disarmament by successive stages."[40]

[37] Cf. Report of the British Representative on the Preparatory Commission of the League of Nations for the Disarmament Conference, *British State Papers,* Cmd. 2888 (1927).

[38] Chairman's address, F. O. Roberts, and Executive Committee resolution, *Report of the Twenty-seventh Annual Conference of the Labour Party,* 1927, pp. 168, 236.

[39] Resolution moved by Arthur Ponsonby, I.L.P. Conference, April 10, 1928, *New Leader,* April 13, 1928, p. 15.

[40] Executive Committee resolution, *Report of the Twenty-eighth Annual Conference of the Labour Party,* 1928, pp. 183–84. Dalton, Brockway, and Lansbury at the L.S.I., Brussels, August 5–11, 1928, supported a resolution demanding that the work of the Preparatory Commission be "accelerated" and a disarmament conference summoned "as soon as possible." *Ibid.,* p. 332. Also cf. Labour motions against estimates, 214 *H.C.Deb.,* March 12, 1928, col. 1607; March 15, 1928, col. 2200; 225 *H.C.Deb.,*

The British government, however, was unwilling to undertake such a comprehensive program as that suggested by the Labour party. Instead of attempting to break the deadlock in the Preparatory Commission and thus facilitate an international agreement on general disarmament, the government preferred a more limited approach to both the scope of the agenda and the number of participants. Consequently, it welcomed the suggestion of the United States for a Three-Power Naval Conference at Geneva to consider the extension of the principles adopted at the 1921 Washington Naval Conference with regard to the ratio in different classes of ships or "in other important ways." In accepting the invitation, the government attached the condition that the "special geographical position" of the British Empire "must be taken into account." The government was confident that the three powers would succeed in concluding a naval limitation pact, whereas all of the powers in the League Preparatory Commission had failed in producing a general disarmament treaty. However, the government failed to anticipate that even a three-power conference with a limited agenda could fail for lack of adequate diplomatic preparation and agreement.[41]

When the conference opened at Geneva, it was apparent that there had been no previous discussions and that the experts had come armed with their own plans based upon the assumption that naval limitation must not be allowed to alter the effective fighting positions of their respective navies. The initial optimism of the governments over the prospects of naval limitation rapidly gave way to despair, for it proved impossible to reach any compromise on the irreconcilable claims submitted by each set of experts. The failure of the conference, according to the chief British delegate, was brought about by the government's insistence upon a "six-inch gun" and its refusal to concede "mathematical parity." The government thought that it would be "most dangerous" to have stated in the treaty that the United States was entitled to mathematical parity in auxiliary vessels; and it "preferred no agreement to one embodying that principle." When the cabinet decided "to insist upon a six-inch gun, even if it meant the breakdown of the negotiations," Cecil said, he chose to resign from the British delegation. He felt that the government had, against his "most earn-

February 28, 1929, col. 2270; 226 *H.C.Deb.*, March 7, 1929, col. 675; March 14, 1929, col. 1389.

[41] The original U.S. suggestion was for a five-power naval conference, but France considered the proposal unacceptable because it threatened to compromise the success of a general disarmament plan and weaken the League of Nations by depriving the Preparatory Commission of a part of its program. Cf. John Wheeler-Bennett, *Disarmament and Security Since Locarno* (New York: Macmillan, 1932), p. 108.

estly expressed protests," taken a course which had caused the failure of such "vitally important negotiations."[42]

The Labour party agreed that the failure of the Three-Power Naval Conference was a "serious setback to the cause of peace in the world." It charged that the British government had caused the breakdown of the conference by its "reactionary demand" for seventy cruisers,[43] which was an actual increase in tonnage, and that it had brought about the resignation of Viscount Cecil by its "general reactionary attitude."[44] To the Labour party, the unfortunate result of the Three-Power Conference was "proof" of the ineffectiveness of disarmament discussions unless they were preceded by agreements for the settlement of possible disputes. It called, therefore, upon the government to reopen negotiations with the United States with a view to the settlement of all outstanding questions between them including the control of the sea in time of war and a "drastic" reduction of naval armaments.[45] If the government could not agree with America upon the limitation of naval armaments, how could the Continental military powers be expected to reduce their armaments? If Britain and the United States failed to agree, it was also doubtful if the League of Nations Disarmament Conference could have much success so far as naval armaments were concerned.[46]

The government did not attempt either to reopen negotiations with the United States or to persuade the Continental powers in the Preparatory Commission to reduce their armaments. Rather, it turned to France for a bilateral agreement recognizing their respective naval and military needs.[47] The Labour party attacked the Anglo-French "compromise" as "an agreement not to limit armaments," conceding to Britain the cruiser program denied at the Three-Power Conference and to France the land armaments refused at the League of Nations Preparatory Commission. Such an agreement would have a "disastrous effect" upon the United States, which had already rejected British naval demands as "unacceptable"; and it would prevent the resumption of the Anglo-American naval discussions. In addition, the new *"entente cordiale"* was denounced as a violation of the British govern-

[42] 69 *H.L.Deb.*, November 16, 1927, cols. 89, 91–93.

[43] Cf. Austen Chamberlain, 209 *H.C.Deb.*, July 27, 1927, cols. 1246–50.

[44] *Report of the Twenty-eighth Annual Conference of the Labour Party*, 1928, p. 183.

[45] *Report of the Twenty-seventh Annual Conference of the Labour Party*, 1927, p. 236.

[46] Lt. Cmdr. J. M. Kenworthy, "The Geneva Naval Conference," *Foreign Affairs*, IX (August 1927), 39–40.

[47] Chamberlain admitted the negotiations with France but not the contents. Cf. 220 *H.C.Deb.*, July 30, 1928, cols. 1837–38.

ment's commitments under the Locarno Treaty to guarantee the security of Germany as well as of France, and to give "sincere co-operation" to the disarmament work undertaken by the League of Nations.[48]

The failure of the disarmament efforts at Geneva reaffirmed the Labour party's conviction that it was impossible to dissociate disarmament from arbitration and the "sense of security."[49] The same conclusion was accepted by the League Assembly when it convened following the deadlock reached in both the Preparatory Commission and the Three-Power Conference. The realization of the relationship of arbitration, security, and disarmament led some of the League members, including France, to attempt a revival of the Geneva Protocol as the most effective means of establishing the security necessary for the achievement of disarmament. However, to forestall this attempt, the British Foreign Secretary made it clear at the outset that Britain had no intention of going beyond the security guaranties already provided in the Locarno Treaty. Obviously it was impossible for the League to restore the Protocol without the co-operation of the British government. However, it was also impossible to continue the disarmament negotiations without the creation of a greater feeling of security. Therefore, a compromise resolution was proposed by the Assembly's Third Committee which, while not reviving the original Protocol, recognized the dependence of disarmament upon arbitration and security. The League Assembly, in accordance with this resolution, agreed to the appointment by the Preparatory Commission of a special committee (Arbitration and Security) to consider "the measures capable of giving all States the guarantees of arbitration and security necessary to enable them to fix the level of their armaments at the lowest possible figures in an international disarmament agreement."[50] The relationship was thus acknowledged by the League Assembly. It remained for the new committee to produce, and the League members to adopt, the measures of arbitration and security deemed

[48] Ramsay MacDonald, *Report of the Twenty-eighth Annual Conference of the Labour Party*, 1928, pp. 185–87. Labour supported a censure motion condemning the "compromise" as endangering "peace in Europe" and "good relations with the United States." However, the Prime Minister and Lord Cushendun denied any commitment to France. Cf. 222 *H.C.Deb.*, November 13, 1928, cols. 721, 738–55; 72 *H.L.Deb.*, November 7, 1928, cols. 61–78.

[49] Ramsay MacDonald regarded the breakdown at Geneva as a "natural failure," for without a security agreement disarmament would not be achieved. 210 *H.C.Deb.*, November 24, 1927, cols. 2089–96.

[50] Arbitration, Security, Disarmament and the Work of the Preparatory Commission for the Disarmament Conference, Report and Draft Resolution Submitted by the Third Committee to the Assembly, Eighth Ordinary Session of the Assembly of the League of Nations, League of Nations, *Documents*, A.108, 1927, ix; A.124, 1927, ix.

essential for the further progress of the Preparatory Commission toward an international disarmament agreement.

Arbitration had been the foundation of the Labour party's program for peace and security. It had, when in office, rejected the Draft Treaty of Mutual Assistance as inadequate regarding arbitration and had attempted to substitute the more comprehensive scheme embodied in the Geneva Protocol. Since 1924, it had reaffirmed its support of the principle of all-inclusive pacific settlement, repeatedly urging the government to accept that same principle.[51] It had declared its own readiness to sign the Optional Clause and to conclude treaties of arbitration with any country, and had submitted to the Labour and Socialist International a model convention of all-inclusive pacific settlement.[52] Therefore, it welcomed the demand made by the members of the League of Nations for the revival of the principles of the Protocol and the decision of the Assembly to consider arbitration and security as a means of attaining international disarmament. However, it realized that since the Conservative government had hitherto neglected every opportunity for advance beyond the position of the Covenant, substantial progress toward a scheme of universal arbitration was unlikely so long as that government remained in power.[53] No fewer than six opportunities had been offered for closing the gaps in the Covenant, wholly or partially, and the Conservative government had rejected five of them and "compromised" the sixth. The policy of the government had been, first of all, to reject the obligation of compulsory arbitration contained in the Geneva Protocol. At Locarno, in spite of the fact that the government had "preached" arbitration to France and Germany, it refused to accept arbitration for itself. When Switzerland had turned to Britain for a bilateral treaty of all-inclusive pacific settlement, the offer had been declined and the same response

[51] Cf. Arthur Henderson, *Second Labour and Socialist International*, Marseilles, August 27, 1925 (London: Labour Party, 1925), pp. 260, 285; Executive Committee resolution, *Report of the Twenty-fifth Annual Conference of the Labour Party*, 1925, p. 252; Arthur Ponsonby, *Now Is the Time* (London: Parsons, 1925), p. 185; I.L.P. Conference, February 13, 1926, *New Leader*, February 19, 1926, pp. 8–9; Executive Committee resolution, *Report of the Twenty-sixth Annual Conference of the Labour Party*, 1926, p. 254; Labour motion of censure, 208 *H.C.Deb.*, July 11, 1927, cols. 1761–62; Executive Committee resolution, *Report of the Twenty-seventh Annual Conference of the Labour Party*, 1927, pp. 235–36; *Labour and the Nation* (London: Labour Party, 1928), pp. 10, 41; Hugh Dalton, *Towards the Peace of Nations* (London: Routledge, 1928), p. 131.

[52] The L.S.I. Congress, Brussels, August 5–11, 1928, adopted a resolution demanding "that all international disputes should be submitted to compulsory arbitration . . . or peaceful settlement." *Report of the Twenty-eighth Annual Conference of the Labour Party*, 1928, p. 332.

[53] Labour Party, *Arbitrate! Arbitrate! Arbitrate!* (London: 1926), p. 12.

had been made to similar proposals by Sweden, Holland, and Spain.[54] The government had neglected to subscribe to the Optional Clause in the instrument establishing the Permanent Court of International Justice—a refusal to surrender the right of private war even for legal disputes with states that would accept compulsory arbitration— although it was committed by a League resolution to settle disputes "of every description" by pacific means.[55] In signing the Kellogg Pact, the government had "compromised" the significance of a declaration "renouncing war" for pacific settlement by reserving, at its own discretion, the right to resort to war for the defense of certain unspecified regions of the world.[56] In view of this record, Labour believed that the Conservative government's attitude toward the pacific settlement of disputes would constitute "the principal obstacle to the extension of the movement for arbitration."[57]

The sixth and final opportunity for closing the gaps in the Covenant was presented to the British government by the Arbitration and Security Committee, which had been established by the Preparatory Commission in accordance with the resolution of the Eighth Assembly. In response to the questionnaire outlining the proposed work of the committee and circulated to the League members, the British government set forth its observations on the further development of arbitration, security, and pacific settlement of international disputes. With regard to arbitration, the government pointed out that there were "limits" beyond which a state could not go in accepting binding obligations. In the government's opinion, the time hardly seemed "ripe" for any general system of sanctions for the enforcement of arbitration treaties. Sanctions should be operated by "knitting together the nations most immediately concerned." Britain had already guaranteed the regions where her "particular interests" were "most vitally affected." She was, therefore, unable to contract further obligations and extend the "tremendous responsibilities" involved in regions where her interests were "less directly concerned." As to the Optional Clause in the Statute of the Permanent Court of International Justice, the

---

[54] Charles Trevelyan, 208 *H.C.Deb.*, July 11, 1927, col. 1877; Chairman's address, F. O. Roberts, *Report of the Twenty-seventh Annual Conference of the Labour Party*, 1927, p. 168.

[55] The resolution had been unanimously adopted by the Eighth Assembly, September 24, 1927, League of Nations, *Documents*, A.119, 1927, ix. The discrepancy was referred to by Ramsay MacDonald, 210 *H.C.Deb.*, November 24, 1927, cols. 2089–92.

[56] W. Arnold-Forster, "Arbitration: The Government's Record," *Socialist Review*, XXXVI (January 1928), 11–15.

[57] Executive Committee resolution, *Report of the Twenty-seventh Annual Conference of the Labour Party*, 1927, p. 236.

government could not agree to accept "definitively" the obligation to arbitrate justiciable disputes. It preferred bilateral to general treaties, and insisted that nonjusticiable disputes should be submitted to conciliation rather than to arbitration. However, even bilateral conciliation treaties, which provided that where the parties did not accept the recommendations of a conciliation commission the dispute should be referred to the Permanent Court of International Justice, should be "discouraged." In commending the need for reservations, the British government concluded that "time" was necessary to overcome the difficulties which had caused these "limitations," and that as the "sense of security" increased, it would become "more easy" for states—even for those whose interests were world-wide—to accept comprehensive engagements to arbitrate justiciable disputes.[58]

It was evident to the Labour party, as well as to the other members of the Arbitration and Security Committee, that in view of the British memorandum, the security provided by the Covenant was not accepted at its full value. The Labour party noted that over and over again there appeared in the memorandum a "rooted objection to the universality of the League's undertakings." The government would not agree "to go to law impartially" with every state willing to accept an equal obligation because it had to take into account "the nature of its general relations with that State." The government regarded the Locarno Treaty as the "ideal type" because it resembled the "old-fashioned treaties" in that it was particular and not universal like the League Covenant. The idea that "particular interests" were to determine whether states resorted "to war or to law" was held to "cut at the very root of the League." The Labour party condemned the Foreign Secretary's "theme of the beauties of elasticity" which made him prefer the politically minded League Council, even for the settlement of justiciable disputes, to a legally minded court of arbitration or of justice. It concluded that "the whole of this deplorable document" had been inspired by the government's desire to avoid as far as possible "any definite obligation to go to law"; to "maintain war as an instrument of national policy"; to favor "certain Powers for particular reasons" instead of co-operating with "all law-abiding peoples"; and to "preserve and widen every loophole" through which "anarchic force" could find a way. If, as the government insisted, "time" was necessary for increasing the respect for international law and the sense of security, how, Labour asked, was the respect for international law to get stronger if Britain refused to strengthen it by frank ad-

[58] Memorandum on Arbitration and Security, *The Times*, January 19, 1928, p. 11.

herence, and how was security to be increased unless the threat of war was abandoned once and for all?[59]

In view of the reservations expressed by the British government in its memorandum, the Arbitration and Security Committee was compelled to exclude from its proposed work the preparation of a general arbitration convention binding upon all members of the League. As a compromise between the attitudes of Britain and the other members of the League, including France, who desired a strengthened arbitration and security system, the committee concluded a series of "model" treaties of conciliation, arbitration, nonaggression, and mutual assistance. Before the treaties were submitted to the League Assembly, the Labour party commented that it seemed extremely unlikely that their adoption would substantially increase security or even facilitate the work of the Preparatory Commission, since they were not general treaties, nor did they provide for unconditional compulsory arbitration, nor did they fill the gaps left by Article XV of the League Covenant.[60] However, when the Ninth Assembly received the model treaties, it agreed to significant modifications which actually met most of Labour's criticisms of the original work of the Arbitration and Security Committee. In spite of the opposition to amendment voiced by the British delegation in the Third Committee, the Assembly succeeded in combining the three multilateral draft conventions (A, B, and C) for arbitration and conciliation into one General Act providing for: the arbitration of nonlegal disputes (A), the judicial settlement or arbitration of disputes of a legal character (B), and the settlement of disputes by conciliation (C). This modification made it possible for states to adhere to the General Act as a whole, and thereby accept the pacific settlement of every kind of international dispute. The General Act, unlike the model treaties, would come into force between any two or more states as soon as they had accepted it, as a whole or in part, to meet their special needs, and would remain open indefinitely to the adherence of all states. The remaining draft treaties were approved by the Assembly and recommended to states as models for adoption. While the British government would have preferred to see the arbitration treaties also remain as models, and not open for signature, it withdrew its opposition to the modifications proposed by the Third Committee when it became evident that approval by the League Assembly did not obligate the members to adhere to the treaties.

[59] H. M. Swanwick, "Elasticity or Rot, a Commentary on the British Government's Memorandum on Arbitration and Security," *Foreign Affairs*, IX (March 1928), 263–64.

[60] "The Ninth Assembly," *ibid.*, X (September 1928), 43.

Although the government was urged by the Labour party to accept "without any reservations which would weaken the obligation to settle all disputes by pacific means,"[61] it refused to sign any part of the General Act of Arbitration, Conciliation, and Judicial Settlement. The Labour party reaffirmed its belief that further progress toward all-inclusive arbitration, and thus toward disarmament, was improbable as long as a Conservative government remained in control of British foreign policy.

In retrospect, the Labour party regarded the period of the Baldwin administration as a time of "missed opportunities" in the international field, when Britain might have played an active part in building up an effective League of Nations, but unfortunately failed to do so.[62] It appealed to the nation in 1929 on the basis of the respective foreign-policy records of the Conservative and Labour parties. Labour claimed that while in 1924 Britain was hailed as a "leader in world pacification," by 1929 she was regarded as "one of the principal impediments to it." The Conservative government, although professing a belief in international arbitration, had refused to commit itself to accepting the Protocol, the General Act, all-inclusive bilateral treaties, and the jurisdiction of the Permanent Court of International Justice. The government had hampered disarmament by obstructing the work of the League of Nations, conducted its negotiations for a naval agreement with the United States in such a manner as to compel its "most distinguished" representative to resign, and brought appreciably nearer a "ruinous competition" in armaments. By resorting to secret diplomacy with the Anglo-French "compromise," the Conservatives had seriously endangered Britain's relations with both Germany and the United States. Finally, "in order to give a semblance of discreditable life to the expiring legend" which had brought it into power, the government had severed diplomatic relations with Russia, and had terminated, "with injurious effects," its trade agreement.[63] In contrast, the Labour party would establish the "largest possible measure of political and economic co-operation among the nations." It would at once take steps to settle all outstanding differences with Soviet Russia, to resume diplomatic and commercial relations, and to encourage a revival of trade. The structure of peace and of Labour's foreign policy would be built upon the foundation of the League of Nations. It would be completed by the party's "six pillars of peace": the renunciation of

[61] Executive Committee resolution, *Report of the Twenty-eighth Annual Conference of the Labour Party*, 1928, p. 183.

[62] John Parker, *Labour Marches On* (Harmondsworth: Penguin Books, 1947), p. 21.

[63] Cf. chapter vi, pp. 71–72.

war, disarmament, arbitration, open diplomacy, economic and political co-operation. As Labour stood for arbitration and disarmament, it would accept the General Act and the Optional Clause, and would "press for the speedy completion" of a general disarmament treaty. The Labour party appealed to the country for approval to resume its work and to regain for Britain the "proud position" which it had held in 1924.[64]

[64] *Labour and the Nation*, pp. 10, 40–43; "Labour's Appeal to the Nation," May 30, 1929, *Report of the Twenty-ninth Annual Conference of the Labour Party*, 1929, p. 306.

6

SIX PILLARS OF PEACE

The Labour party was granted the opportunity to resume its work in the international field as a result of the General Election of 1929. The party succeeded in increasing its popular support by over three million votes, as well as its representation in the House of Commons. This election, in contrast with that of 1923, gave Labour a larger number of members of Parliament than the Conservative party.[1] However, Labour was still in a minority in the House of Commons, as the Liberals held a balance of fifty-seven seats. The Labour party, therefore, called upon the Liberals to provide the necessary parliamentary majority. Again, as in 1923, Ramsay MacDonald consented to the formation of a minority Labour government dependent upon the support of the Liberal party in the House of Commons. Although the Labour party was aware that dependence upon Liberal approval would mean the surrender of a socialist policy at home, it also realized that the alternative of refusing to form a minority government would mean the sacrifice of its international, in addition to its domestic, program. There was some basis for Labour's hope of Liberal support in the international field, in spite of the fact that the two parties had split in 1924 over the issue of Anglo-Russian relations. Since that time, they had co-operated to a considerable extent in opposition to the foreign policy pursued by the Conservative government.[2] An additional factor for Labour's optimism was the recently issued Liberal party program on "World Peace" endorsed by Lloyd George and Herbert Samuel. According to this statement, the Liberals were committed to many of the international policies advocated by Labour: the "complete suppression of war as a means of settling disputes between nations"; the acceptance of the Optional Clause and all-inclusive arbitration as the "most hopeful approach to the linked problems of security and disarmament"; the "immediate and stringent limitation and reduction of armaments" and the repudiation of any idea of competition in naval construction with the United States; the restoration of diplomatic and commercial relations with Russia; and the "whole-

[1] In 1929, Labour obtained 8,364,883 votes and 288 seats as compared with 4,348,379 votes and 191 seats in 1923.

[2] The Liberals and Labourites co-operated on a motion of censure against the Anglo-French naval "compromise." Cf. 222 *H.C.Deb.*, November 13, 1928, col. 721.

hearted support of the League of Nations as the arbiter of international peace and order, in preference to the basis of peace upon separate pacts, *ententes* and alliances."[3]

The Labour government had no intention of abiding by the principle of continuity, so far as its predecessors' foreign policy was concerned. Instead, its aim was continuity in the foreign policy which it had initiated in 1924 and advocated throughout the five-year period in the Opposition. The task for the new Labour government was a twofold one: to complete the international program which had been interrupted by its resignation from office at the end of 1924, and to settle the outstanding issues in the international field which had been inherited from the previous Conservative administration. Remaining from 1924 were the problems of arbitration, security, and disarmament, unsolved because of the repudiation of the Geneva Protocol, and relations with Russia, embittered by the rejection of the Anglo-Soviet treaties. Since that time, diplomatic relations with Russia had been severed, relations with the United States strained by the naval rivalry, reconciliation with Germany threatened by the Anglo-French "compromise," and international disarmament prevented by the deadlock in the Preparatory Commission and the failure to achieve a system of universal arbitration and security. The undertaking of this task was shared by Arthur Henderson, at the Foreign Office, and the Prime Minister himself, who took a personal interest and played an important role in the conduct of diplomatic negotiations. Henderson had had considerable administrative experience, serving in the Coalition war cabinet and as Home Secretary in the first Labour government. He had been active in the international socialist movement, and in recognition of his efforts in reconstituting the Labour and Socialist International after the war, had been elected president by the International Congress of 1923. Assisting Henderson at the Foreign Office, respectively as Undersecretary and Private Secretary, were Hugh Dalton and Philip Noel-Baker, both of whom had made significant contributions toward the formulation of the party's foreign-policy program.[4] In the Ministry were such leading Labour spokesmen on international affairs as Arthur Ponsonby, Charles Trevelyan, F. W. Pethick-Lawrence, H. B. Lees-Smith, Arthur Greenwood, Noel Buxton, J. R. Clynes, Herbert Morrison, and Emanuel Shinwell.

The Labour party came into office pledged to establish the "largest

---

[3] "Liberal Foreign Policy," *Foreign Affairs*, XI (May 1929), 123.

[4] Cf. Hugh Dalton, *Towards the Peace of Nations* (London: Routledge, 1928); Philip Noel-Baker, *The Geneva Protocol* (London: King, 1925), *League of Nations at Work* (London: Nisbet, 1926), and *Disarmament* (London: Hogarth, 1927).

possible measure of political and economic co-operation among the nations." One of the first steps which it undertook in fulfillment of this program was the resumption of diplomatic and commercial relations with Russia. Since the Labour party's resignation from office in 1924, relations with the Soviet Union had progressively deteriorated, beginning with the rejection of the treaties and culminating in the severance of diplomatic relations.[5] While in the Opposition, the Labour party had repeatedly challenged the government's policy with regard to Russia, demanding that negotiations and friendly relations be resumed. During the three years in which the government pursued a policy of neither breaking nor carrying on relations with the Russian government, the Labour Opposition persisted in its efforts to convince the government that the negotiation of the outstanding grievances between the two governments would lead to an economic agreement producing increased trade and commerce, and to full diplomatic relations contributing to the establishment of international peace.[6] The break with Russia finally came in 1927 when the government, after instigating a search of Arcos Limited, the Russian trading organization, and the Trade Delegation of the Russian government, charged the Soviet Union with "military espionage" and "subversive activities." The accusation was promptly followed by the government's demand for the termination of the trade agreement, the withdrawal of the Soviet Trade Delegation and Mission from London, and the recall of the British Mission from Moscow.[7] The Labour party condemned the government's raid on Soviet premises in London as "unjustifiable and fruitless" and demanded that the government's allegations be proved and the truth revealed by an examination of all relevant documents and a full inquiry into the facts. The termination of the trade agreement and the severance of diplomatic relations, Labour pointed out, would have "serious international consequences" and "close a promising avenue to the restoration of trade and industry." Through its Russian policy, Labour claimed, the government had

[5] Cf. Selections of Papers Dealing with the Relations Between His Majesty's Government and the Soviet Government, 1921–27, *British State Papers*, Cmd. 2895 (1927).

[6] Ramsay MacDonald, 203 *H.C.Deb.*, March 3, 1927, cols. 624–25; Arthur Ponsonby, "The Need of a Russian Settlement," *Foreign Affairs*, VI (March 1925), 196–98.

[7] 206 *H.C.Deb.*, May 24, 1927, cols. 1842–54. The way was prepared for a break by the government's note protesting against Soviet propaganda. Cf. Note from His Majesty's Government to the Government of the U.S.S.R. Respecting the Relations Existing Between the Two Governments, February 23–26, 1927; Documents Illustrating the Hostile Activities of the Soviet Government and the Third International Against Great Britain, *British State Papers*, Cmd. 2822, 2874 (1927).

"committed a wanton act of self-injury to British trade, introduced a new and disturbing issue in international relations, encouraged the spread of war alarms in Soviet Russia, and provoked serious counter-charges of espionage and other reprisals."[8] The Labour party promised that it would re-establish normal political and trading relations between Great Britain and Russia at the earliest possible moment "on the basis of reciprocal recognition of non-interference with each other's internal affairs." Labour, when in power, would again, as in 1924, "hold out the hand of friendship to the people of Russia."[9]

The opportunity of negotiating with Russia came in 1929. Shortly after the Labour government was formed, the cabinet decided that the Foreign Secretary should "take the matter in hand" and seek by conversations to lay down the conditions upon which a new treaty could be concluded. With the opening of conversations, the first point of procedure to be settled was the immediate exchange of ambassadors between the two countries. As preliminary conditions for the resumption of diplomatic relations, the Labour government insisted upon an exchange of reciprocal guaranties relating to propaganda and a mandate from the House of Commons.[10] As soon as an agreement on propaganda was reached, the government requested parliamentary approval of the procedure for the settlement of the questions outstanding between the two countries, including those relating to propaganda and debts. The sanction of the House of Commons was granted, but not without a protest from the Conservative Opposition "deploring" the failure to maintain the conditions laid down for the resumption of diplomatic relations. The Foreign Secretary assured the House that the guaranties relating to propaganda would be exchanged no later than the date on which each ambassador presented his credentials, and that with the consent of Parliament both of the conditions preliminary to the restoration of diplomatic relations would be fulfilled. As a result of the conversations, the government had received "a very definite commitment" from Russia that all forms of debts and claims would be negotiated immediately upon the resumption of diplomatic relations. This time, however, the government did not recommend to Parliament that it "pledge the credit of the British taxpayer to any loan raised by the Soviet Government."[11] Consequently, the censure

[8] Motion of censure, 206 *H.C.Deb.*, May 26, 1927, col. 2195.

[9] Executive Committee resolution, *Report of the Twenty-seventh Annual Conference of the Labour Party*, 1927, p. 236; Chairman's address, George Lansbury, *Report of the Twenty-eighth Annual Conference of the Labour Party*, 1928, p. 154; *Labour and the Nation* (London: Labour Party, 1928), pp. 10, 43.

[10] Cf. Correspondence Regarding the Resumption of Relations with the Government of the U.S.S.R., *British State Papers*, Cmd. 3418 (1929).

[11] Arthur Henderson, 231 *H.C.Deb.*, November 5, 1929, cols. 895–910. The Con-

of the Conservative Opposition was limited to condemning the "careless drafting" of the protocol of agreement.[12]

The Labour government's mandate for restoring diplomatic relations with Russia was fulfilled before the end of 1929 by the formal exchange of ambassadors between the two governments.[13] With the conclusion of this first point of procedure, negotiations were begun on the settlement of the questions relating to propaganda and debts. During the course of the negotiations, the government was convinced by the rank and file of the Labour party of the "vital importance" of doing "everything within reason" to facilitate trade in view of the grave state of unemployment, particularly in the heavy industries, and the "imperative need" for new markets for British goods. The government was requested to explore every avenue which would lead to increased trade with the Soviet Union and to arrange a commercial agreement "at an early date" in order that such trade might be placed "on a stable basis."[14] Accordingly, the government was influenced toward "pushing forward" a temporary commercial agreement, to serve as a *modus vivendi* pending the completion of a full treaty of commerce and navigation, and a temporary agreement with regard to fisheries. The effect of the Commercial Pact was the exchange of reciprocal "most-favored-nation" agreement with respect to commerce and national treatment, increased export credit facilities for Russian trade, and the establishment of a Soviet trade delegation in London.[15] The government's action was assured of parliamentary support in view of the attitude of its own party and the commitment of the Liberal party to reverse the decision of the preceding administration severing relations with Russia. Nevertheless, the Conservative Opposition continued its protest against the government's policy and, during the period between the signature of the protocol of agreement and the commercial *modus vivendi*, raised almost seven hundred parliamentary questions regarding the negotiations with the Soviet Union. The gov-

servative amendment to the government motion seeking parliamentary approval was defeated 324–199, the Liberals supporting the government.

[12] 233 *H.C.Deb.*, December 18, 1929, col. 1447. The Conservatives' second censure motion was defeated 254–107.

[13] Cf. Notes Exchanged on the Occasion of the Resumption of Diplomatic Relations with the U.S.S.R., London, December 20, 1929, *British State Papers*, Cmd. 3467 (1929).

[14] Motion on "Trade with Russia" submitted by Ellen Wilkinson and carried by the government, 243–139. 234 *H.C.Deb.*, February 5, 1930, col. 1923.

[15] Temporary Commercial Agreement Between His Majesty's Government in the United Kingdom and the Government of the U.S.S.R., London, April 16, 1930; Temporary Fisheries Agreement Between the Government of the United Kingdom and the U.S.S.R., London, May 22, 1930, *British State Papers*, Cmd. 3553, 3583 (1930).

ernment, however, refused to be deterred from a policy which, it claimed, had already resulted in an increased export trade and improved relations between the two countries. It was determined to promote friendship with Russia because it was the policy of the Labour government to do everything within its power "to facilitate and expedite the highest possible standard of good relations with all countries."[16]

Labour's policy of securing peace through international co-operation was also directed toward seeking a reconciliation between Germany and the Allied Powers. The Labour party had consistently supported the political and economic recovery and the restoration of Germany, with full equality, to the community of nations. For that reason, it had welcomed the evacuation of the First Rhineland Zone by the Allied troops, the admission of Germany to the League Council, the Preparatory Commission for the Disarmament Conference, the Locarno Agreements and the Pact of Paris, and the appointment of a "Committee of Experts" to prepare a final settlement of reparations. It had noted with concern, however, the Anglo-French "compromise" and the serious repercussions of such an agreement upon relations with Germany. To ensure the good will of Germany, the Labour party had advocated the ending of the *"entente fraternelle"* with France, the complete settlement of the reparations issue, the "immediate and unconditional" withdrawal of all foreign troops from the Rhineland, and the disarmament of the Allied Powers in fulfillment of their pledges to Germany under the peace treaties. The achievement of this program, Labour believed, would result in the reconciliation of Germany and the general pacification of Europe.[17]

When the Labour party came into office, it was enabled to carry out its reparations and Rhineland policies by the completion of the Young plan by a committee of independent financial experts presided over by the American member, Owen D. Young. The proposed plan, as submitted for the consideration of the governments concerned, concluded the process of transferring reparations from the political to the economic sphere begun with the Dawes plan, by the final reduction and fixation of the German debt, by the establishment of a progressive

---

[16] Arthur Henderson, 239 *H.C.Deb.*, June 6, 1930, cols. 2626–31.

[17] As early as 1922, the British, French, German, Italian, and Belgian socialists had formulated proposals regarding "the final settlement of the Reparations Problem in connection with the debt problem; the withdrawal of the foreign troops from the Rhine; and disarmament by sea, land and air, which were subsequently confirmed by Congresses of the entire International at Hamburg (1923) and Brussels (1928)." Resolution of Executive Committee of L.S.I., Zurich, July 28–29, 1929, *Report of the Thirtieth Annual Conference of the Labour Party*, 1930, p. 313.

scale of annuities, and by the provision of a bank for international settlements replacing the Allied Reparations Commission and offering facilities for the collection and transmission of the German annuities.[18] After careful consideration, the Labour government announced that it felt unable to accept the recommendations of the Young committee in their entirety. It could accept the experts' proposals with regard to the amount of the German annuities and the method and condition of payment. It could accept the constitution of the proposed international bank and agree to the connection between debts and reparations. But it could not agree to the experts' proposal that in the distribution of the German annuities the rights of Great Britain under existing agreements should be altered to the detriment of that country.[19] Supported in its policy by the other major political parties,[20] the Labour government attempted to obtain agreement to a modification of the plan during the international conference convened at The Hague to give effect to the report of the Young committee.

Since the issues before The Hague Conference were both financial and political, the Labour government was represented by the Chancellor of the Exchequer, Philip Snowden, and the Foreign Secretary, Arthur Henderson, who participated respectively in the committees set up to deal with the two sets of questions before the conference. The financial negotiations were the most difficult task for the conference since they involved an alteration of the Young plan to comply with the views of the British government. The Chancellor of the Exchequer recapitulated the position of the British delegates, emphasizing that they objected to the alteration of the percentages of German annuities accorded to Great Britain at the Spa Conference (1920), the distribution of unconditional and conditional payments to the disadvantage of Britain, and the provision for deliveries in kind harmful to British trade. Under the proposed scheme, Snowden pointed out, Britain would lose £200,240,000 a year; and no allowance would be made for the arrears of £200,000,000 due to Britain from her debtors, which Britain had paid to the United States before receiving any payment of Allied debts. The British government was prepared to "wipe the slate clean" of all international debts and reparations, as promised in the Balfour Note (1922); but so long as reparations and debts were payable, Britain would insist upon "being fairly treated in this matter."[21]

[18] Cf. Report of the Committee of Experts on Reparations, *British State Papers*, Cmd. 3343 (1929).

[19] Arthur Henderson, *Report of the Twenty-ninth Annual Conference of the Labour Party*, 1929, p. 208.

[20] Cf. 230 *H.C.Deb.*, July 26, 1929, cols. 1667–90.

[21] Snowden gave Parliament a complete account of the government's position

The British objections were met by a compromise arrangement increasing the total payments and unconditional annuities due to Britain, restricting the deliveries in kind, and guaranteeing the payment of certain annual sums toward the Allied debt owed to Britain. With this modification of the Young proposals, the conference was able to conclude the financial agreement for the final settlement of German reparations.[22] The British government was convinced that the "momentary and temporary disagreements and misunderstandings" which had "obscured the real issues of the Conference" would "not survive the settlement reached," but, on the contrary, would "strengthen good relations."[23]

The political questions concerning the evacuation of the Rhineland necessarily depended to a considerable extent upon the progress made in the financial sphere. Consequently, it was only when agreement was reached on the financial issue that it was possible finally to complete the political agreements which had been prepared. The Foreign Secretary had made it known at an early stage of the conference that the British government was insistent upon the withdrawal of its troops from the Rhineland and felt that the time had come for the complete evacuation of German occupied territory. Although French opinion differed from British opinion on this matter, the conciliatory policies pursued by the French Foreign Minister, M. Briand, and the German, Dr. Stresemann, facilitated an accord upon the political issues before the conference. As a result, an agreement was adopted for the complete evacuation of the Rhineland by the troops of the Allied Powers. The withdrawal of British troops and the evacuation of the Second Zone would be concluded before the end of 1929; the Third Zone would be free of all occupation forces in June of 1930. By that date, five years in advance of the period of occupation specified by the Versailles Treaty, there would not be a single soldier in any of the occupied parts of German territory.[24] The British Foreign Secretary emphasized the "real importance" of the evacuation arrangements' being obtained not piecemeal, not by each power acting singly, but through the common agreement of all concerned. By this "great act of reconcilia-

---

before the opening of the conference. Cf. 229 *H.C.Deb.*, July 9, 1929, cols. 683–85; 230 *H.C.Deb.*, July 26, 1929, col. 1667.

[22] Cf. Protocol with Annexes Approved at the Plenary Session of The Hague Conference, August 31, 1929; Agreements Concluded at The Hague Conference, January 1930, *British State Papers*, Cmd. 3392 (1929), 3484 (1930).

[23] Ramsay MacDonald, League of Nations, *Official Journal*, Special Supplement 75, Records of the Tenth Ordinary Session of the Assembly, Third Plenary Meeting, September 3, 1929, p. 33.

[24] Cf. International Agreement for the Evacuation of the Rhineland Territory, The Hague, August 30, 1929, *British State Papers*, Cmd. 3417 (1929), 3796 (1931).

tion," the powers participating in The Hague Conference had "at long last taken the final step for bringing the world war to an end."[25]

The Labour government was satisfied that the co-operation of the European powers and the participation of Germany as an equal partner in The Hague settlements had contributed toward a Franco-German reconciliation and had ended the notion of an exclusive Anglo-French entente. As evidence of the good will resulting from the agreements, the French Foreign Minister, after the conclusion of the conference, suggested the establishment of a "bond of solidarity" among the European nations which would enable them "to get into touch at any time, to confer about their interests, to agree on joint resolutions and, if need be, to meet any grave emergency."[26] The favorable response of the German Foreign Minister and the interest indicated by twenty-six European states who were members of the League[27] encouraged M. Briand to submit to the European powers on May 17, 1930 (the date on which the Young plan and the last stage of Rhineland evacuation came into operation), a proposal for the organization of a European federal union.[28] In reply to M. Briand's memorandum, the British government expressed its "fullest sympathy" with the endeavor to "promote closer co-operation among the nations and Governments of Europe, and thus strengthen the safeguards against another European war." It agreed with M. Briand that it was "primarily in respect of economic relations" that European association was "urgently to be desired."[29] As to the methods proposed by the French for the realization of their purpose, Britain felt that the machinery required for the promotion of closer co-operation should be League machinery, without incurring the risks and difficulties which a system of new and independent institutions might involve. An "exclusive and independent European Union of the kind proposed might emphasise or create tendencies to inter-continental rivalries and hostilities" which it was "important in the general interest to diminish and avoid." Moreover, the British government was inclined to believe that the purpose which

[25] Arthur Henderson, League of Nations, *Official Journal*, Special Supplement 75, Records of the Tenth Ordinary Session of the Assembly, Seventh Plenary Meeting, September 6, 1929, p. 57.

[26] *Ibid.*, Sixth Plenary Meeting, September 5, 1929, p. 52.

[27] The British delegate, William Graham, referred in complimentary terms to what had been said about a United States of Europe by Briand and Stresemann, stressed the importance of European economic unity, and proposed a two-year tariff holiday. *Ibid.*, Tenth Plenary Meeting, September 9, 1929, pp. 79–81.

[28] Cf. text in Despatch to His Majesty's Ambassador in Paris Enclosing the Memorandum of the French Government on the Organization of a System of European Federal Union, *British State Papers*, Cmd. 3595 (1930).

[29] Cf. Ernest Bevin's resolution for European economic unity, *Report of the Fifty-ninth Annual Conference of the T.U.C.*, 1927, pp. 391–96.

the French government had in view could be effectively secured by so adapting the proposals put forward in the memorandum as to bring them fully within the framework of the League of Nations.[30]

The British government's view of the Briand plan, shared by the other League members, was reflected in a resolution submitted to the Assembly by the French government on behalf of the delegations of forty-five member states. The resolution, as adopted by the Eleventh Assembly, recognized that close co-operation between the governments of Europe in every field of international activity was "of capital importance for the preservation of peace"; and that such co-operation, whatever form it might assume, "should be within the framework of the League of Nations, in complete accord with the League and in the spirit of the Covenant." The governments of the European members of the League were invited to participate in a commission of inquiry to pursue the study which had already been begun with the circulation of the Briand memorandum and to prepare "definite proposals" for submission to the next League Assembly. The commission, duly constituted under the presidency of M. Briand, included in its membership the foreign ministers of the principal European powers. The British Foreign Secretary expressed the hope that as a result of the discussions for securing a full and complete examination of this important question and preparing a detailed scheme, any final decision would be taken "only on the authority of the League of Nations." Henderson believed that whatever course was adopted should permit the governments to satisfy themselves on two points: that the final plan proposed would be "wholly consistent" with the international obligations undertaken in the Covenant and that the plan would facilitate the disarmament policy of the League of Nations.[31]

Although the Labour government sympathized with French efforts to increase European co-operation and strengthen the guaranties against war, its immediate concern was not the creation of new machinery but the more effective operation of that which already existed. It was convinced that within the framework of the League Covenant, as supplemented by the Pact of Paris, it was possible to achieve security through the fulfillment of the obligations with regard to the pacific settlement of disputes and the reduction and limitation of armaments. The League had thus far been unable to accomplish its prime task—a

[30] Reply from the British Government, July 16, 1930, League of Nations, *Documents*, Relating to the Organization of a System of European Federal Union, A.46, 1930, vii, pp. 52–53.

[31] League of Nations, *Official Journal*, Special Supplement 84, Records of the Eleventh Ordinary Session of the Assembly, Fourth Plenary Meeting, September 11, 1930, p. 40.

general disarmament agreement—because the nations had not been willing to reduce their armaments without adequate guaranties of security. It was the Labour government's belief that the acceptance of obligatory and comprehensive arbitration would be "the greatest of all factors" in providing the security which would enable the powers to disarm in accordance with Article VIII of the Covenant. Only through arbitration, Labour insisted, would it be possible "to take the next step towards real security from war"—the step which would be taken when a general treaty of disarmament was finally concluded.[32]

The Labour party had always stood for the principle of arbitration in international disputes. While in office, it had supported the adoption of the Geneva Protocol and in the Opposition had consistently attacked the Conservative government for its "backwardness" in accepting compulsory arbitration. For that reason, the Labour government decided to make a "complete break with the Conservative past" by declaring its intention of signing the Optional Clause in the statute of the Permanent Court of International Justice. Labour regarded the acceptance of the Optional Clause as the "logical consequence" of the commitment under the Pact of Paris that the settlement of international disputes should never be sought except by pacific means. The Optional Clause had removed the "defects" in the prewar conventions of pacific settlement by conferring upon the Permanent Court jurisdiction in all international disputes which could be settled by means of law and by eliminating the requirement of a special agreement for the submission of the dispute. Adherence to the Optional Clause was an obligation to accept the jurisdiction and the verdict of the Permanent Court. Moreover, with regard to justiciable disputes, a signatory state was no longer free to refuse to allow a dispute to go before the Court if another party which had also signed the Clause desired to obtain a legal verdict. The Labour government believed that a general acceptance of the Clause by all members of the League of Nations would be a "most powerful factor" in international security against war and the "surest way of giving a new direction in international relations."[33]

Before fulfilling the pledge of ratification contained in its Electoral Manifesto and its Address from the Throne, the Labour government, in accordance with the principle of parliamentary control of foreign policy, requested the approval of the House of Commons. The gov-

[32] Arthur Henderson, *ibid.*, 75, Records of the Tenth Ordinary Session of the Assembly, Seventh Plenary Meeting, September 6, 1929, p. 58.

[33] Declaration Made on Behalf of His Majesty's Government in the United Kingdom at the Time of Signature of the Optional Clause, Geneva, September 19, 1929, *British State Papers*, Cmd. 3421 (1929).

ernment was criticized for having signed the Optional Clause at all, for having excluded too many classes of disputes from the Court's jurisdiction, or for not attaching enough reservations to acceptance. Although the Conservative party had itself refused to accept the Clause, its chief concern, according to its amendment against the government's motion for approval, was that ratification should be subject to the additional reservation relating to the Laws of War on Sea, "as being absolutely necessary to safeguard the freedom of action of the British Navy."[34] In reply to the criticisms of the Opposition, the government insisted that the three classes of disputes excluded from the declaration of acceptance—those arising prior to ratification, those falling exclusively within domestic or Commonwealth jurisdiction, and those in which the parties preferred to resort to the League Council or other methods of peaceful settlement before the dispute reverted automatically after twelve months to the Court—were "wholly reasonable and proper" reservations. As to the reservation suggested by the Conservative party, the government believed that the Council of the League was "most suited" to deal with naval action. The question came, therefore, under the reservation already attached regarding the suspension of the Court's jurisdiction whenever a "better settlement" might be obtained by the dispute's being handled under the "conciliatory spirit" of the League Council. In addition, the government maintained that the ordinary arguments against submitting British naval action to arbitral decision had ceased to be relevant to any discussion of the Optional Clause, since it had been established under the Covenant and the Pact of Paris that a member of the League did not possess any right to carry on commerce with a state with which the League was at war and, therefore, was no longer obliged to rely on the old rules governing the relations of belligerents and neutrals. In other words, as between members of the League there could be no neutral rights because there could be no neutrals. So far as the Labour government was concerned, its "whole policy" was based upon a determination to comply with its obligations under the Covenant of the League and the Pact of Paris.[35]

The Labour government's signature of the Optional Clause had given a "fresh impetus" to the cause of arbitration. When it had announced its intention to sign, only some nineteen states had ratified their signatures; by the time that ratification had been approved in

[34] 234 H.C.Deb., January 27, 1930, cols. 653, 666. The amendment was defeated and the government motion accepted, 278–193.

[35] Memorandum on the Signature of His Majesty's Government in the United Kingdom of the Optional Clause of the Statute of the Permanent Court of International Justice, *British State Papers*, Cmd. 3452 (1929).

Great Britain, twenty-six states had completed their ratification and sixteen others had signed the Clause with the intention of ratification. Although the Labour government regarded the acceptance of the Optional Clause as a "great step forward," it was only a beginning. The Clause covered only those classes of disputes which lent themselves to settlement by the application of recognized rules of international law; hence there remained that class of disputes which was not amenable to those methods and which, failing settlement by the League Council, might lead to war. The government looked forward to the acceptance by all states of the principle that disputes not only of a justiciable nature but of every kind should be settled by pacific means. The solution of that further problem required the acceptance of means for the peaceful settlement of all classes of disputes as an alternative to the war forever renounced under the Pact of Paris.[36]

The discrepancy between the renunciation of war under the Pact of Paris and the recognition of the right to engage in war under the Covenant had been viewed by the Labour party as one of the chief obstacles to the further extension of a system of all-inclusive arbitration. The Labour government was anxious that the Kellogg Pact should be not only a "declaration on paper," but "translated into constitutions and institutions" that would ensure pacific settlement as the alternative to war. Therefore, it suggested to the League Assembly, at the same time that it announced its intention to sign the Optional Clause, that the "dead wood" should be "pruned" out of the Covenant in order to bring it into line with the Kellogg Pact by which nations had renounced the right of private war.[37] The amendments proposed by the British delegation were directed toward closing the gaps in the Covenant by eliminating the right of resort to war recognized as legitimate in Article XIII, "three months after the award by the arbitrators or the judicial decision or the report of the Council," and in Article XV, if the Council failed to reach a report unanimously agreed to by the members not parties to the dispute. The Assembly responded favorably to the British lead in agreeing to the examination of the terms of the Covenant, recognizing the right of League members to have recourse to war, with a view to modification. In accordance with the British resolution, reports on the amendments to the Covenant were prepared by a Committee of Eleven (Jurists) and by the First (Legal and Constitutional) Committee of the Assembly and submitted

[36] Arthur Henderson, League of Nations, *Official Journal*, Special Supplement 84, Records of the Eleventh Ordinary Session of the Assembly, Fourth Plenary Meeting, September 11, 1930, p. 41.

[37] Ramsay MacDonald, *ibid.*, 75, Records of the Tenth Ordinary Session of the Assembly, Third Plenary Meeting, September 3, 1929, p. 34.

to the governments of the members of the League for their observations.[38]

The discussion of the proposed amendments to the Covenant produced a protest from the Conservative Opposition against the commitment of the British government "to an extension of the obligations
under Article XVI of the Covenant in a manner which would be welcomed by most of the nations of Europe as a reinsurance of their own
security at the cost of the British Empire." The Conservative view
was that Britain had already undertaken the "formidable obligation"
to apply sanctions only against a nation which resorted to war without
submitting its dispute to investigation and report during the period
specified by the Covenant. Under the proposed amendments, however,
Article XVI would legally come into force against any nation which
resorted to war in "any circumstances"; and that was a "much wider
obligation" than the Conservatives cared to assume. They might be
willing to undertake the obligation to institute economic sanctions in
the first case, where they might "reasonably" refuse to bind themselves
to use them in the second.[39] The Labour government, on the other
hand, accepted the judgment of the League Committee of Eleven that
the amendments to Articles XII, XIII, and XV would not, in practice,
add to the burden of the obligations contracted by League members
under Article XVI of the Covenant. The proposed amendments were
aimed at securing the pacific settlement of disputes with greater cer-
tainty and more effectively; to that extent they would reduce the possibility of war and thereby the burden of sanctions.[40] Hence, the
British delegation announced its intention of acceptance and expressed
the hope that the other members of the League Assembly would consent to the adoption of the proposed amendments. If that were done, it
would take out of the Covenant the right of legitimate private war
which under its present stipulations still remained. War would then
become in law what in morality it had always been, "an international
crime against mankind at large."[41]

In fulfillment of its policy of strengthening the provisions for the

[38] Cf. Papers Regarding Proposed Amendments of the Covenant of the League
of Nations in Order to Bring It into Harmony with the Pact of Paris of 27th of
August 1928, September 1929–November 1930, British State Papers, Cmd. 3748
(1930).

[39] Lord Lothian, letter to The Times, February 20, 1930, p. 15; and reply by
Viscount Cecil, ibid., February 25, 1930, p. 15; Austen Chamberlain, letter, ibid.,
February 27, 1930, p. 15.

[40] Cf. Report of the Committee of Eleven, League of Nations, Documents, A.8,
1930, v.

[41] Arthur Henderson, Report of the Twenty-ninth Annual Conference of the
Labour Party, 1929, p. 208.

pacific settlement of disputes contained in the League Covenant, the Labour government played an important part at Geneva in the preparation of the Convention for Financial Assistance and the General Convention to Improve the Means of Preventing War. Although the latter convention was not actually completed until after the resignation of the Labour government, its progressive development from the status of a model treaty was primarily due to the efforts of the British delegation. The original suggestion for a General Convention to Improve the Means of Preventing War had been made by the German government to the Arbitration and Security Committee for the purpose of "strengthening" the powers of the League Council, under Article XI of the Covenant, to prevent the occurrence of war. Under Article XI, the decision of the Council, in any case of war or threat of war, required unanimous approval including that of the parties to the dispute, and no obligation was imposed upon the contestants to act in accordance with the "advice" rendered by the Council. However, as supplemented by the proposed convention, in case of a dispute or threat of war, the signatory states would undertake in advance to accept and execute the recommendations of the Council. The Arbitration and Security Committee hesitated, nevertheless, to prepare such a convention in view of some of the observations which it had received in response to the questionnaire which it had circulated to the government members of the League. The British Conservative government, which had specifically stated its opposition to both general treaties and compulsory arbitration in its "Memorandum on Arbitration and Security," would not be likely to support the adoption of the new convention. Consequently, the committee drew up a model treaty, instead of a general convention, "to Strengthen the Means of Preventing War," and submitted it, as one of the ten model treaties on arbitration and security, to the Ninth Assembly of the League. It was not until the Tenth Assembly in 1929, however, that action was taken to implement the model treaty. At that time, the British Labour Foreign Secretary, Arthur Henderson, suggested that the model treaty be made the basis for a General Convention to Improve the Means of Preventing War open to the signature of all the members of the League. The Assembly endorsed the British resolution and the task of drafting the proposed convention was begun;[42] but by the time

[42] A preliminary Draft Convention which contained two texts, owing to division of opinion on the compulsory character of the Council's military proposals in the event of war or threat of war, the supervision of these, and the application of sanctions to powers which might refuse to adopt them, was submitted by the Arbitration and Security Committee to the Eleventh Assembly. The Assembly's Third Committee and its subcommittee found it impossible to produce a single text, however, and a

that the final draft was completed for submission to the Assembly, the British Labour government was no longer in office. The text of the General Convention was accepted by the Twelfth Assembly and opened for accession until February 2, 1932 (the date fixed for the convening of the Disarmament Conference). Approval by the Assembly, however, placed no obligation upon the members to attach their signatures, and the succeeding British Conservative government did not consent to ratification.

In the case of the Convention on Financial Assistance, the Labour government was able to realize the completion of its initial efforts to strengthen the means for the pacific settlement of disputes. The provision of financial aid to states which were the victims of aggression had been suggested at the first session of the Preparatory Commission in 1926. As a result of the work of the commission's Arbitration and Security Committee and the League's Financial Committee, a Draft Convention was submitted in 1929 for the consideration of the members of the League Assembly. The principle embodied in the convention was that a state attacked in violation of international obligations had a right to financial assistance from the other signatory members. Discretionary power was retained by the League Council to grant financial aid to the party accepting mediation if one of the parties to an international dispute refused to take measures to safeguard peace or submit the dispute to pacific settlement. The financial assistance was to take the form of an international loan secured by the borrowing government, all the governments subscribing to the convention and certain governments as "special" guarantors bearing the risk of any delay in the payments of amounts due from the ordinary guarantors. In accordance with the suggestion of the British delegation, financial assistance was also to be granted in the case of a "threat of war"—an additional safeguard against the outbreak of hostilities. The convention was to come into force upon the conclusion of a general treaty for the reduction of armaments.[43]

During the course of the discussions at Geneva on the Draft Convention on Financial Assistance, the British government's support of the plan was assailed by certain sections of the Conservative press which had made no such protest when the proposed convention had

special committee was appointed at the request of the Assembly to complete the drafting of the convention. Cf. League of Nations, Eleventh Assembly, Third Committee, General Convention to Strengthen the Means of Preventing War, *Report of the Third Committee to the Assembly*, September 26, 1930.

[43] League of Nations, Eleventh Assembly, Third Committee, Convention on Financial Assistance, *Report of the Third Committee to the Assembly*, September 26, 1930.

received the approval of the preceding Conservative administration. The chief objection to the convention was based upon the assumption that Britain would be bound to assume a new and heavy responsibility to "pay for other people's wars," and thereby incur serious financial burdens.[44] In reply to this objection, Labour pointed out that the assistance envisaged in the plan would not be provided in any instance without the unanimous consent of the League Council, on which the British government had a permanent seat. Since the obligation to come to the assistance of a state attacked in violation of the provisions of the Covenant was an obligation undertaken by every member of the League, the proposed convention would do no more than provide machinery for the fulfillment of that obligation. Financial assistance would be granted only to a state which was the victim of aggression or the threat of aggression and used against a state which was placed under the ban of the whole League by the terms of Article XVI. Since the Covenant empowered the Council to recommend to all members the provision of financial, and even military, assistance, it was from the Covenant and not from the proposed convention that the obligation arose. The Labour government believed that the convention would be a strong weapon in the hands of the Council to establish, before hostilities began, which party to the dispute would be the aggressor by the test of refusal to agree to mediation. The threat of the Council to grant financial support to the state willing to submit to mediation or arbitration would exercise great pressure in the direction of the pacific settlement of international disputes. On the basis of this belief, the Labour government supported the adoption of the convention by the League Assembly and attached its signature, along with twenty-seven other governments, before the close of the Eleventh Assembly.[45]

When the Labour government announced, at the Eleventh Assembly, that it would support both the amendments to the Covenant and the Convention on Financial Assistance, it also declared that it had always been favorably disposed toward the principles of the General Act and always believed that true security could only be obtained by co-operative action.[46] Following the adoption of the General Act for the Pacific Settlement of International Disputes by the Ninth Assembly, the Labour party had advocated British approval and had promised, in its Electoral Manifesto, that a Labour government would

[44] Criticism of the convention was made by the *Daily Mail, Daily Express, Daily Telegraph*, and *Observer*. Cf. "Paying for Other Peoples Wars," *Foreign Affairs*, XI (October 1929), 207.

[45] League of Nations, *Official Journal*, Special Supplement 84, Records of the Eleventh Ordinary Session of the Assembly, Fourth Plenary Meeting, September 11, 1930, p. 41; Seventeenth Plenary Meeting, September 29, 1930, p. 142.

[46] Arthur Henderson, *ibid.*, Fourth Plenary Meeting, September 11, 1930, p. 41.

sign the Act. The Labour government regarded adherence to the General Act as the "logical consequence of the Pact of Paris" and the "logical consequence of the Optional Clause." Since the government had already accepted the Optional Clause for the arbitration of justiciable disputes, its accession to the General Act would provide for the arbitration of nonjusticiable disputes as well and thus complete its acceptance of the pacific settlement of international disputes of every class, in accordance with the pledge undertaken in the Pact of Paris. In presenting the motion for parliamentary approval of the accession, the government asserted that it was "simply carrying into practice" the policy to which its predecessors in office were committed. The General Act was such a collective agreement as that "hinted at" in the resolution unanimously adopted by the Eighth Assembly calling for "measures capable of giving all States the guarantees of arbitration and security necessary to enable them to fix the level of their armaments at the lowest possible figures in an international disarmament agreement." Nevertheless, the Conservative party opposed the policy to which it was allegedly "committed" by declining to accept an act which "diminished the authority of the Council of the League" and substituted "a procedure tending to encourage international disputes."[47] In reply, the Foreign Secretary denied that the authority of the League Council would be "diminished" in any way since the government had, by the terms of its proposed accession, "specifically reserved the right to bring any case before the Council," and provided that Chapter III of the Act (arbitration of disputes of a nonlegal nature) would not be applied unless the Council had failed to reach a settlement.[48] With regard to the second criticism, the Foreign Secretary pointed out that, since there had already been "dozens of bilateral treaties" of arbitration and "under none of them" had international disputes been "provoked," he saw no basis for the charge that under the General Act disputes would be "encouraged." The Act had received the unanimous approval of the League Assembly, and the Labour government intended to fulfill Britain's obligations as a member of the League of Nations by its accession to the General Act.[49]

[47] Austen Chamberlain moved an amendment on behalf of the Conservative Opposition "reaffirming its adherence to the Covenant of the League of Nations and the Pact of Paris," but declining "to accept the General Act." 249 *H.C.Deb.*, March 9, 1931, col. 832.

[48] The government attached substantially the same conditions to its accession to the General Act as it had to the signature of the Optional Clause. Cf. Memorandum on the Proposed Accession of His Majesty's Government in the United Kingdom to the General Act of 1928 for the Pacific Settlement of International Disputes, *British State Papers*, Cmd. 3803 (1931).

[49] 249 *H.C.Deb.*, cols. 826–30, 895, 935. The Conservative amendment was defeated, and the government motion carried, 231–139.

The Labour government had approved the General Act, as it had all of the other measures for arbitration and security, with the belief that states would be prepared to reduce and limit their national forces in proportion to their confidence in the constructive machinery of peace. When the Labour party assumed office in 1929, progress toward international disarmament had thus far been obstructed by Anglo-American naval rivalry and the failure of the members of the Preparatory Commission to reach the basis of agreement necessary for the summoning of an international disarmament conference. The Labour party had proclaimed, in its Electoral Manifesto, that since a "drastic reduction of armaments" was "long overdue," it would welcome the initiative of the United States and "press for the speedy completion of the Disarmament Treaty and the convocation of a General Disarmament Conference." The prospect of breaking the deadlock in the disarmament negotiations had been presented to the Labour government with the reopening of the question of naval armaments by the American representative on the Preparatory Commission. The failure of the Three-Power Naval Conference had shown "conclusively" that until the question was approached in a "wholly different spirit," no way existed of solving the problem. The general acceptance of the Kellogg Pact had provided that "fresh spirit" and an "unprecedented" opportunity for advancing the cause of disarmament. As a result, the United States government had been prompted to announce its readiness to accept a compromise on the "paramount difficulty" of establishing the ratio of equality between two cruiser fleets having, according to their different requirements, a different proportion of the large, heavily armed type of cruiser to the smaller, more lightly armed type. It had been left to the British Labour government to take up this offer in the "spirit" in which it had been made and "to turn it to practical account."[50]

The Labour Prime Minister, immediately after assuming office, initiated conversations on the subject of naval disarmament with the new United States Ambassador, General Dawes, and the American representative on the Preparatory Commission, Hugh Gibson. MacDonald was convinced that a preliminary agreement on Anglo-American differences was essential to a general agreement on naval building. He assured the other governments that had been represented at the 1921 Washington Naval Conference that they would be informed of the conversations and invited to a preliminary conference as soon as the way was "cleared." The final agreement would then be reported

[50] Arthur Henderson, *Report of the Twenty-ninth Annual Conference of the Labour Party*, 1929, p. 210.

to the Preparatory Commission as a "contribution" to the disarmament work of the League of Nations. Throughout the course of the negotiations, MacDonald emphasized the point that an Anglo-American understanding would be a preparation for a larger and more comprehensive international compact rather than an alliance excluding others—"a board round which the other nations might ultimately sit in co-operative fellowship, study the arts and the ways of peace, gaining a sense of security, not by arms, but by the absence of arms."[51] Rapid progress toward Anglo-American agreement was facilitated by the decision of the Labour government to suspend all work on the two cruisers under construction, to cancel the submarine depot ships and two contract submarines, to slow down dockyard work on other naval construction, and to postpone the 1929–30 program until the matter had received further consideration. In addition, the government had agreed upon the principle of naval "parity" with the United States, allowing for "a measure of elasticity" to meet the peace requirements of the two nations. The Prime Minister was determined not to allow "technical points to overrule the great public issues" involved in reaching an agreement. He therefore proposed to make this matter his chief concern until a settlement was reached. A meeting with the President of the United States would take place, he announced, when it would be most helpful to promote the cordial relations of the two countries and, in particular, to advance the ends of disarmament and peace which they held in common.[52]

By the time that MacDonald conferred with Hoover, the preliminary conversations with General Dawes had already removed every fear that at an international conference the "unbridgeable differences" between Britain and the United States would "doom such a conference to failure." MacDonald was able, therefore, to study with Hoover the "ways and means of filling in the narrow gaps still remaining in a programme of building which would at the same time recognise parity in strength and variety in the use of tonnage." As a result of the personal conference, it was agreed to adopt the principle of parity in each of the several categories, with such parity to be reached by the end of 1936. Anglo-American negotiations were thus brought to the stage at which it was possible to announce that there was no point outstanding of such serious importance as to prevent an agreement. It was recognized, however, that no final settlement on such questions as battleship strength and replacement and submarine limitation could be reached except in consultation with the other principal naval powers.

[51] Address at Lossiemouth, June 18, 1929, *Foreign Affairs*, XI (July 1929), 154.
[52] 230 *H.C.Deb.*, July 24, 1929, cols. 1305–6.

The British government, therefore, issued an invitation to the governments of France, Italy, Japan, and the United States to be represented at a conference to consider naval disarmament with regard to the categories not included under the 1921 Washington Treaty. Acceptance was received from the governments concerned, and the Five-Power Naval Conference convened in London in January 1930.[53]

In preparation for the conference, the British government had relied upon the Kellogg Pact as the basis for its negotiations. It was convinced that, as a result of the new position and improved political conditions brought about by the "renunciation of war" on the part of the principal naval powers, the possibilities of naval disarmament had been considerably increased. With regard to its own intentions, the Labour government had given ample demonstration by suspending the construction of the Singapore naval base, reducing the cruiser claims from the 1927 figure of seventy to fifty and deleting from the 1929 naval program two cruisers, four destroyers, and three submarines.[54] As a result of these concessions, together with the thorough preliminary preparations between Great Britain and the United States and the successful conversations between the United States and Japan, agreement by the three principal naval powers was assured.[55] However, general agreement was prevented by the irreconcilable views of the two Mediterranean powers: the determination of Italy to secure naval parity with France, and the resistance of France to naval reduction without additional guaranties of security. Consequently, it was decided that a three-power naval treaty covering all categories of ships would be concluded, supplemented by a five-power treaty following the settlement of the Franco-Italian differences. The treaty between Britain, the United States, and Japan reduced the existing battleships of these three powers by nine, stopped the building of new battleships until 1936, and fixed the minimum level for cruiser, destroyer, and submarine categories for Britain and the United States at 541,000 tons as compared with the demands of the Conservative government at the Geneva Conference of 1927 for 737,000 tons. Since the other two powers had accepted four of the five parts of the treaty, full agreement had thus been reached on the postponement

[53] Ramsay MacDonald, 231 *H.C.Deb.*, November 5, 1929, col. 886.

[54] Cf. A. V. Alexander, First Lord of the Admiralty, *ibid.*, November 13, 1929, col. 2012; 232 *H.C.Deb.*, November 20, 1929, cols. 463–68; 234 *H.C.Deb.*, January 29, 1930, cols. 1019–20; February 5, 1930, col. 1919; 236 *H.C.Deb.*, March 12, 1930, cols. 1298–1300.

[55] Cf. Memorandum on the Position of the London Naval Conference, 1930, of His Majesty's Government in the United Kingdom, London, February 4, 1930, *British State Papers*, Cmd. 3485 (1930), which was in harmony with the United States position.

of replacement of capital ships and the disposal of overage vessels
(Part I), the limitation of submarine tonnage and special vessels not
subject to limitation (Part II), the regulation of submarine warfare
(Part IV), and the duration period of the treaty (Part V). With
regard to the remaining part (the allocation of tonnage in auxiliary
vessels), the two powers were to continue their efforts to reach a settlement accommodating their building in the future to the standardiza-
tion in Part III of the treaty. The treaty was to be in force until the
end of 1936, subject to the further consideration of the naval powers
in 1935.[56]

The Labour government was satisfied that a "real beginning" had
been made at the London Naval Conference and that the result would
be "further reductions, more stringent limitations upon competition
and closer relations between the Powers." However, a hostile reception was given to the treaty by the Conservative Opposition which
disclaimed "any responsibility for it" and demanded that a select committee be appointed to examine and report upon the proposals contained in the international agreement. The chief concern of the Conservatives was that the "parity" which had been conceded to the United
States would result in actual "inferiority" for Great Britain. They
felt that the security of the British Empire had been seriously compromised by the reduction in cruiser strength from the seventy which
they had demanded at Geneva and by the lack of adequate provision
for replacements.[57] In reply, the Labour government reiterated the
belief that armaments did not provide security, and that under the
present international conditions, resulting from the "outlawry of
war," the number of fifty cruisers could be regarded as adequate to
meet Britain's commitments under the League Covenant. The Labour
party emphasized that the Conservative demand for seventy cruisers
had wrecked the Geneva Conference and that a Labour government
had succeeded in 1930 where a Tory government had failed in 1927:
with the London treaty, the three greatest navies in the world had
been strictly limited in every class of warship. By halting the competition in naval construction and reducing the naval strength of the three
principal powers, the government had assured a total financial saving
of £67,000,000 which would have been spent on the replacement of
battleships and on the Conservative program for cruisers, destroyers,

[56] Memorandum on the Results of the London Naval Conference from January 21–April 15, 1930, *British State Papers*, Cmd. 3547 (1930).

[57] The treaty was attacked on this basis by Churchill and Amery, 238 *H.C.Deb.*,
May 15, 1930, cols. 2111–14, 2188; but the Conservative motion was defeated, 283–201
(239 *H.C.Deb.*, June 2, 1930).

and submarines. That "notable achievement," Labour claimed, would take a "foremost place in the history of disarmament efforts."[58]

As a result of the London Naval Conference, the Labour government felt that it could go to Geneva with "very much more confidence" and a "fair case for pressing for disarmament on land and in the air."[59] When the Labour government came into office, the Preparatory Commission, after three years of negotiations, had suspended its sixth session without agreement on the Draft Disarmament Convention. One of the principal reasons why the Commission had hitherto been unable to complete its work was that, although there were those who contended that disarmament in all three spheres was a single problem, progress in the naval sphere had been held up by the inability of Great Britain and the United States to solve their particular differences. As a result, when the Preparatory Commission had received the suggestion of the American representative for a renewed attempt at naval limitation, it had decided to adjourn its proceedings until further progress among the principal naval powers had been recorded. Although the Labour government had welcomed the prospect of a naval agreement arising out of the American proposal, it was convinced that a reduction in naval armaments alone, leaving land armaments potentially as threatening as ever, would not bring either peace or security. It therefore informed the League Assembly that the British government, while desiring and working for "the production of actual, concrete results" in the field of naval armaments, would "do all in its power to hasten the preparations for a general disarmament conference."[60]

With this objective in view, the Labour government decided to make a fresh start on the problem of land armaments by bringing the issue before the Tenth Assembly of the League of Nations. The British delegation submitted to the Third Committee of the Assembly a draft resolution expressing the hope that the Preparatory Commission would finish its work "at the earliest possible moment," and in concluding the Draft Convention would consider the application of the same principles to land, sea, and air disarmament; the limitation of

[58] Chairman's address, Susan Lawrence, *Report of the Thirtieth Annual Conference of the Labour Party*, 1930, p. 157; *The Record of the Second Labour Government* (London: Labour Party, 1935), p. 2. The treaty was defended by Ramsay MacDonald (237 *H.C.Deb.*, April 10, 1930, col. 2473; 238 *H.C.Deb.*, May 15, 1930, cols. 2088–96; 239 *H.C.Deb.*, June 2, 1930, cols. 1800–10), and by Lord Parmoor (77 *H.L.Deb.*, May 8, 1930, cols. 468–82; 78 *H.L.Deb.*, July 1, 1930, cols. 201–14).

[59] A. V. Alexander, 238 *H.C.Deb.*, May 15, 1930, col. 2193.

[60] League of Nations, *Official Journal*, Special Supplement 75, Records of the Tenth Ordinary Session of the Assembly, Third Plenary Meeting, September 3, 1929, p. 34.

land effectives and war matériel; and the recognition of an international authority to supervise the execution of the disarmament provisions.[61] It was at once evident to the other members of the Assembly that the Labour government, by reopening the question of land forces, intended to reverse the disarmament policy of its Conservative predecessors. At the last session of the Preparatory Commission, the representative of the Conservative government, Lord Cushendun, had admitted that "land armaments did not constitute the branch of the subject in which Great Britain was most interested." As Britain "was not and did not pretend to be a military Power in the Continental sense of the term," she recognized that "in this sphere the lead could and should be taken by the military Powers."[62] In contrast with this attitude, the Labour government was very much interested in land armaments and did not propose to allow the Continental powers the opportunity to evade the limitation of land forces. The British resolution met with strong opposition from the large military powers, including France, who objected to the raising of such issues as the limitation of military effectives and the matériel of land warfare. As a result, a compromise resolution was accepted by the League Assembly whereby the statements made in the Third Committee with regard to the principles upon which the final work of the Preparatory Commission should be based would be communicated to the Preparatory Commission "for any necessary action." Although the compromise resolution did not include the specific instructions to the Commission embodied in the original British resolution, it provided the opening for "any necessary action." The British delegation would thus be able to raise the whole question of the reduction of land forces at the next session of the Preparatory Commission.[63]

The opportunity for the Labour government to present its proposals to the Preparatory Commission was delayed for another year in view of the Commission's decision to postpone the resumption of its sixth session until after the London Naval Conference and the Franco-Italian naval settlement. With the conclusion of the London Naval Treaty, the date for the last session of the Preparatory Commission was set for the end of 1930. However, by the time the Eleventh Assembly of the League convened in September 1930, the

[61] League of Nations, *Official Journal*, Special Supplement 78, Records of the Tenth Ordinary Session of the Assembly, Minutes of the Third Committee, September 19, 1929, pp. 72–75.

[62] Cf. Declaration by the British Delegation to the Preparatory Commission, April 19, 1929, League of Nations, Tenth Assembly, *Report on the Work of the League Since the Last Session of the Assembly*, A.6, 1929.

[63] Cf. League of Nations, *Official Journal*, Special Supplement 75, Records of the Tenth Ordinary Session of the Assembly, Nineteenth Plenary Meeting, September, 24, 1929, p. 162.

other obstacle which had prevented the meeting of the Preparatory Commission—Franco-Italian naval differences—had not yet been removed. The British Foreign Secretary expressed the anxiety of many of the League members that further delay in the proceedings of the Commission would compromise the success of any disarmament efforts. Though recognizing that some progress had been made during the previous year with regard to naval armaments, Henderson reminded the Assembly that it had been ten years since the disarmament work of the League had begun, yet the "sacred" obligation undertaken in Article VIII of the Covenant had not been honored. Unless disarmament could be made general, unless it could be completed by the reduction and limitation of land forces, the peace treaties would not have been executed, the Covenant would not have been fulfilled, and the peace of Europe and of the world would not be safe. The time for "practical results" had now arrived, and Henderson hoped that when the Preparatory Commission resumed its efforts it would "press on vigorously" to the completion of its task.[64] The Assembly concurred with the views of the British Foreign Secretary and agreed upon a resolution expressing the conviction that, during its session in November, the Preparatory Commission would be able to finish the drawing up of a preliminary Draft Convention and thus enable the League Council to convene a conference on the reduction and limitation of armaments "as soon as possible."[65] Henderson's plea was realized, for within two months of its convening, the Commission had completed the text of a Draft Convention.

The final session of the Preparatory Commission imposed a serious responsibility upon the British Labour government. Although it had some assurance of co-operation in the naval sphere from the United States and Japan, there still remained the Franco-Italian naval differences to be settled to a point at which a general naval agreement would be possible. In the field of land armaments, the problem of meeting the French claim for security and the German demand for equality had been magnified by the recent German elections resulting in a victory for the extremist parties pledged to destroy the Versailles peace settlement. The German delegation was thus subject to the pressures of the Nationalist and National Socialist parties for the achievement of a level of arms equality with the other Powers. France, on the other hand, was more determined than ever to retain her su-

[64] *Ibid.*, 84, Records of the Eleventh Ordinary Session of the Assembly, Fourth Plenary Meeting, September 11, 1930, p. 42.

[65] *Ibid.*, September 30, 1930, pp. 163–68. Also cf. *ibid.*, Special Supplement 87, Records of the Eleventh Ordinary Session of the Assembly, Minutes of the Third Committee, September 24, 1930, pp. 73–79.

periority in armaments in view of the menace to her security involved in a revival of German militarism. An additional obstacle to successful negotiations was the Russian delegation, which, having failed to convince the Commission to accept its proposals for "total" disarmament, proceeded to obstruct any alternative suggestions. The task of undertaking these difficult negotiations was entrusted to Viscount Cecil, who had consented to return to the Preparatory Commission as a representative of the British Labour government. In view of Cecil's record as a sincere supporter of general disarmament, both at the Geneva Naval Conference and at the Preparatory Commission, he was most likely to succeed, if anyone could, in gaining the co-operation of the other delegations.

The British delegation took advantage of the Tenth Assembly's resolution instructing the Preparatory Commission to take "any necessary action" by reopening the whole issue of the limitation of land forces and matériel, many aspects of which had already been left to the discretion of the Continental military powers by the preceding Conservative government. The decisions which had been reached at the previous session of the Preparatory Commission had the effect of weakening the limitation of land armaments by the exemption of trained reserves and the exclusion of any direct control of expenditure. It was therefore the objective of the British delegation to bring before the Commission a reconsideration of these issues as well as the principles contained in the resolution which it had submitted to the Third Committee of the League Assembly as the basis for a disarmament convention. The British delegation was determined that the final draft should not exclude the possibility of the reduction of any of the matériel of warfare. Consequently, it was largely because of its efforts that a Draft Convention covering the whole field of military, naval, and air armaments was adopted by the Preparatory Commission. The Commission succeeded in proposing a classification of armaments and the methods by which they were to be limited. Thus the Draft Convention provided that armies were to be restricted through limiting the total number of men serving, both conscript and professional, and the period of military service in those states retaining the conscription system. In the case of navies, the number of ships, the number of officers and enlisted men, and the amount of money allocated in the national budgets for naval armaments were to be subject to limitation. In the air forces, the personnel, the number of airplanes, and their horsepower were to be restricted. There was also to be limitation of the total budget expenditure on all armaments in all countries. This provision, Viscount Cecil believed, would allow for the control of the cost of matériel of air forces which he had not been able to have included in the draft. In addition, there was to be established a Permanent Disarmament Commission to supervise the loyal execution of the terms of the disarmament treaty. The agreement to accept a supervisory Commission was, in Cecil's opinion, "the most encouraging thing that happened at Geneva" and "the greatest reform that had ever been started." Within the ambit of the present draft, Cecil claimed, "almost any degree of reduction" was possible.[66]

In view of the repeated but unsuccessful attempts of the previous decade, the conclusion of the preparatory negotiations was a considerable achievement and an important step toward general disarmament. The Preparatory Commission had provided only the framework, however; it remained for the governments participating in the World Disarmament Conference to insert the actual figures of limitation or reduction for all categories of effectives and armaments. The Labour government realized that the year 1931 would be a critical one for the League of Nations in that the movement of public opinion during that year would determine whether the first World Disarmament Conference would be "a farce or a reality." Unless the Conference resulted in a treaty which would stop competition in all forms of armaments, subject them to effective limitation, and bring about such substantial reductions as were clearly intended by Article VIII of the Covenant and anticipated by the defeated Powers at Versailles from the promises made to them by the Allies, "the whole edifice of international peace" would be "shaken to its foundations."[67] The international conference was to meet this challenge the following year—February 2, 1932—and in recognition of the leading part played by the British Labour government in completing the preparations for, and in securing the summoning of, the Disarmament Conference, its Foreign Secretary, Arthur Henderson, was chosen to preside over the proceedings.

In addition to its work in the fields of arbitration, security, and disarmament, the Labour government did much to strengthen and improve the general machinery of international co-operation in many other ways. It secured the status and independence of the League

[66] Despatch from Viscount Cecil of Chelwood enclosing the Report of the Preparatory Commission for the Disarmament Conference and the Draft Disarmament Convention, Geneva, December 10, 1930, *British State Papers*, Cmd. 3757 (1931).

[67] This warning was issued by the Labour government's representative on the Preparatory Commission, Cecil, who had sufficient evidence from the hostile attitude of the German delegation that Germany would repudiate the disarmament provisions of Versailles unless equality of armaments for Germany was recognized. *Foreign Affairs*, XIII (January 1931), 444.

Secretariat by guaranteeing the rights of its members in a statute adopted by the Assembly in 1930. It secured the adoption of proposals for the more rapid ratification of general conventions drawn up under the auspices of the League and attached its own ratification to the Arms Traffic Convention. It proposed a new convention for the limitation of the manufacture of dangerous drugs which was adopted by an international conference in June 1931. It contributed to the preparatory work for future international economic co-operation and for further progress toward the reduction of barriers to international trade by signing the treaty for the creation of an international agricultural mortgage bank and by proposing a "tariff truce" to prevent an increase of European tariffs during the dangerous period of the world slump. It convened a conference representing twenty-seven maritime states which concluded an International Convention establishing for the first time uniform safety rules for all the cargo ships of the world. The Labour government's policy of fostering good will and co-operation with all nations, but exclusive alliances with none, was applied to improving relations with the Great Powers—Russia, Germany, France, Japan, and the United States. In addition, it took the lead in settling with China the outstanding differences—the Boxer indemnity and the return of Weihaiwei—between the two governments; and in concluding with Iraq a treaty providing for the termination of the mandate, the grant of full self-government, and membership in the League of Nations. Thus, by 1931, the Labour government had realized in the international sphere all but one of the objectives contained in its Electoral Manifesto and in its party program, *Labour and the Nation*—the adoption of a general disarmament treaty by the Powers participating in the World Disarmament Conference.[68]

The Labour government did not survive the opening of the Disarmament Conference, however, and was thereby deprived of the opportunity of completing its final task. The downfall of the second Labour government was brought about partly by the world-wide economic crisis but primarily by the political crisis within the Labour movement itself. The inability of a minority Labour government to deal with the financial emergency on socialist lines eventually led to the disillusionment of its supporters and the defection of its chief leaders to the Opposition. The final break came with Ramsay MacDonald's decision, on the plea of financial stringency, to cut down unemployment allowances and other forms of social expenditure and to

---

[68] Cf. *Two Years of Labour Rule* (London: Labour Party, 1931), pp. 42–46; Hugh Dalton, *Report of the Thirty-first Annual Conference of the Labour Party*, 1931, p. 184.

head a "National" government with a predominantly Conservative membership pledged to carry out such a program of economies. Although only a handful of Labour members of Parliament, including Snowden, Thomas, and Jowitt, and no local Labour parties or trade-unions followed MacDonald, the party was severely shaken by the split. With Arthur Henderson as leader, the party appealed to the country on the basis of its foreign-policy record and its program for solving disarmament through arbitration and security.[69] Labour's success in the international field was completely overshadowed, however, by the claims of the "National" government to save the country from the dangers of the world slump. As a result, the election practically destroyed the parliamentary Labour party, reducing its membership to the prewar level of forty-six and its popular support by almost two million votes. The crisis within the British Labour movement had shown that it was in the domestic sphere, not in the international, that Labour had failed to produce a fully developed program.[70]

[69] "Labour's Call to Action," October 27, 1931, *Report of the Thirty-second Annual Conference of the Labour Party*, 1932, p. 321.

[70] Cf. John Parker, *Labour Marches On* (Harmondsworth: Penguin Books, 1947), pp. 22–24.

7

YEAR OF CRISIS

The year 1931 was one of crisis for the Labour party itself and for the international peace system which it had constructed. After the General Election, the Labour party returned to the House of Commons greatly weakened, in numbers as well as by the loss of almost all of its prominent leaders in the field of international affairs. As a parliamentary Opposition, the tiny minority was practically impotent in the face of the preponderent strength of the "National" government and its supporters. Its effectiveness in matters of foreign relations was further compromised by the fact that the leadership of the parliamentary party had passed to George Lansbury, an outstanding pacifist whose views on foreign policy were at variance with the majority of his party. Lansbury himself admitted that when he became leader of the parliamentary party, he was "up against the difficulty of squaring pacifist principles with the policy of the Party." During the years since the war, the party's policy had been based upon the principle embodied in the League Covenant that peace could be maintained only through collective security, a policy which he could not support. It was his belief that if collective security were operated to such an extent as to impede an aggressor, it would undoubtedly mean a return to the "universal war and destruction" of 1914. Lansbury's own road to peace was through "collective justice, equity and freedom between nations"; and during the brief period of his leadership he tried his utmost to direct the thoughts and actions of the party along that line.[1] Though the party resisted Lansbury's pacifist persuasions, it was unable for almost four years to produce a leader to challenge them. In the interval, it was content to agree with Lansbury upon an international program rejecting the balance of power and the use of force as an instrument of national policy and aiming at the subordination of national sovereignty to world loyalty, the reduction of all national armaments to the lowest possible level, the substitution of arbitration for war, and the removal of the economic causes of war. The compromise proved to be an unsatisfactory one, however, and the parliamentary group suffered from the lack of leadership to express its views. The inadequacy of Lansbury's program to meet the challenges to international

[1] George Lansbury, *My Quest for Peace* (London: Michael Joseph, 1938), pp. 16–17, 55.

peace and security after 1931 only confirmed the view of his colleagues that no system of international co-operation could endure unless it were founded upon a basis of law upheld with the same vigor and success as the law of a national state.[2]

Disillusionment as well as disagreement threatened the survival of the Labour party after the desertion of its leaders. The hatred and resentment resulting from the feeling that MacDonald and his personal following had betrayed the Labour movement and had sacrificed its socialist principles were so intense as to detract from the immediate necessity of reconstructing the party under new leadership. Instead of mending its party ranks, Labour lost confidence in itself and for some years was inclined to look at all of its leaders with suspicion.[3] In addition, the fact that MacDonald had split the Labour movement by accepting the policies of its capitalist opponents served to reinforce the views of that section of the movement which had always ruled out the possibility of any collaboration with capitalist parties either at home or abroad. MacDonald's deception provided valuable ammunition for the "class war" enthusiasts to attack the gradualism of the party and its willingness to compromise with capitalism to achieve domestic reform and international co-operation. It was the conviction of this minority that there was only one real struggle, that of the workers against the capitalists; and that co-operation with nonsocialist parties or states detracted from the main objective of the working-class movement. The influence of this opinion reached its climax at the Hastings Conference when the Labour party recorded its distrust of capitalist governments by adopting a resolution calling upon the National Executive to seek consultation with the trade-union and co-operative movements with a view to deciding and announcing to the country what steps, including a general strike, were to be taken to organize the opposition of the working class in the event of war or threat of war. Although Labour's acceptance of this resolution indicated the hopelessness and disillusionment which had permeated the party and caused it to regard with suspicion the motives of capitalist governments, its simultaneous endorsement of a policy of international co-operation through disarmament and collective security illustrated the confusion and disagreement which had swept over the movement as a result of the cleavages within its ranks.[4] Actually, Labour's brief excursion into the realm of direct action was contrary to the

[2] Cf. Clement Attlee, *The Labour Party in Perspective* (London: Gollancz, 1937), pp. 215–16.

[3] John Parker, *Labour Marches On*, p. 23.

[4] Cf. *Report of the Thirty-third Annual Conference of the Labour Party*, 1933, pp. 186, 192.

traditional beliefs and attitudes of the party; and after 1933 such a policy was advocated primarily by the Independent Labour party, which had disaffiliated from the Labour party to work for a program of "socialism in our time."[5] The Labour party's traditional policy of constitutional opposition to capitalist governments at home and international co-operation with all nations, socialist or nonsocialist, eventually survived the onslaught of the pacifist and the class-war advocates, but not until the future leaders of the party were able to revitalize the traditional principles to meet the changed circumstances resulting from the domestic and international crisis of 1931.

The survival of the peace system which the Labour party had played such an important part in creating was threatened in 1931 with the breakdown of world economy and the menace of war. When the peace system was constructed, it was assumed that political democracy would be the prevailing system of government, that the League would be universal and would impose all-round limitation and reduction of armaments, that the cult of war was dead, and that the prevailing economic system would continue to function successfully. On the basis of these assumptions, it was possible to provide a reasonable sense of security with the conclusion of the Kellogg-Briand Pact, the treaties to strengthen the means of pacific settlement and prevention of war, The Hague Settlements on reparations and the Rhine, the Three-Power Naval Treaty, and the Draft Disarmament Convention. All of these assumptions were destroyed, however, by the world economic crisis which engendered a wave of political reaction in the form of nationalism, imperialism, and militarism. As a result of this challenge to the survival of democracy and to the idea of peace throughout the world, Labour found it necessary after 1931 to reorient its foreign policy to an international situation which was marked by the failure of the League members to uphold the principles of the Covenant, the rise of Fascism and dictatorship, the growth of armaments, and the steady drift toward world war.

The Labour party believed that the essential condition for overcoming the world crisis was the re-establishment of international confidence, which had been so severely shaken by the combined forces of nationalism and militarism. The means proposed by Labour to restore such confidence were an agreed solution to the problem of international debts, an end to the growing excesses of protectionism, a guaranty of peace in the Far East against Japanese imperialism, and a "serious

[5] The reasons for disaffiliation were presented to the Bradford Conference of the I.L.P. and the conference approved the decision to disaffiliate on July 30, 1932. Cf. *New Leader*, August 5, 1932.

step" in the direction of international disarmament. Labour emphasized that all of these questions were closely interrelated. It would be impossible to solve the problem of debts, for example, unless a "serious move" were made toward international disarmament. Without international disarmament, it would be impossible to put a stop to protectionism, which derived its strength from armaments. And unless determined steps were taken against the warlike policy of Japan in the Far East, it would be impossible to give the nations the feeling of security essential for international disarmament. The questions of disarmament, reparations, and war debts, Labour insisted, were "too closely connected financially and politically for a final settlement to be possible without a general settlement." It was Labour's aim to bring pressure to bear upon the government with a view to a European agreement on a plan of economic reconstruction and on the joint action to be taken to curtail protectionism, co-operate in the permanent stabilization of currencies, secure the cancellation of war debts, and prepare the way for disarmament by preserving international security against aggression.[6]

While Britain was involved in the midst of the financial crisis which brought about the formation of the "National" government, the first serious challenge to the international peace system was undertaken with Japan's invasion of Manchuria. The preoccupation of the Western world with the problem of economic salvation provided the Japanese militarists with the opportunity of averting the internal consequences of their own economic depression by embarking upon a policy of imperialism and conquest. The British government's responsibility for the policy to be adopted toward the conflict after China, the victim of the aggression, had appealed to the League Council, was clearly defined by the obligations embodied in the Covenant and further clarified by the fact that Britain was the only member of the League that was a first-class Power in the Far East. The Labour party reminded the government of its responsibilities as a member of the League Council and warned that Manchuria was the "test case" which would decide whether the League dare act against a Great Power.[7] When Japan showed no intention of heeding the League Council's directive for the evacuation of its troops and the pacific settlement of the dispute, Labour criticized the government for not taking a stronger line at the Council meetings and for not supporting

[6] Statement by General Council of T.U.C. and National Executive Committee of the Labour Party, May 25, 1932, endorsing Declaration by Joint Disarmament Conference of L.S.I. and I.F.T.U., Zurich, May 19–20, 1932, *Report of the Thirty-second Annual Conference of the Labour Party*, 1932, p. 60.

[7] George Lansbury, 260 *H.C.Deb.*, November 25, 1931, cols. 462–63.

the American declaration of the "nonrecognition" of territorial conquest by a similar announcement. Labour called upon the government to take a "bold lead" at Geneva in proposing vigorous action against the Japanese aggression. The aggression was "unusually clear," Labour held, and the circumstances were favorable for action against Japan as she stood alone, without allies, and the League had the assistance of the United States. If the League failed under these circumstances, it would be "wholly impotent" to deal with an outbreak of war and to "shield the weaker from the stronger." All that had been done to draft a Covenant, to construct a World Court, and to sign the Kellogg Pact would have been a "waste of energy"; and the Kellog Pact would be a "scrap of paper" and the League Covenant an "antiquarian relic."[8]

The government admitted the validity of the principle contained in the Covenant that nations should submit their disputes to peaceful settlement, but seemed more concerned with the proposition that while the League Council was doing its utmost to promote that result, the members should "abstain from what might be regarded as partial judgment." It would be "wholly improper," in the government's opinion, to express by action on its own account, independent of the League, its judgment on a matter that was under investigation by a League Commission. Although the government would "certainly not agree to seeing the terms of the Nine-Power Treaty flouted," it could see no justification for assuming that anything of the kind was likely to take place "in the face of the assurance given by the Japanese Government."[9] The Foreign Secretary, Sir John Simon, insisted that the action of the Japanese army in Manchuria did "not in the least resemble the invasion by a foreign force of some other country" because Japan, in fact, had "exceptional rights over strips of territory there." The government had done its utmost at Geneva "to hold the scales fairly" and "to carry out faithfully the principles of the League of Nations." It had agreed to the appointment of a League Commission of Inquiry, presided over by Lord Lytton, and would await the results of that investigation. As world opinion became "sufficiently strong," Simon asserted, sanctions would not be needed.[10]

[8] H. N. Brailsford, "The Test of the League," *New Leader*, November 13, 1931, p. 7; "The League in Retreat," *ibid.*, November 27, 1931, p. 7.

[9] Anthony Eden, Undersecretary of State for Foreign Affairs, 262 *H.C.Deb.*, February 29, 1932, cols. 917–18.

[10] 260 *H.C.Deb.*, November 25, 1931, col. 466; 263 *H.C.Deb.*, March 22, 1932, cols. 919–23. Simon stressed the importance of "conciliation," not sanctions, and the necessity for "impartiality" before the League of Nations. *Official Journal*, Special Supplement 101, Records of the Special Session of the Assembly, I, Fourth Meeting of the General Commission, March 7, 1932, pp. 62–63.

The Labour party protested that while the Lytton Commission proceeded with its investigation, the Japanese armed forces, in "flagrant violation" of Japan's many treaty obligations and with a complete disregard of pledges given to the Council of the League, invaded, occupied, and established a virtual protectorate over the vast Chinese provinces of Manchuria. These war operations had been undertaken by Japan "on unsubstantial grounds, satisfaction for which could easily have been obtained if Japan had made full use of the methods of peaceful settlement provided in the Covenant." On the other hand, Labour recognized, as the League Council had done, that from the beginning of the conflict China had put her case in the hands of the League and agreed to accept its proposals for a peaceful settlement. Political disorder in China was no justification for the invasion of her territory, Labour held, for Japan had undertaken, in the Nine-Power Treaty signed at Washington in 1922, "to provide the fullest and most unembarrassed opportunity to China to develop and maintain for herself an effective and stable Government." The Labour party emphasized that any war or threat of war was a matter of concern to the whole League; wars could not be localized, nor the range of their influence limited. If the nations of the world took no action to uphold the Covenant of the League, they would thereby destroy the collective system of world law; they would be unable to appeal for its aid in one part of the world if they allowed it to be defied in another; they would leave armed force as the determining factor in Asia and elsewhere; they would gravely increase the existing sense of international insecurity; and they would shatter all hopes for the reduction of armaments in the West as well as in the East. The National Council of Labour therefore urged the government to request the League Council to call upon the League members and signatories of the Kellogg Pact to withdraw their ambassadors from Tokyo. If Japan, in defiance of world public opinion, continued the war, then the British government would be obliged, in conformity with its undertakings as a signatory of the Covenant (Article XVI), to propose to the Special Assembly of the League whatever co-operative and graduated measures of financial and economic constraint might be necessary—in association and agreement with the United States and the members of the League—to restore peace and to ensure a just settlement of all outstanding questions between Japan and China, on the basis of the Covenant of the League of Nations, the Nine-Power Treaty, and the Pact of Paris.[11]

[11] "The Far Eastern Situation: British Labour's Declaration," National Joint Council of the Labour Party, February 23, 1932, *Report of the Thirty-second Annual Conference of the Labour Party*, 1932, p. 68.

The Labour party's pleas for action against Japanese aggression had thus far been met by the government's refusal to act independently of the League, thereby interfering with the proceedings of the Commission of Inquiry. Therefore, as soon as the League Commission submitted its report, the Labour party urged the government to do everything in its power to vindicate the authority of the Covenant and the Kellogg-Briand Pact by supporting the findings of the Lytton Commission on the Sino-Japanese dispute. The Labour party believed that the report of the League Commission provided a "great opportunity" to maintain the principles of the League Covenant and "perhaps the last chance" to prevent failure over the Manchurian conflict. The government, however, refused to take a stand on the findings of the Commission until the Japanese document of reply had been considered by the League.[12] When the League finally decided, after seventeen months of investigation and discussion, that Japan was the aggressor and that her conduct was not consistent with the obligations imposed upon her by the Covenant, the Pact of Paris, and the Nine-Power Treaty, the Labour party demanded immediate action. Now that the League had declared who was the aggressor, "all the sanctions, all the obligations of the Covenant ought to be carried through." The leader of the parliamentary party called upon the government to declare at once a complete embargo against the aggressor, prohibiting from export everything—arms, ammunition, finance, and credit—that would "aid and abet Japan." The long delay had already enabled the Japanese government to consolidate its conquests in Manchuria and to get a "jumping-off place further into China."[13] In response to Labour's request for sanctions, the Foreign Secretary, entirely overlooking the fact that Japan had been condemned by the League as the aggressor and had rejected the Lytton Report, stated that it was impracticable for a single country like Britain "acting alone to differentiate between one combatant and another." International consideration was "no doubt the best process," but pending international consultation, the government would not authorize the issue of licenses for export to either China or Japan of any article mentioned in the Arms Export Prohibition Order-in-Council of May 1931. Simon maintained till the end that if the British government stopped the export of

[12] Sir John Simon, 270 *H.C.Deb.*, November 10, 1932, cols. 537–38, in reply to Labour motion of censure, cols. 525–28.

[13] George Lansbury, 275 *H.C.Deb.*, February 27, 1933, cols. 37–48. The General Council of the T.U.C. and National Executive of the Labour party called for an economic boycott in accordance with Article XVI, February 22, 1933, *Report of the Thirty-third Annual Conference of the Labour Party*, 1933, p. 51.

arms to both countries, it would not be "favouring one more than the other."[14]

The Labour party concluded that the "National" government's repeated declaration that it would not take sides in the Sino-Japanese conflict had been a definite encouragement to Japanese aggression. Labour believed that Japan's "cynical dishonouring of her own pledged word, the contemputous disregard of international right and justice, the incredible barbarity of her military aggression and the forcible seizure of Chinese territories" constituted "one of the blackest pages in the history of international brigandage." It was not only against Japan's wanton acts that Labour felt compelled to protest; unhappily, the governments of the world had "all been accessories to the crime." Co-operatively, through the League of Nations, they were "the custodians of world peace, international justice and the rights of nations." On one pretext or another they "wriggled out of their responsibilities, leaving peace to its fate, and China to her ravishers." Instead of "mobilizing all the vast economic and moral resources at the disposal of the League, they rendered it impotent, and by so doing connived at an act of international aggression." In this "tragic and ignoble surrender of Right to Might," Labour declared, "the British Government—the 'National' Government—played the chief guiding part."[15]

The Labour party had warned the government that if Japan succeeded in aggression, it would be impossible to persuade the world that this would not be the method adopted in every dispute in which a Great Power was involved. Throughout the Manchurian conflict, Labour had stressed the link between security and disarmament and had insisted that, until every nation could count upon mutual aid, there would be no disarmament. Labour believed that a failure in Manchuria would make it impossible for the Geneva Disarmament Conference to "get France to go in whole-heartedly for disarmament," to "get Germany to reject all idea of rearmament," or to "get Japan to give up her Imperialist desire." The Labour party had "pinned its faith to the League," but feared that because the League had denied its duty of mutual aid, it had in advance condemned its Disarmament Conference to failure.[16]

The Labour party had looked forward to the World Disarmament Conference as "one of the most momentous events in the history of

[14] 275 *H.C.Deb.*, February 27, 1933, cols. 57–58, 155.

[15] Chairman's address, Joseph Compton, *Report of the Thirty-third Annual Conference of the Labour Party*, 1933, p. 134.

[16] Clement Attlee, 270 *H.C.Deb.*, November 10, 1932, cols. 526–29; H. N. Brailsford, "The League Is Dead," *New Leader*, February 19, 1932, pp. 1–2; "Sir John Simon Fails," *ibid.*, February 26, 1932, p. 2.

the world" and had expressed its confidence that the participating governments would co-operate in a policy of "progressive, simultaneous and supervised reduction of armaments by mutual agreement." It had reaffirmed its belief that the present expenditure on armaments by the nations of the world was a "danger to peace and to the security of the peoples" and had urged the government to put forward "proposals for drastic and far-reaching reductions, by international agreement, in numbers and equipment of all armed forces and in military, naval and air expenditure."[17]   In addition, British Labour had joined the Socialist and Trade Union Internationals in concluding a series of demands to be presented to the Disarmament Conference of the League of Nations. In its five-point disarmament program, International Labour declared that there should be equality of rights and duties for all nations; a substantial, immediate, and general reduction of armaments; an extension of reduction to cover all forms of armaments, including peacetime effectives, reserves, all classes of military expenditure, navies, fortifications, and arms and munitions for land and sea forces; a system of strict international control; and a permanent international disarmament organization. In connection with the World Disarmament Conference, an International Petition Campaign in favor of disarmament was organized by the International Labour movement, and the petition calling upon the governments represented at Geneva "to take some positive action" was submitted during the opening meetings of the Disarmament Conference.[18]

By the time the Disarmament Conference convened, the Japanese invasion of Manchuria had been extended to Shanghai, and the governments participating in the Conference were anxiously awaiting League action against the aggressor. The British Labour party reaffirmed the declaration of the International Labour movement that, so long as the Great Powers did not prevent Japan from continuing her campaign of plunder in China, and did not make use of the possibilities already existing to oblige her to respect treaty obligations, they would not have the right to make this lack of security, which they themselves had provoked, "a pretext for the sabotage of disarmament." It agreed that "the greater the danger of the Disarmament Conference being wrecked, the greater the duty of the Industrial and Political Sections of the Labour Movement and their Press to intensify their propaganda against War and for Disarmament." British

---

[17] National Executive Committee resolutions, *Report of the Thirty-first Annual Conference of the Labour Party*, 1931, pp. 42, 184.

[18] "The Fight for Disarmament and Against the Dangers of War," Joint Resolution of the L.S.I. and I.F.T.U., *Fourth Labour and Socialist International*, Vienna, July 25–August 1, 1931 (London: Labour Party, 1932), Section X, pp. 1–3.

Labour also consented to co-operate with the labor organizations in all countries "to continue to organise meetings and demonstrations in order thus to bring the strongest possible pressure to bear upon the Governments to compel them to conclude a Disarmament Treaty putting into effect as the first step towards total disarmament, the demands of the Labour and Socialist International and the International Federation of Trade Unions."[19]

Accordingly, the Labour party urged the British government to make definite disarmament proposals as Britain's contribution to the discussions at Geneva. The initiative, however, came not from Britain but from the United States, with a scheme submitted by President Hoover for the immediate scrapping of one-third of the existing battleships of the great naval powers, the reduction of cruiser, destroyer, and submarine tonnage, and the abolition of big guns, tanks, and bombing aircraft. The Labour party welcomed the plan as a substantial first step toward total disarmament and as a practical challenge to the representatives of the nations assembled in the Disarmament Conference at Geneva and expressed the hope that everything would now be done to secure the immediate adoption of President Hoover's proposals as a minimum program. In spite of Labour's warning that a rejection of the American proposals would destroy the hopes for the success of the Disarmament Conference and would also throw upon the European governments the responsibility for having compromised the collaboration of the United States, the British government "torpedoed" the Hoover plan by refusing to scrap battleships immediately.[20] The government's reply to the American initiative was characterized by the Labour Opposition as an offer to give up submarines which it did not want, tanks over twenty tons which it did not have, and aerial bombing, except in certain areas. Although the government was committed to "qualitative disarmament"—the abolition of the offensive weapons prohibited to Germany—this was made "farcical," Labour declared, by Admiral Pound's statement that battleships were "more precious than rubies" and could never be regarded as "aggressive" weapons. Labour felt that it was a "grave mistake" to go into a disarmament conference "surrounded by a retinue of military and naval experts."[21] According to the Foreign Secretary's explana-

[19] Resolution of the Joint Conference of the L.S.I. and I.F.T.U., Zurich, May 22–23, 1932, reaffirmed by the General Council of the T.U.C. and National Executive Committee of the Labour Party, May 25, 1932, *Report of the Thirty-second Annual Conference of the Labour Party*, 1932, pp. 60, 311.

[20] H. N. Brailsford, "Simon Torpedoes the Hoover Plan," *New Leader*, July 1, 1932, p. 2.

[21] Clement Attlee, 270 *H.C.Deb.*, November 10, 1932, cols. 530–31.

tion, what the government had all along attempted to do was "in no sort of way to set up a rival to anybody else's plan," but to be sure that there were no commitments which were "contrary to the essential convictions of anyone." Consequently, the first phase of the Disarmament Conference closed with no progress recorded and with the withdrawal of the German delegation from the conference.[22]

Viewing with grave concern the serious deterioration in the international situation, the Labour party warned that "the failure of the Disarmament Conference would be fraught with the gravest dangers to the peace of Europe and the world." It held that the government, by the "narrow nationalism of its outlook," by the "surrender to those who desired to maintain inflated armaments," and by its "indifference or hostility to the League of Nations," had facilitated this deterioration. Labour condemned the doctrine that armaments provided security and declared its "unqualified hostility to the rearming of any country in any circumstances." At the same time, it recognized that the victors in the last war could not evade their solemn responsibility and obligations toward the former Central Powers and the world. If Britain and France continued to reject any substantial measure of disarmament, their responsibility for a situation which might have the most serious consequences would be very grave. The Labour party called upon the government, "at this critical moment, to give a bold lead to the Disarmament Conference and thus endeavour to avoid a catastrophe of incalculable gravity."[23]

During the second year of the conference, the British government finally produced a plan which it claimed would assist the conference by meeting the respective claims of Germany for equality and France for security. The two essentials of the British Draft Convention, according to the Prime Minister, were that it contained for the first time figures regarding various arms and provided for "a stage of progress towards equality" during which equality itself would not be carried out, but there would be no question of rearmament.[24] The Labour party denied that the British Convention provided for either disarmament or security. The Prime Minister's proposals started too high, more or less stabilizing armaments at those high levels, and leaving room for considerable reduction before any marked advance

[22] 270 *H.C.Deb.*, November 10, 1932, col. 548. Cf. speech of Rt. Hon. Sir John Simon at Opening of Disarmament Conference, February 8, 1932; Declaration of British Disarmament Policy; Declaration of the Policy of His Majesty's Government in the United Kingdom on Disarmament in Connection with Germany's Claim to Equality of Rights, *British State Papers*, Cmd. 4018, 4122, 4189 (1932).

[23] National Executive resolution, *Report of the Thirty-second Annual Conference of the Labour Party*, 1932, p. 228.

[24] Ramsay MacDonald, 276 *H.C.Deb.*, March 23, 1933, col. 514.

was made in the direction of disarmament. The plan pointed not to a reduction of the armaments of others to Germany's low level, but to an increase of Germany's arms to equal the higher level elsewhere. Labour did not attach much importance to the prospect of merely controlling poisonous gas and submarines unless there were also proposals for permanently reducing the personnel and war matériel of all countries. As for security, the Convention made no provision beyond "consultation" and left untouched the questions of supervision and control.[25]

Although the British Draft Convention was accepted by the Disarmament Conference as a basis for discussion, it did not advance beyond a "first reading" because of the reservations and conflicting interpretations attached by the governments represented at the conference. When the United States intervened with a proposal accepting the British Draft as a first step toward the abolition of all aggressive weapons and providing for the conclusion of a "consultative pact" to implement the security proposals contained in the British plan, the Labour party hoped that some real progress would follow. Though the British government "warmly welcomed" President Roosevelt's declaration, it did not take up the American offer either to participate in a security plan or to further the reduction and limitation of armaments. Instead, within a few days of the American declaration to the Disarmament Conference, the British government "dropped a bombshell" by refusing to consider the abolition of aerial bombing. In spite of the possibility of a new race in air armaments, the British government claimed that a monetary saving would be accomplished by bombing from the air rather than by sending a land expedition to police an outlaying area of the Empire. It was "terrible to think," Clement Attlee declared, "that for these considerations we should hold up the Disarmament Conference."[26] The Labour party, on the other hand, was "resolutely" in favor of the total abolition of air warfare and military aircraft, and the international control of civil aviation. It therefore demanded that the government at the Disarmament Conference abandon its "retrograde attitude on the question of air bombing."[27] It was too late, however, to hope for any modification of the government's position, for the Disarmament Conference adjourned in June 1933 to allow the Powers to negotiate the differences which

[25] David Grenfell, ibid., cols. 521–23. Cf. Draft Disarmament Convention Submitted to the Disarmament Conference at Geneva on March 16, 1933, by the Rt. Hon. J. Ramsay MacDonald, British State Papers, Cmd. 4279 (1933).

[26] 279 H.C.Deb., June 13, 1933, col. 35.

[27] George Lansbury, 280 H.C.Deb., July 5, 1933, col. 342.

had thus far prevented the achievement of a disarmament convention.

After the adjournment of the conference, British Labour joined the International Labour movement in a campaign "to support every loyal effort made to avoid failure of the Disarmament Conference." The International warned that at a time when the Fascist governments were creating "uneasiness and mistrust," it was "the imperative duty of the democratic Governments not to show any spirit of accommodation in regard to these violations of international agreements and to refrain from associating themselves with any weakness in the task of disarmament." It insisted that the World Disarmament Conference resume its work without delay, with the determination to secure an effective reduction of armaments, which alone was capable of diminishing the dangers of war. "A substantial disarmament convention under rigorous supervision," it held, was "a guarantee of universal security" and "must be concluded."[28] The British Labour party, impatient with the "long-drawn-out delay" in the disarmament negotiations, decided to submit to the government a series of proposals to break the deadlock among the Powers. It suggested an eight-point program for presentation to the Disarmament Conference including the following provisions: the complete abandonment of all air bombing; general abolition of all weapons forbidden to Germany; international control of civil aviation; reduction by all nations in expenditure on arms; supervision of private manufacture and trade in armaments; international inspection and control of armaments in all countries; creation of an international police force; and definition of aggression on the basis of the proposals made by the Committee of the Disarmament Conference.[29] Labour's plan was rejected by the government, with Sir John Simon's explanation that Britain had already taken an "active lead" throughout the conference and had been the one Great Power to set an example by a unilateral reduction of armaments, by producing a connected scheme, and by "daring to mention a figure." The government was determined to continue its negotiations outside the Disarmament Conference because it was convinced that the key to a disarmament arrangement lay in the finding of an accommodation between Germany and France.[30]

During the course of these "parallel and supplementary conversa-

[28] Resolution of Joint Disarmament Commission of the L.S.I. and I.F.T.U., *Fifth Labour and Socialist International*, Paris, August 1933 (Zurich: L.S.I., 1933), p. 24.

[29] 281 *H.C.Deb.*, November 13, 1933, col. 579.

[30] *Ibid.*, cols. 691–700. For the negotiations with Germany on the question of equality of rights, cf. Proceedings of the Bureau of the Disarmament Conference, Geneva, October 14, 1933, *British State Papers*, Cmd. 4437 (1933).

tions," the British government produced a memorandum attempting to provide a basis for prompt agreement. The government admitted that it was not an "ideal or spectacular" program, but under the circumstances of Germany's final withdrawal from the Disarmament Conference and from the League of Nations, certain concessions had to be made to realize a convention which contained some disarmament and which faced the realities of the present time. In "approaching the whole thing in a spirit of realism," the government had reached "the inevitable deduction from two positions": that Germany's claim to equality of rights in the matter of armaments could not and ought not to be resisted and that no practical solution could be found on the basis that all nations throughout the world immediately abandon all weapons denied to Germany by the Versailles Treaty. The objective of the government's memorandum was to show how it was possible for highly armed powers progressively to get rid of their heaviest weapons.[31] The memorandum was regarded by the Labour party as a proposal for the recognition of the rearmament of Nazi Germany. German equality had been recognized too late and conceded "not to reason but to force." In view of the German intention of rearmament and the French fear for security, it was not likely that any degree of disarmament would follow from the British memorandum. The "real failure" of the Disarmament Conference, according to the Labour Opposition, was not primarily due to the differences over tanks or air forces but to the fact that there had been "no acceptance of the principle of the disuse of force in world affairs."[32]

If any possibility of disarmament remained after the circulation of the British memorandum, it was "jeopardized" by the government's decision, despite the negotiations for a Disarmament Convention and for European pacts of nonaggression and mutual assistance, to enter upon a policy of rearmament which Labour claimed was "neither necessitated by any new commitments nor calculated to add to the security of the nation." The government's White Paper on Defence marked a complete change of policy which Labour believed was "completely at variance with the spirit in which the League of Nations was created to establish a collective world peace." So far from ensuring national safety, it would lead to international competition, the insecurity thereby engendered, and ultimately to war. Condemning the rearmament program as a return to the prewar atmosphere of alliances

[31] Sir John Simon, 285 *H.C.Deb.*, February 6, 1934, col. 992; Anthony Eden, 287 *H.C.Deb.*, March 14, 1934, col. 391. Cf. Memorandum on Disarmament Communicated by His Majesty's Government in the United Kingdom to the Governments Represented at the Disarmament Conference, *British State Papers*, Cmd. 4498 (1934).
[32] Clement Attlee, 285 *H.C.Deb.*, February 6, 1934, cols. 1000–1001.

and rivalries and an arms race, Labour opposed the policy of the "National" government in seeking security by piling up huge competitive armaments.[33] However, in view of the threatening attitude of the dictatorships, which were increasing their armaments at an unprecedented rate, flouting international law, and refusing to co-operate in the work of organizing peace, Labour declared that "the armed strength of the countries loyal to the League of Nations must be conditioned by the armed strength of the potential aggressors." The policy of the Labour party, reaffirmed until the outbreak of the war, was to maintain such defense forces as were consistent with "the country's responsibilities as a Member of the League of Nations, the preservation of the people's rights and liberties, the continuance of democratic institutions and the observance of International Law." At the same time, "realising the relation between foreign policy and armaments, and having regard to the deplorable record of the Government," Labour declined "to accept responsibility for a purely competitive armaments policy" and reserved "full liberty to criticise the rearmament programme of the present Government."[34] Consequently, the Labour Opposition consistently voted against the arms estimates "in order to mark its entire opposition to the international policy of the Government," of which the rearmament program was "an integral part." A vote against the estimates was not a vote for the abolition of the services concerned, but a vote in opposition to the policy of which the estimate was the expression. Labour did not advocate unilateral disarmament. On the contrary, it definitely declared its willingness to provide such defense forces as were required for Great Britain to do her part in a system of collective security through the League of Nations.[35]

The failure of the disarmament efforts and the reversion to militarism in Europe and Asia had prevented the restoration of the international confidence which Labour regarded as an essential condition for overcoming the economic crisis. During the disarmament negotiations, the Labour party had insisted that unless a serious move were made toward disarmament it would be impossible to solve the prob-

[33] Motions of censure, 292 *H.C.Deb.*, July 30, 1934, col. 2325; 299 *H.C.Deb.*, March 11, 1935, cols. 35–46.

[34] National Executive resolution, *Report of the Thirty-sixth Annual Conference of the Labour Party*, 1936, p. 182; National Council of Labour, "International Policy and Defence," *Report of the Sixty-ninth Annual Conference of the T.U.C.*, 1937, p. 473; *Report of the Thirty-seventh Annual Conference of the Labour Party*, 1937, pp. 181-84, 279.

[35] The Parliamentary Party's Manifesto on Armaments and Foreign Policy, July 1936, New Fabian Research Bureau, *The Road to War* (London: Gollancz, 1937), pp. 192–93.

lems of reparations, war debts, international trade, and commercial relationships. Labour had repeatedly declared that the economic consequences of the policy of reparations and war debts had been "most disastrous to Europe and throughout the world," and had urged "a new settlement of the entire problem" with a view to establishing the conditions under which reparations and inter-Allied debts might be canceled and "the fabric of European economic life restored."[36] The recognition that under existing economic conditions Germany would be incapable of fulfilling the obligations assumed under the Young plan at the end of the year of the Hoover moratorium and the hope that a satisfactory solution to the problem of reparations would pave the way for a war-debts settlement with the United States finally prompted the British government to consult upon these questions with the other European powers at an International Conference at Lausanne. The result of this conference was an agreement to abolish German reparations and to settle upon one capital payment due from Germany, subject to a three-year moratorium from the date of the settlement. The Labour party gave its "wholehearted support" to the Lausanne Agreement "as the first step towards clearing away the tangle of financial and political injustices of the War."[37] On the other hand, it viewed with disapproval the "secret agreement" between Britain and France, claiming that it restored the *entente cordiale* and aroused the suspicions of the German government as to the intentions behind the agreement. It also condemned the "Gentlemen's Agreement" between Britain and the other European powers not to ratify the Convention until a "satisfactory settlement" had been reached between them and their own creditors as an ultimatum to the United States to release the European powers from their obligations. The Labour party felt that the British government, by its "secret agreements" at Lausanne and by its disarmament policy at Geneva, had compromised a future settlement of war debts with the United States. In view of the American attitude that it was unfair that Europe should expect the war-debts question to be settled if that settlement were to release money to be spent on more armaments, Labour believed that the British government's response to the Hoover disarmament plan had "destroyed not merely the faint hope of cancellation, but the pros-

[36] Cf. Statement of General Council of the T.U.C. and National Executive of the Labour Party, May 25, 1932, *Report of the Thirty-second Annual Conference of the Labour Party*, 1932, p. 60; resolutions adopted, *ibid.*, p. 253; and *Report of the Thirty-first Annual Conference of the Labour Party*, 1931, p. 179.

[37] Sir Stafford Cripps, 268 *H.C.Deb.*, July 11, 1932, cols. 923–24. Cf. Final Act of the Lausanne Conference, July 9, 1932, *British State Papers*, Cmd. 4126 (1932).

pect of any really generous reduction."[38] As George Lansbury pointed out, the conference at Lausanne and the conference at Geneva were "irrevocably mixed up" and the reduction of debts proved to be dependent upon the progress toward the reduction of armaments.[39]

Although welcoming the "first step" taken at Lausanne, the Labour party noted that even if the Lausanne Agreement had been a final settlement of reparations and war debts, which it was not, it would still be a very small part of the work necessary to overcome the world economic crisis. Labour believed that it was "useless to clear away the wreckage unless some better system" were put in its place and that the cause of world economic distress was not merely reparations and war debts but economic nationalism. It therefore looked forward to the meeting of the World Economic Conference which had been decided upon at Lausanne as an opportunity for reaching "a great new international agreement" and removing some of the causes of militarism and dictatorship. It also expressed the hope that nothing would be done at the forthcoming Imperial Conference at Ottawa to prejudice the success of the later conference at London and that the British government would not allow any postponement of the World Economic Conference. It warned, however, that an essential preliminary to the success of the World Economic Conference was that the British government should give clear and unequivocal support to an immediate universal and substantial reduction of armaments on the basis of equality of status for all nations. The World Economic Conference could not succeed without a great measure of success at the Disarmament Conference; and the United States was most unlikely to co-operate in the economic reconstruction of Europe unless she were convinced that the European states were in earnest about disarmament. Again, Labour insisted that the question of world recovery was bound up with the settlement of debts and dependent upon the achievement of disarmament. These two things—debts and disarmament—Clement Attlee predicted, might yet "kill the World Economic Conference."[40]

During the preparatory stage of the conference, the Labour party

[38] H. N. Brailsford, "Europe's Cobweb," *New Leader*, July 27, 1932, p. 8. Actually, the two "secret" agreements were published, but not until considerable suspicion had been aroused as to their content. Cf. Declaration Issued by His Majesty's Government in the United Kingdom and the French Government Regarding Future European Co-operation, July 13, 1932; Further Documents Relating to the Settlement Reached at the Lausanne Conference, June 16–July 9, 1932, *British State Papers*, Cmd. 4131, 4129 (1932).

[39] 267 *H.C.Deb.*, June 28, 1932, col. 1773.

[40] 279 *H.C.Deb.*, June 13, 1933, col. 39. Also cf. George Lansbury, David Grenfell, 268 *H.C.Deb.*, July 12, 1932, cols. 1150, 1224.

repeatedly demanded from the government a statement of its aims and proposals. The leader of the Labour Opposition claimed that the country was entitled to know, after nearly two years of office by the present government, what its policy in regard to the various questions to come before the Economic Conference really was. Lansbury complained that there had not been a single concrete proposition nor a clear and coherent statement of the government's own policy.[41] Some indication of the government's intentions was provided, however, by its rejection of the policy resolution supported by the Labour Opposition. The proposed program, recognizing that the chief factor in producing world-wide economic distress was to be found in the financial and economic restrictions placed upon international trade, urged the government "to lay before the forthcoming World Economic Conference definite proposals for the all-round reduction of tariffs and the removal or reduction of other obstacles to trade, to take the initiative in the formation of a group of free trade or low tariff countries and to make agreements for such modifications in the most-favoured-nation clauses of existing treaties as may be necessary." In response, the government pointed out that one of the factors in aggravating world economic distress had been "the consistent raising of tariffs by the vast majority of the countries of the world since the War and the exploiting of the free market of Great Britain, which provided the dumping ground for the surplus products of those countries, with disastrous results to British industry and workpeople." The government maintained that it had established a "reasonable tariff policy" which had ended the "defenceless condition" of Great Britain, rendered it possible to secure trade agreements with friendly countries, and provided the power to bargain with, and, if necessary, to retaliate against countries with hostile tariffs. In considering these matters in connection with the World Economic Conference, the government was ready so to modify existing treaties as to give tariff advantages to those countries which were ready to reciprocate in the promotion of freer trade and to raise tariffs against those countries which did not desire to reciprocate. From this reply the Labour Opposition concluded that the government had no ideas of its own, no constructive policy, and believed that the best way of getting rid of economic nationalism was "to be as nationalist yourself economically" as possible.[42]

The Labour party attributed the failure of the London Economic

[41] 277 *H.C.Deb.*, May 9, 1933, cols. 1378, 1381.

[42] Sir Stafford Cripps, 275 *H.C.Deb.*, March 15, 1933, col. 2026. The Opposition motion was defeated, 203–58, and the government's policy as stated in the amendment was approved. *Ibid.*, cols. 1971, 1985.

Conference to the fact that without political pacification there could be no recovery from the world crisis. Holding economic nationalism to be "really a form of armament," Labour contended that it was impossible to achieve any measure of economic disarmament while there was military armament and aggression in Europe and Asia. In spite of Labour's warning, the conference had been postponed for over a year, during which time the Japanese conquest of Manchuria, the breakdown of the disarmament negotiations, and the Nazi revolution in Germany had had the worst possible effect upon the international economic situation. Having also asked for the World Economic Conference before the Imperial Conference was called, Labour believed that it was a "profound mistake" to have delayed the Economic Conference and to have made the Ottawa Agreements before the London Conference came into being. At Ottawa, the government committed itself to a policy of economic nationalism which, Labour insisted, was one of the factors that led to the failure of the World Economic Conference. As a result of the Imperial Agreements, Labour pointed out, the British representative on the Preparatory Commission of the Economic Conference, Sir Walter Layton, had resigned from the Commission, stating that the British government's economic policy made it impossible for the World Economic Conference to succeed. The Labour party concluded that the London Conference failed because there had been neither adequate preparation nor any real co-operation among the governments in an effort to solve their common economic problems. There had been only an attempt by each country to try to make every other country fall in with the plans suitable for its own area, whether it was the United States and the question of currency, or the bloc of gold countries and the gold standard, or Britain and tariffs, quotas, and restrictions. In this failure, Labour charged, the British government had its "very large share," for it had given an impetus to economic nationalism by its Imperial Agreements at Ottawa and had compromised international co-operation with Europe and the United States by its Far Eastern and disarmament policies at Geneva.[43]

[43] Sir Stafford Cripps, 280 *H.C.Deb.*, July 26, 1933, cols. 2622–31. For the government's policy at the conference, cf. Statement by the Chancellor of the Exchequer at the Monetary and Economic Conference on 14th June 1933; Monetary and Economic Conference, Declaration by Delegation of British Commonwealth, *British State Papers*, Cmd. 4357, 4403 (1933).

8

THE TURNING POINT

The international situation resulting from the failure of the nations to banish the fear of war, to achieve a substantial measure of disarmament, and to grapple with the economic problems of the new age called for a restatement of the principles of Labour's foreign policy which would take full account of the changed circumstances in the world. During the past three years, the Labour party had endeavored to strengthen and develop its organization and membership and to review and expand its policy in the light of experience and needs of the times. By 1934, the National Executive Committee felt that the time had arrived for it to circulate to affiliated organizations for consideration and to submit to the annual conferences of the Trades Union Congress and the Labour party for adoption a considered statement of its general policy under the title, *For Socialism and Peace*. In presenting the new policy statement and the Executive's report on "War and Peace," Arthur Henderson wanted it to be "very clearly understood" that the Executive was not putting forward a new policy but was restating Labour's aims and Labour's policies and indicating the methods by which that policy might be applied. The methods adopted by the National Executive Committee had already been either seriously discussed by the Labour Party Conference or brought before the movement in the literature of the party, especially in the pamphlet prepared by Henderson the previous year, *Labour's Foreign Policy*. Thus the Executive had kept well within the decisions of the Party Conference. At the Hastings Party Conference, there had been two foreign-policy resolutions carried: one was exclusively concerned with propaganda and resistance to war; the other touched on the wider aspects of Labour's policy for preventing war by organizing peace. Neither resolution, according to Henderson, contradicted nor invalidated the other, nor was ever intended to supersede the long-continued foreign policy of the party upheld by both minority Labour governments. Labour's foreign policy, in the fullest sense of the term, was not actually discussed at Hastings, although the conference had before it the pamphlet *Labour's Foreign Policy* and had indicated its approval "in no unmistakable fashion" of the speech delivered by Henderson on the question of war and peace. In preparing its report, the National Executive had to consider how to give effect to the instructions in the

"War and Peace" resolution agreed upon at Hastings. These instructions included consultation with the co-operative, trade-union, and international labor movements with a view to deciding what steps, including a general strike, were to be taken to organize the opposition of the working class in the event of war or threat of war.[1] The Executive very soon found that it was difficult to separate the question of war resistance from the wider question of preventing war by organizing peace. It was therefore obliged to show how the two resolutions at Hastings supplemented each other and how they both fitted into Labour's foreign policy as a whole. To do this it was necessary not only to prepare a restatement of that policy, so framed as to incorporate the developments introduced by the two Hastings resolutions, but also to take account of the present international situation and tendencies. That was why, Henderson insisted, the declarations in the Executive's report on "War and Peace" and in the manifesto *For Socialism and Peace* were "really a restatement of Labour's old policy and attitude in international relations."[2]

The result of the National Executive's efforts was a proclamation of "aims and policy for permanent world peace and good international relations," including criteria by which they were to be applied. In its report on "War and Peace," the Executive went further by pointing out that, in the event of threat of war, a special Trades Union Congress would be held to decide how to deal with the situation in the circumstances of the moment. This was in harmony with the decision of the Weymouth T.U.C. (September 1934), taken under the Standing Orders of the T.U.C., providing that in the event of there being a danger of an outbreak of war the General Council would call a special congress to decide on industrial action, and "strictly consistent" with the decision of the Labour Party Conference under the Hastings resolution. The Executive, however, having given very serious consideration to this position, was definitely of the opinion that the trade-union movement alone should not be expected to bear the responsibility for stopping war. The lack of a strong and independent trade-union movement in such countries as Germany, Italy, and Japan made the calling of a general strike against their governments an impossibility. In addition, since it was quite possible that aggressive action might come

[1] Cf. *Report of the Thirty-third Annual Conference of the Labour Party*, 1933, pp. 186–92. A resolution of the Joint Disarmament Commission of the L.S.I. and I.F.T.U. called upon the workers to organize a general strike and a boycott against an aggressor state, defined as a state refusing arbitration. *Fifth Labour and Socialist International*, Paris, August 1933 (Zurich: L.S.I., 1933), p. 24.

[2] *Report of the Thirty-fourth Annual Conference of the Labour Party*, 1934, pp. 152–53.

from some of those countries, a general strike under such circumstances could not possibly be made effective by the trade-unions in those countries. Not only the trade-union movement, but every section of the Labour movement and every citizen who wanted to preserve peace should therefore share the responsibility of any organized action that might be taken to prevent war. The Executive had not abandoned the idea of a general strike nor in any way repudiated the Hastings resolution. It had devised a war-resistance policy consistent with the whole of Labour's foreign policy. It believed that there was no alternative to the collective peace system except a relapse into international anarchy, a race in armaments, and, sooner or later, war or revolution. Development of the collective peace system was the only policy that held out any hope of producing a warless world, of preventing war by organizing peace.[3]

In the statement *For Socialism and Peace*, the Executive provided the "positive and constructive policy which any Labour Government would seek to apply in all its international relations." Labour's policy was directed toward "the abolition of war, through the League of Nations, and the strengthening of the Collective Peace System, by expanding and clarifying the undertaking not to resort to war; by non-aggression treaties backed by a definition of aggression and the ultimate revision of the Covenant; by arbitration, and the provision of machinery for the final settlement of all disputes by peaceful means; and the substitution of an international police force under the League's authority for national armed forces." The "great dominating aim" was the organization of peace through the League of Nations and the removal of the causes of war. To realize its aims, Labour proposed to pass a "Peace Act of Parliament," which would make it impossible for any British government to use force as an instrument of national policy without violating the law of the land and would empower the government to apply any economic and financial measures necessary to take its share in collective action. In addition, Labour would "create machinery and obligations for settling all international disputes by pacific methods; promote drastic disarmament by rapid stages through international agreement, with the ultimate object of the abolition of national armed forces and their replacement by an international police force; abolish the weapons of aggression forbidden to Germany; abolish the private manufacture and sale of armaments, abolish national air forces, internationalise civil aviation, and create an international air force; develop friendly relations, commercial and political, with the Soviet Union and the United States; combat economic na-

3 "War and Peace," *ibid.*, pp. 245–46.

tionalism, particularly tariffs, and press for international agreement in economic and financial questions, transport, travel and communications, raw materials, loans, hours and conditions of labour, public health, etc., using to the utmost the League of Nations and the International Labour Office." Labour was determined to "abjure once and for all the old negative, backward-looking, competitive idea of maintaining the balance of power as the final goal of British foreign policy," substituting "the constructive, positive forward-looking of a Co-operative World Commonwealth." That was why Labour's whole approach to the question of international relations was "fundamentally different from that of the Conservatives." Since 1918, the Labour party had "never wavered in its loyalty to the policy of the League of Nations, of compulsory arbitration of international disputes, of disarmament, of international economic co-operation, and of pooled security by mutual guarantees against aggression"; and it had "never shirked the fundamental difficulties" involved in the principle of international co-operation.[4]

The Executive's foreign-policy statement received the overwhelming support of both the Trades Union Congress at Weymouth and the Labour Party Conference at Southport. Even the severest critics of the Executive's policy recommended in their amendments that Britain should remain in the League of Nations and that the next Labour government should strive to make effective, on as wide a front as possible, the principle of collective security. The dissenting minorities at both conferences represented the two streams of opinion which had been repeatedly expressed in opposition to the party's foreign policy. One of these views, held by the pacifists and expounded by Lord Ponsonby, advocated a program of complete and unilateral disarmament irrespective of the armaments of the other countries. The other opinion, put forward by Sir Stafford Cripps and the Socialist League, warned of the dangers of co-operation with capitalist states and insisted upon lining up the socialist countries apart from the other countries of the world. According to the class-war advocates, neither Arthur Henderson nor any other individual could ensure peace under an organized competitive capitalist system, and to justify armaments and war preparations by the fear of an aggressor meant "helping the bloody ferocious rule of British imperialism."[5] The replies of Arthur Henderson, Philip Noel-Baker, Ernest Bevin, and Clement Attlee left

[4] *For Socialism and Peace* (London: Labour Party, 1934), pp. 8–15. Also cf. Arthur Henderson, *Labour's Foreign Policy* (London: Labour Party, 1933), p. 3.

[5] Cf. *Report of the Thirty-fourth Annual Conference of the Labour Party, 1934*, pp. 159–74; *Report of the Sixty-sixth Annual Conference of the T.U.C., 1934*, pp. 321–28.

the conference in no doubt at all regarding the League obligations undertaken. Even the opposition had to admit that on this issue there was certainly no ambiguity: the Labour party had given its solemn pledge that, in accordance with League commitments, it was "prepared to go to war as an ally of other capitalist Powers, if need be in defence of a capitalist nation, should the League at any time declare such a nation to be the victim of an act of aggression."[6] According to the overwhelming vote against the critical amendments, the Labour party had refused to accept the view that the attempt to secure international co-operation must await the triumph of socialism throughout the world. On the contrary, it had held that whatever kind of governments might exist in different countries, it was none the less the duty of the Labour movement to work with all its power to develop the beginnings of peace. Clement Attlee expressed this belief when he said that "ultimately we shall not get peace until we have world socialism, but we have to deal with things as they are today."[7]

In supporting the policy outlined in *For Socialism and Peace*, the Labour party accepted the inevitable consequences of honoring all the obligations of the League Covenant and making a reality of the collective peace system: peaceful settlement of disputes, renunciation of war, collective determination of an aggressor, and collective action against an aggressor so determined. Labour recognized that disarmament would not be possible unless a solid system of collective defense within the League of Nations was established and also that the danger of war would not be averted unless it was fully realized that any act of aggression would be resisted by collective strength sufficiently powerful to restore peace. To this end, it was necessary for every member of the League to co-operate loyally and effectively in support of the Covenant and in resistance to any act of aggression. In order to prevent war, it was essential "to restore faith in the sincerity of the declarations of the Briand-Kellogg Pact and in the reality of the Collective Peace System." Labour advocated the conclusion of a treaty of nonaggression and mutual assistance associated with the sanctions system of the Covenant and including a definition of the aggressor in an international conflict which would cover the whole of Europe. When a general pact was concluded with provisions sufficiently wide and precise to constitute an effective guaranty of collective action

---

[6] Jennie Lee, "What I Saw at the Labour Party Conference," *Labour Leader*, October 5, 1934, pp. 1, 5.

[7] *Report of the Thirty-fourth Annual Conference of the Labour Party*, 1934, p. 174. The Socialist League amendment was defeated, 2,146,000–206,000; the Executive's report on "War and Peace" was adopted 1,953,000–269,000; and the appendix on "War and Peace" was adopted, 1,519,000–673,000. *Ibid.*, pp. 165, 178.

against an aggressor, special pacts would cease to be necessary. Until then, Labour was determined that any special treaties should be compatible with the rights and obligations of members of the League, should respect the functions and jurisdiction of the duly constituted organs of the League, and should be open for signature to any other state in the same region and upon the same terms. Labour was convinced, however, that no system of security, nor the Covenant of the League of Nations itself, would "produce its full effect" until the world had "courageously entered upon the path of general disarmament."[8]

When it came to applying its foreign policy, Labour was faced with an international situation fraught with the danger of a new race in armaments and a threat of aggression to which the events in the Far East had given the initial impulse. Labour held that the government's Far Eastern policy consisted, in its essentials, of preferring the risk of disregarding its obligations under Articles X and XVI of the Covenant to the risk of honoring these obligations. Consequently, "the tentacles of Japanese imperialism" had been extended beyond Manchukuo into northern China and Mongolia, thus creating a major menace to world peace in the Far East. The perils of the Far Eastern situation had for the present, however, been somewhat obscured by the position in Europe resulting from German rearmament and the Nazi regime's open reversion to power politics and international anarchy. The Labour party asserted that the verdict of history would assign to the British government "a not inconsiderable share of responsibility" for the Nazi menace in so far as it had been created by external circumstances. If, from the outset of the Disarmament Conference, the present British government had offered, at least to all European members of the League, a treaty of nonaggression and had declared that it subscribed loyally and wholeheartedly to the minimum obligations of the collective system—the renunciation of war as the means of changing the status quo and the boycott of the aggressor— while urging German equality of rights through general disarmament, the present situation would have been very different. This was not done, however. Instead, the British government at Geneva had opposed all plans for the drastic reduction of armaments and had acquiesced in clandestine German rearmament. In the realm of security, the Conservatives' policy had been one of "no further commitments" and a refusal to define existing commitments. Labour claimed that its warnings had been disregarded and its prophecies fulfilled. Nazi Ger-

---

[8] Manifesto of the Bureau of the L.S.I., Brussels, May 7, 1935, *Report of the Thirty-fifth Annual Conference of the Labour Party*, 1935, p. 314.

many had left the Disarmament Conference and the League of Nations. Through its lack of a positive foreign policy, the British government had allowed Hitler and Mussolini to assume the initiative in European politics and to compel Great Britain to treat with them "not on the basis of collective security, but on the basis of unlimited national sovereignty."[9]

The Four-Power Pact initiated by Mussolini had been the first step in this direction. The "National" government had given sufficient indication of its impatience with the role of the smaller members of the League to encourage Mussolini to broach the subject of a European Concert of Great Powers. During the Sino-Japanese conflict, it had been evident that the British government, annoyed by being compelled by the smaller powers to acknowledge that Japan was the aggressor state in the dispute, felt that the Covenant gave excessive rights to these powers. A similar attitude had been revealed in the British Draft Disarmament Convention (Articles 1 to 5) which gave the Great Powers (including the aggressor Japan) the monopoly of the right even to summon a conference. This "consortium of Great Powers," substituted for the League Council as the executive and consultative organ under the Treaty, was to consult, in the event of a danger to the peace, under the Kellogg Pact instead of under the Covenant. The British project had been defeated by the other League members, as had its opposition to condemning the Japanese aggression, but the intent in both cases had not been overlooked by the Italian dictator.[10] Immediately following the submission of the British Draft Convention, Mussolini issued an invitation to the British Prime Minister and Foreign Secretary to confer in Rome on their way back from Geneva and upon their arrival presented the proposal. In its original form, the pact recognized the preponderant authority of the four Great Powers (Britain, France, Germany, and Italy) in determining the affairs of Europe. It provided for the revision of the territorial provisions of the peace treaties and the rearmament of Germany to the level of the other Great Powers in the event of a breakdown of the Disarmament Conference. The British government welcomed Mussolini's plan and agreed that Article XIX of the Covenant regarding treaty revision was not meant to be dormant. According to the Prime Minister, there was no greater danger than that, when the inevitable nationalist revival occurred, the peace treaties would be the subject of challenge. Believing, however, that there were certain difficulties in the form of the

[9] "The International Situation," Report of the National Executive Committee, 1934–35, *ibid.*, pp. 3–4.

[10] Vigilantes, *Inquest on Peace* (London: Gollancz, 1935), pp. 246–47.

draft which might arouse the suspicions of France and the smaller powers, the British government felt that provision should be made for recognition of the corresponding obligations of the Covenant— namely, the sanctity of treaties—and for consultation with the smaller powers whenever their special interests were concerned. Britain's objective in supporting the plan, according to Sir John Simon, was to endeavor by consultation, co-operation, and communication to prevent the formation of two opposing blocs in which one or other of these Great Powers would find themselves opposed. It was not in the least, Simon asserted, "that they should combine together to impose their will on other people"; the only alternative to the co-operation of the Four Powers was "that they should go different ways."[11]

The alternative to the Four-Power Pact, the Labour party insisted, was co-operation within the League of Nations in accordance with the obligations of the Covenant. Opposing the Great Power concept completely, Labour viewed the Four-Power bloc as "a great menace to the League of Nations" and "a super-dictatorship of Europe." The British government, in supporting this pact, was departing from the conception of the maintenance of world peace by the action of a number of nations, great and small operating together, to a world in which the League of Nations would be dominated by a number of Great Powers. Labour could see no desirable basis for the scheme, particularly if the real reason for the Four-Power Pact was to barter something in exchange for Germany's promise not to rearm. The Labour party had always believed that the peace treaties should be revised by joint action of all nations rather than in the interests of a few powers. But Labour would not countenance for a moment "yielding to Hitler and force what was denied to Stresemann and reason." If now, after ten years, recognition were given to force by concessions to this new Germany, the whole of what had been done since the war to set reason and justice above force would be definitely set back. The revision of the territorial settlement in favor of Germany, Attlee said, "would be an ironical pendant to the rape of China by Japan."[12]

British Labour's apprehensions of Great Power hegemony and territorial concessions to the dictators were shared by France and the smaller powers of Europe. As a result of the pressure of the French bloc of Little Entente Powers, the Four-Power Pact was amended to such an extent that the essence of Mussolini's original proposal was eliminated in the final draft. The provisions for the predominant authority of the Great Powers, opposed by the smaller states, and for

[11] 276 *H.C.Deb.*, April 13, 1933, cols. 2816–21.
[12] *Ibid.*, cols. 2741–43.

territorial concessions, opposed by France, did not appear at all in the text of the concluded treaty. The question of treaty revision (Article XIX) was merely recognized, along with the corresponding obligation of the sanctity of treaties (Articles X and XVI), and provision was made for the high contracting Powers only to "examine the position." As to the reference to Articles X and XVI of the Covenant, the British government insisted upon noting that its adherence to the agreement did not imply "any extension" of British obligations in European affairs and that it was "no part of the policy of Great Britain to assume further and additional obligations of this character." When the Labour party read the five articles of the final pact, it saw that they amounted to nothing more than that the Four Powers would agree to consult together before taking action, which, it noted, they were bound to do already under the Covenant. The point emphasized by the Prime Minister was that the pact's "big and almost only detail was the revision of treaties"; but Labour observed that revision seemed "rather to have slipped out of the Pact" now that it was "lumped together" with Articles X and XVI as subject to further examination. Without revision, Labour wondered if there was anything effective about the pact at all.[13] The only practical result of the Four-Power Pact was that it convinced Mussolini that the "National" government shared his own views of the machinery of the League of Nations and that among the Great Powers, the League had no convinced supporters except France who could be relied upon to uphold the obligations of the Covenant. Throughout the negotiations, the British government had shown its preference for conducting its diplomacy outside the League of Nations and for evading its obligations under the Covenant.[14]

The Four-Power Pact was the prelude to what the Labour party regarded as the government's policy of yielding to "the dictation of the Hitlers and the Mussolinis."[15] The next stage in this procedure opened with the London Agreement of February 3, 1935, by which the "National" government, having rejected the idea of an all-European treaty, associated itself with a plan of regional pacts covering Western, Eastern, and Central Europe, the conclusion of which was to be followed by Germany's return to the League of Nations and the limitation of armaments.[16] The Labour party was strongly opposed to any such

[13] Clement Attlee, 279 *H.C.Deb.*, June 13, 1933, col. 36. Cf. Despatch to His Majesty's Ambassador at Rome in Regard to the Agreement of Understanding and Co-operation Between France, Germany, Italy, and the United Kingdom, London, June 7, 1933, *British State Papers*, Cmd. 4342 (1933).

[14] *Inquest on Peace*, pp. 252–53.

[15] Clement Attlee, 304 *H.C.Deb.*, July 11, 1935, col. 539.

[16] Cf. Joint Communiqué Issued on Behalf of His Majesty's Government in the

local agreements or to any pact of the kind involving military commitments unless it were part of the League system of collective security. Such regional pacts had only a limited utility, and, at the worst, they tended to weaken the Covenant and the wider loyalty to the League and particularly the whole idea of the universality of peace. Labour felt that it should have been made perfectly clear from the start that Britain would sign no such convention with any state which was not a member of the League or which was not prepared to carry out all the obligations of the Covenant. The German government obviously had no intention of returning to the League of Nations or of concluding an Eastern or a Danubian security pact, as it had answered the British government's proposals by the frank and defiant avowal of German rearmament on a scale equivalent to military preponderance in Europe. The Labour party reminded the government that, by the London Declaration of February 3, it had been agreed that neither Germany nor any other Power whose arms had been defined by the peace treaties was entitled by unilateral action to modify these obligations and that this agreement had been repeated at the Stresa Conference and at the meeting of the League of Nations Council. In spite of these pledges, the British government "tore up entirely" the Treaty of Versailles by concluding a naval agreement with Germany which was "tantamount to a final admission by the British government of the abandonment of the basis of negotiations agreed upon at London on February 3, 1935," and a "final ironical commentary" upon the government's statement of policy to Germany (September 18, 1932) that the correct position under the Treaty of Versailles was that Part V (relating to German disarmament) was still binding and could only cease to be binding by agreement. On what ground, Labour asked, could the government argue that it was entitled to go to Stresa and denounce Germany for violating the Treaty of Versailles by introducing conscription when it entered into a private arrangement recognizing German naval rearmament in violation of that same treaty? By conceding German naval rearmament, Labour declared, the government had "yielded to power politics and blackmail" what it had "refused to international justice and co-operation."[17]

The Labour party vigorously denied the government's claim that

United Kingdom and the Government of the French Republic as the Result of the Conversations Between the French and British Ministers in London, February 1–3, 1935, *British State Papers*, Cmd. 4798 (1935).

[17] George Lansbury, 301 *H.C.Deb.*, May 2, 1935, col. 579; Clement Attlee, *ibid.*, cols. 673–75, 304 *H.C.Deb.*, July 11, 1935, cols. 538–39; Seymour Cocks, *ibid.*, cols. 587–89. For Treaty cf. Exchange of Notes Between His Majesty's Government in the United Kingdom and the German Government Regarding the Limitation of Naval Armaments, London, June 18, 1935, *British State Papers*, Cmd. 4953, 4930 (1935).

the London Agreement had given "general satisfaction all over Europe" and that the Anglo-German naval treaty had made "a contribution to world peace and international appeasement."[18] It pointed out that the entire London Plan had miscarried: none of the proposed security pacts had been concluded; Germany had repudiated the collective system and disarmament; the project for a Western air pact, based on the idea that peace was a direct concern of the British government in Western Europe only, had been reduced to "a surviving fragment of the moribund Agreement" by the new race in air armaments. The Labour party could see no use in suggesting, as the government had done, that it could get any safety from an Eastern pact, a Danubian pact, an air pact, or a German pact when the series of broken pacts had already impeded the Foreign Offices of Europe.[19] Instead of contributing to international security or disarmament, as the government had maintained, the German naval agreement had convinced the other Powers that the aims of British policy were "to strengthen Germany so as to counter-balance French and Russian influence, to avert German naval competition and German colonial ambitions by giving Hitler a free hand in Eastern Europe and to encourage German and Japanese aggressive designs against Soviet Russia."[20] The agreement had given a further impetus to the new naval race initiated by the failure to support the collective security system in the Far East and the breakdown of the Disarmament Conference. Japan had denounced the Washington Naval Treaty and the British government had in consequence abandoned the system of naval ratios, which meant the end of the Washington and London naval treaties and the hope of any international limitation of naval armaments. The Anglo-German Naval Pact, Labour asserted, had been "a further step in the disintegration of the collective peace system of Europe."[21]

The immediate effect of the "National" government's concession to Nazi Germany was to encourage the aggressive ambitions of the Italian dictator. Italian mobilization for the Abyssinian campaign began as early as February 1935. Even at the Stresa Conference, in April, when Britain, France, and Italy, confronted with the accom-

---

[18] Cf. Ramsay MacDonald, 301 *H.C.Deb.*, May 2, 1935, col. 570; First Lord of the Admiralty, Bolton Eyres-Monsell, 303 *H.C.Deb.*, June 21, 1935, cols. 705–8.

[19] Clement Attlee, 304 *H.C.Deb.*, July 11, 1935, col. 539. For the government's efforts at a settlement, cf. Correspondence Showing the Course of Certain Diplomatic Discussions Directed Towards Securing a European Settlement, June 1934–March 1936, *British State Papers*, Cmd. 5143 (1936).

[20] Robert Dell in *Time and Tide*, quoted in *Inquest on Peace*, p. 120.

[21] National Executive Committee, *Report of the Thirty-fifth Annual Conference of the Labour Party*, 1935, p. 5.

plished fact of German rearmament, found themselves in complete agreement in opposing, by all practicable means, any unilateral repudiation of treaties, neither the British nor the French governments warned Mussolini that his military expedition was a strange commentary upon the foreign policy of a Power, the object of whose professed policy was "the collective maintenance of peace within the framework of the League of Nations."[22] At that time, the Labour party pointed out, the policy of the British government was not directed, as it should have been, to making it clear to Mussolini that, if he went to war, Britain would ask the co-operation of the other members of the League in honoring their obligations under Articles X and XVI of the Covenant. On the contrary, the government attempted to make a deal with Italy and France and to persuade the Abyssinians, subject to the intimidation of the Italian military preparations, to sacrifice their territorial integrity and alienate their political independence in favor of Italy as the price of peace. Instead of supporting the efforts of the League to deal with the conflict, the British government brought strong pressure to bear upon Abyssinia to enter into bilateral negotiations with Italy and to adjourn the proceedings before the League Council. The January adjournment was followed by a further adjournment in April and by a "face-saving" arrangement in May, which did not touch the real issue but merely made well-nigh inevitable the situation which subsequently arose. When these direct negotiations broke down, the Labour party stated that there was no longer any doubt that such negotiations had been used by Italy "to circumvent the normal procedure of the League, to despatch troops to the frontiers of Abyssinia and to prepare for a war of conquest to the end of transforming Abyssinia into an Italian colony." The National Council of Labour called upon the government to make immediate proposals in an open meeting of the League Council, with the view of defining the responsibilities of Italy and Abyssinia under the Covenant, and to declare that it would discharge its duties and obligations as a member of the League "without fear or favour."[23] British Labour joined the Socialist and Trade Union Internationals in declaring that it would be intolerable if the Council of the League, after having only recently condemned unilateral breaches of treaties, were now to allow an open breach of treaties and of the League's own Covenant by Fascist Italy. International Labour warned that if, in this

[22] Cf. Joint Resolution of the Stresa Conference including the Anglo-Italian Declaration and the Final Declaration, Stresa, April 14, 1935, *British State Papers*, Cmd. 4880 (1935).

[23] Statement, July 24, 1935, *Report of the Thirty-fifth Annual Conference of the Labour Party*, 1935, p. 12.

clear-cut case of aggression, the League of Nations failed to employ the methods which its Covenant provided to guarantee peace and to apply sanctions against the aggressor, its already seriously diminished authority would receive a "fatal blow" and the foundations of a collective peace system would be destroyed.[24]

Labour's demands for a strong League of Nations stand against aggression were reinforced by public opinion as expressed in the "National Peace Ballot," which had been sponsored by the nonpartisan League of Nations Union and supported by the National Council of Labour. With over eleven and a half million persons voting in this plebiscite, an overwhelming majority declared that Britain should remain a member of the League of Nations and promote, by international agreement, the all-round reduction of armaments, the all-round abolition of national military and naval aircraft, and the abolition of the manufacture and sale of armaments for private profit. The voters were almost unanimous (sixteen to one) in asserting that, if a nation insisted upon attacking another, the other nations should combine to compel it to stop, at least by economic and nonmilitary measures, and there was even a considerable majority (three to one) of the votes cast in the ballot for taking military measures also, if necessary, in such an eventuality. The Labour party hailed the Peace Ballot as "a significant experiment in democratic control of foreign policy" and as "an overwhelming popular mandate to Labour's Foreign Policy." It felt that it now had sufficient grounds for asserting that the policy which it had advocated throughout the Italo-Abyssinian dispute was supported by the great majority of the British people.

The Labour party hoped that the British government would act in accordance with the opinion expressed in the Peace Ballot and saw some indication of the government's moving in this direction by the pronouncements of the leading ministers following the revelation of the results of the poll. When questioned in the House of Commons, the new Foreign Secretary, Sir Samuel Hoare, reversed his previous admission of the need for Italian expansion by announcing that the government was fully conscious of its obligations under the Covenant and certainly intended to uphold them.[25] This same pledge, also made by the Minister for League of Nations Affairs, Anthony Eden, at the previous session of the League Council, was repeated by Hoare at the League Assembly in September. Encouraged by this sudden reversal of policy on the part of the government, the Labour party renewed its efforts for the adoption of sanctions against the aggressor. In co-

[24] Joint Resolution of I.F.T.U. and L.S.I., Brussels, July 31, 1935, *ibid.*, p. 315.
[25] 304 *H.C.Deb.*, July 11, 1935, col. 519; August 1, 1935, col. 2926.

operation with the Labour and Socialist International, British Labour agreed to use all the political means at its disposal to persuade the government to fulfill its duties as a member of the League of Nations and "to put an end to the deplorable failure of the League," thus obliging it

a) to draw the requisite consequences from Mussolini's aggression and to take the measures necessary to safeguard Peace, a duty prescribed by Article 11 of the Covenant, if necessary by closing the Suez Canal to Italian war transports;

b) to make arrangements for arbitration which would not be derisory, as is the case with the present arbitration proceedings, that do not even permit any investigation as to the territory upon which the Wal-Wal frontier incident occurred;

c) to guarantee the independence and territorial integrity of Abyssinia in any event, as all the Members of the League of Nations are pledged to do by Article 10 of the Covenant, and, accordingly to reject unconditionally any partition of Abyssinia, a full Member of the League of Nations, into spheres of influence for the Great Powers, and any protectorate by a Great Power over Abyssinia, even when they are given the appearance of economic and administrative concessions.[26]

British Labour also participated in a special conference to confirm the "unwavering allegiance" of the two Internationals to the cause of peace and to condemn the aggressive attitude of Fascist Italy toward Abyssinia. The conference made a supreme appeal to the League of Nations to fulfill its mission to preserve peace and to ensure that "the Covenant, the whole Covenant be now applied, including the sanctions provided for in the Covenant." The pledge of the conference, in the name of millions of workers, to support any measure taken by the League for the effective application of whatever sanctions might be necessary against the aggressor was communicated to the president of the League Council and to the Secretariat for transmission to the members of the Council and presented to the delegates representing their respective countries in the League Assembly.[27]

In full accord with the views expressed by organized labor, wherever freedom of expression existed, the Labour party urged the British government, in co-operation with the other nations represented at the Council and Assembly of the League, "to use all the necessary measures provided by the Covenant to prevent Italy's unjust and rapacious attack upon the territory of a fellow Member of the League." The party pledged "its firm support of any action consistent

[26] Resolution of Executive of the L.S.I., Brussels, August 18, 1935, *Report of the Thirty-fifth Annual Conference of the Labour Party*, 1935, p. 316.

[27] Resolution of Joint Conference of General Council of I.F.T.U. and Executive of L.S.I., September 6, 1935, *ibid.*, p. 10.

with the principles and statutes of the League to restrain the Italian government and to uphold the authority of the League in enforcing Peace." At the annual Party Conference at Brighton the debate on this resolution, which had been jointly framed by the Executive Committees and overwhelmingly endorsed by the Trades Union Congress at Margate,[28] was regarded as "the biggest discussion, and one of the vastest importance, that the Conference had ever had to deal with."[29] The real issue in the Abyssinian debate was whether the Labour party was willing to stand firm for the policy to which it had been pledged since the Geneva Protocol and which it had recently reaffirmed in the policy statement *For Socialism and Peace*, in the resolutions of the Socialist and Trade Union Internationals, and in the support which it had given to the National Peace Ballot. Facing the challenge of the Abyssinian conflict as the first test of the security program embodied in *For Socialism and Peace*, the conference was virtually unanimous in its view that the obligation to support sanctions was an inescapable result of membership in the League of Nations and that a government which refused to meet this obligation had no business belonging to the League. The minority opposing sanctions did so, either as Ponsonby, Salter, and Lansbury did, because they feared that sanctions would mean a war in which Great Britain would be compelled to supply the major part of the force, or, as Cripps and the Socialist League did, because they believed that the League had become "nothing but the tool of the satiated imperialist Powers." In response to these "fallacies" and "shallow arguments," the Labour party clearly indicated, by a majority of over two million votes, that it was in favor of the proper use of force for ensuring the rule of law. In passing this resolution, it did so in the light of Labour's comprehensive policy on foreign affairs. Sanctions were not the only methods of preventing war mentioned in the Covenant and, for the Labour party, sanctions were not enough. The Covenant also contemplated that steps would be taken for disarmament, for the control of international aviation, for the peaceful revision of treaties. Labour did not separate these policies from the issue of sanctions, it did not take the Covenant "piecemeal," and it did not intend to be allowed "to drift into sanctions and nothing but sanctions." Labour's policy looked far beyond the government's policy, "striving to abolish altogether international armies, to abolish the idea of the sovereign State, to develop unity on the political and economic side." The party had emerged from the "great

[28] The T.U.C. adopted the resolution by 2,962,000–177,000. *Report of the Sixty-fifth Annual Conference of the T.U.C.*, 1935, pp. 345–71.

[29] Chairman, W. A. Robinson, *Report of the Thirty-fifth Annual Conference of the Labour Party*, 1935, p. 153.

debate" with its unity unimpaired, but the policy adopted by the conference called for a new type of leadership. Consequently, the dissenting minority was relegated to the back benches with the resignation of Cripps from the National Executive and Lansbury from the leadership of the parliamentary group and with the selection of Attlee to head the parliamentary party. As a result of these decisions, the party felt that it was prepared to go before the electorate to answer for its policy and for what it had said in the past.[30]

The Labour Party Conference was immediately followed by the decision of the "National" government to support a policy of sanctions at Geneva and to appeal to the country on a program of upholding the authority of the League of Nations. The Labour party's first reaction to the government's co-operation with the League in declaring that Italy was the aggressor in the Abyssinian dispute was to record its satisfaction. In association with the Socialist and Trade Union Internationals, it repeated its pledge of wholehearted support for the League's efforts to restore peace, requesting "that prompt and effective sanctions be taken to check and swiftly put to an end this monstrous outrage upon international law." It also urged that no delay should occur in specifying the extent of the sanctions to be applied and that the Italian government should be firmly informed that in the ultimate terms of settlement it would derive no benefit from its acts of aggression.[31] At the same time, the National Council of Labour, "having regard to the gravity of the situation," requested the recall of Parliament without delay in order that the government might inform the House of Commons what steps it proposed the League should take in order to bring the hostilities to an end.[32] When Parliament reassembled at the end of October, the leader of the Opposition repeated the request for information on the government's plans at Geneva, noting that sanctions had still not been applied. The Labour Opposition, frankly disturbed by the line taken by the government, pointed out that the delay in applying sanctions was being utilized by the aggressor to get everything he wanted. The second matter that gave Labour great concern as to whether the government was really in earnest was that, in the midst of this international crisis, it was "plunging into a general election." There had been some very recent conversions to collective security, the leader of the Labour Opposition

---

[30] For the debate, cf. *Report of the Thirty-fifth Annual Conference of the Labour Party*, 1935, pp. 154–93. The resolution was defended by Dalton, Lees-Smith, Trevelyan, Bevin, Noel-Baker, Attlee, Shinwell, and Morrison, and carried 2,168,000–102,000.

[31] Resolution of Joint Meeting of the L.S.I. and I.F.T.U., Brussels, October 12, 1935, *Report of the Thirty-sixth Annual Conference of the Labour Party*, 1936, p. 302.

[32] Statement of October 4, 1935, *ibid.*, p. 32.

observed, but he hardly liked to put them down to the Peace Ballot. Labour was under the impression that the government, in deciding upon an election, was "out to win the election and not to make secure the peace of the world."[33]

The Labour party was convinced that the government, "fully aware that its prestige had waned and that there was a growing distrust of its handling of international affairs," was determined "to take electoral advantage of the public's preoccupation with the grave international situation produced by aggressive Fascism and to exploit the genuine mass feeling in support of the policy of collective security which had been demonstrated so remarkably in the Peace Ballot." In support of this view, the Labour party pointed to the policy of the "National" government during the past four years:

It had lost the initiative in the cause of Peace. It had taken a leading part in the slow strangulation of the World Disarmament Conference. It had been shifty and irresolute when the League was confronted with the wanton aggression of Japan in China. It had convened a World Economic Conference which it had allowed to disperse barren of any practical results, and which it had made no serious endeavour to recall to life, though Sir Samuel Hoare, before the General Election, found it expedient to emphasise at Geneva the vital importance of collective consideration being given to urgent economic problems.

Yet, in spite of this "disastrous record," the Conservatives were able to obtain a majority at the polls by their pledge to uphold the Covenant of the League and to stand firmly by the principle of collective responsibility for the defense of peace against unprovoked aggression. The attention of the people had been successfully distracted from the domestic scene and from the "National" government's "many sins of omission and commission." As the "avowed defender of collective peace," the government was re-elected, "only to betray the cause to which it was pledged."[34]

Considerably strengthened by the increase in its representation as a result of the General Election, the Labour party returned to Parliament determined to see that the government fulfilled its pledge to the electorate to support the system of collective security at Geneva. Labour had also appealed to the people on a "collectivist" program based upon the foreign-policy principles contained in the policy statement *For Socialism and Peace*. On this basis, it had recovered its popular support of 1929, actually receiving a higher proportion of the total votes cast than it had in any previous election. The combined

[33] Clement Attlee, 305 *H.C.Deb.*, October 22, 1935, cols. 36, 41–44.
[34] Chairman's address, Jennie Adamson, *Report of the Thirty-sixth Annual Conference of the Labour Party*, 1936, p. 158.

electoral efforts of the Conservatives, "National" Liberals, "National" Labourites, and "Nationals" had, however, assured the Baldwin government of a sizable parliamentary majority.[35] When the new Parliament assembled, the Labour Opposition noted that, according to the "King's Speech," the government was committed to a foreign policy based, "as hitherto," on a firm support of the League of Nations and prepared to fulfill, in co-operation with the other members of the League, the obligations of the Covenant. At the same time, however, the government was to continue to exert its influence in favor of a peace acceptable to the three parties in the dispute, namely, Italy, Ethiopia, and the League of Nations. Finding a "fatal dualism" in the government's statement on foreign policy, Labour denied that it was possible, at one and the same time, to fulfill the Covenant and to make a settlement acceptable to the three parties in the dispute. The vindication of public law could not be achieved by making agreements with an aggressor who was "actually perpetrating a crime." The Labour party felt that the government was not carrying out its obligations under Article XVI of the Covenant and had been neither prompt nor effective in the application of sanctions. It hoped that when the Foreign Secretary conferred with M. Laval he would make it clear that Great Britain was not favorable to, and not even interested in, any terms of settlement which would allow the Italian dictator to profit by reason of his aggression.[36]

The Labour party's suspicion that the government had "always hankered after doing a deal" was confirmed within a month of the General Election by the revelation of the Hoare-Laval proposals for the settlement of the Abyssinian conflict. The National Council of Labour recorded its emphatic protest and repudiated the proposals as "a gross violation of the Covenant of the League of Nations and as a betrayal of the Abyssinian people." Although the National Council earnestly desired to see the war in Abyssinia brought to an end, it unhesitatingly condemned any form of settlement which awarded territorial and political and economic advantages to the aggressor at the expense of the victim. Such a settlement, it believed, would encourage further aggression and would be destructive of the collective system of security.[37] In Parliament the Opposition moved a vote of

[35] Baldwin had replaced MacDonald as Premier and Hoare had replaced Simon as Foreign Secretary in June 1935. The Government had obtained 431 members as against Labour's 154 members.

[36] Hugh Dalton, 307 H.C.Deb., December 5, 1935, cols. 323–28. Cf. King's Speech, ibid., December 3, 1935, col. 45.

[37] Statement of December 17, 1935, Report of the Thirty-sixth Annual Conference of the Labour Party, 1936, p. 32.

censure stating that the terms put forward by the government as a basis for an Italo-Abyssinian settlement conflicted with the expressed will of the country and with the Covenant of the League of Nations, to the support of which the honor of Great Britain was pledged, and demanding that these terms be immediately repudiated. The question raised by the leader of the Opposition was whether the action taken by the Foreign Secretary "squared with the declared policy of the Government, with the declared intentions of the Government to support collective security and with the declared policy of the Government to make the collective system a success." The Labour party could not accept Sir Samuel Hoare as the scapegoat for acts for which the government had taken collective responsibility. If the resignation of the Foreign Secretary was right, then the cabinet as a whole ought to resign, having in the first instance endorsed the Foreign Secretary's actions. In putting forward this motion of censure, Labour believed that it had behind it an immense volume of support both at home and abroad, including the majority of members of the House of Commons. Labour observed that large numbers of government supporters were "alarmed and disquieted" and saw no reason to doubt the accuracy of *The Times* report that "these proposals had created an unfavourable impression on the rank and file of Government supporters in the House of Commons."[38] Both of the motions submitted by Conservative members, "implictly, though not explicitly," conceded Labour's case by recognizing, in the motion of Brigadier General Spears, that these proposals were "unacceptable," and in the motion of Earl Winterton, that any terms for settling the Italo-Abyssinian conflict should be such as the League could accept. However, because the latter motion (as an amendment to the Labour motion) also assured the government of "full support in pursuing the foreign policy outlined in the Government Manifesto and endorsed by the country at the recent General Election," the government insisted that that was its policy and asked the House of Commons to endorse it.[39] While the government retained its parliamentary majority, it surrendered its Foreign Secretary as well as his peace proposals.

In view of the fact that the government was now committed to its own party supporters in Parliament as well as to the electorate to pursue the foreign policy outlined in its Election Manifesto, the Labour party demanded that the government adhere firmly to the application of effective sanctions against the treaty-breaking Power and

[38] Quoted by Pethick-Lawrence, 307 *H.C.Deb.*, December 10, 1935, col. 851.

[39] Neville Chamberlain, *ibid.*, December 19, 1935, col. 2120. The votes against the Labour motion and for the government amendment were 397–165 and 390–165.

refuse to recognize the invasion and conquest of any portion of Abyssinian territory as the basis of settlement. In conjunction with the Socialist and Trade Union Internationals, the party drew attention to the fact that the system of sanctions provided for by Article XVI of the Covenant imposed upon each member of the League precise and strict duties and called in particular for the immediate application of the embargo upon oil, coal, iron, and steel.[40] When the war appeared to have reached its most critical phase, the National Council of Labour issued a statement declaring that the invasion of the territory of a fellow member of the League of Nations by a Great Power constituted a grave warning of the peril to which civilization would be exposed if the states represented in the League permitted Italian Fascism "to gather the fruits of its lawless and brutal aggression." It was the duty of all members of the League, Labour insisted, to intensify and extend the measures adopted against Fascist Italy until the authority of the League was vindicated.[41] With the fall of Addis Ababa and the flight of the Abyssinian Emperor, the parliamentary Labour party initiated a debate on the situation for the purpose of ascertaining the government's views, particularly with regard to the continuation of sanctions and the Italian declaration annexing Abyssinia. Although the government refused to reveal its intentions until the meeting of the League Council, many of its supporters advocated the discontinuance of sanctions. The Opposition nevertheless pressed very strongly that sanctions should be maintained and intensified by an embargo on oil.[42] While the future policy of the members of the League, and particularly of the British government, was still uncertain, the National Council of Labour repeated that the invasion of Abyssinia by Fascist Italy constituted and still remained a threat to the League of Nations and to the future of civilization. Labour did not consider the dispute between the League and Italy settled by the present military situation in Abyssinia, but felt that it was more than ever the duty of all loyal League members to maintain the measures adopted against the aggressor.[43] There remained, however, no doubt as to the British government's intentions after the Chancellor of the Exchequer, Neville Chamberlain, expressed the opinion that a continuation of sanctions would be "midsummer madness." Chamberlain's opinion was confirmed by the Foreign Secretary's announcement in the House of Com-

[40] Resolution of Bureau of L.S.I. and Executive of I.F.T.U., Paris, January 16, 1936, *Report of the Thirty-sixth Annual Conference of the Labour Party*, 1936, p. 79.

[41] Declaration of April 21,, 1936, *ibid.*, p. 33.

[42] Cf. 311 *H.C.Deb.*, May 6, 1936, cols. 1713–1841.

[43] Declaration of May 5, 1936, and resolution of L.S.I., May 18, 1936, *Report of the Thirty-sixth Annual Conference of the Labour Party*, 1936, pp. 33, 301.

mons that the government had decided that there was no longer any utility in continuing sanctions as a means of pressure upon Italy and that steps would have to be taken so to organize the League that any efforts in the future would be more successful. The Labour Opposition replied, in a motion of censure, that the government, by its lack of a resolute and straightforward foreign policy, had lowered the prestige of Britain, weakened the League of Nations, and imperiled peace.[44] To give expression to the popular indignation which had been evoked by the decision of the government to support the withdrawal of sanctions against Italy, the National Council of Labour, together with the representatives of the Co-operative party, requested all sections of the movement in every town and village to organize demonstrations of protest. At the London demonstration, the mass meeting condemned the government's abandonment of sanctions, declaring that such action was a betrayal of Abyssinia, condoned the action of the aggressor, and destroyed the effectiveness of the League of Nations in the building up of a system of collective security. It affirmed that peace could be safeguarded only by strengthening the present constitution of the League of Nations so as to ensure that all states stood unitedly against an aggressor and viewed with deep dismay the indications of the "National" government's intention to evade its obligations for the preservation of peace.[45]

[44] 313 *H.C.Deb.*, June 23, 1936, col. 1605. The motion was defeated, 384–170.
[45] Resolution of June 28, 1936, *Report of the Thirty-sixth Annual Conference of the Labour Party*, 1936, p. 34.

9

A MENACE TO PEACE

The Labour party regarded the Italo-Abyssinian affair as the turning point for the League and collective security. Up till then the Covenant was still officially the basis of British foreign policy and Geneva the place where the British government did business with other governments. After the failure of sanctions against Italy, even the pretense of basing British foreign policy on loyalty to the League was abandoned. The "National" government's preference for appeasement of the dictators, rather than collective security against their aggression, was already evident from the Four-Power Pact and the Hoare-Laval plan. The final stage in the collapse of collective security was the failure even to mention it, let alone apply it, against Fascist intervention in Spain and German dismemberment of Austria and Czechoslovakia.[1]

The Labour party's determination to uphold the collective peace system received its strongest expression in the case of the Fascist attack upon the Spanish republic. Labour had heralded the birth of the Spanish republic as a ray of light and hope at a time when Fascism was trampling out liberty all over the world.[2] Consequently, its sympathies were, from the outset of the civil war, with the Loyalist government of Spain. Shortly after the Fascist revolt against the republic, the leader of the parliamentary party, at a conference of the Labour and cooperative movements, secured the adoption of a resolution pledging "all practical support to our Spanish comrades in their struggle to defend freedom and democracy in Spain." Another manifestation of support for the Loyalist cause was the dispatch of a telegram to the Spanish premier, signed by several Labour members of Parliament, expressing their admiration of "the heroic fight being put up by the Spanish people against the attack of Fascists who aimed at the destruction of the democratically-elected People's Government of Spain." These sentiments, voiced by leading members of the Labour party, were echoed at local Labour and trade-union meetings, at the international labour and socialist congresses, in the Labour press and on

---

[1] Cf. Diplomaticus, *Can the Tories Win the Peace?* (London: Gollancz, 1945), p. 73.

[2] Telegram of the National Executive Committee to the new Spanish republic, July 8, 1931, *Report of the Thirty-first Annual Conference of the Labour Party*, 1931, p. 43.

the floor of Parliament.[3] However, in view of the fact that the British government was determined to follow, in co-operation with the French, Italian, German, and Russian governments, a policy of nonintervention, the Labour party was compelled to revise its original course of action. In Labour's opinion, the nonintervention policy was a "second-best solution." It would have preferred to render all possible assistance to the Spanish government in accordance with the policy dictated by the general practice of international law. Nevertheless, it believed that nonintervention, if effectively applied, would be cumulatively valuable to the Spanish republic, whose position would be strengthened if the embargo were made the means of depriving the Franco rebels of the outside resources on which they were dependent. It was on the basis of this conviction that Arthur Greenwood, deputy leader of the parliamentary party, declared, "Let us, if we can, get a neutrality agreement, all nations standing aside."[4]

As soon as it became evident that the nonintervention system was not being upheld by the Fascist powers, the Labour party reversed its support for the neutrality policy by calling upon the government to take the initiative in securing an international agreement giving the Spanish government the right to obtain the means for its own defense.[5] The Labour Opposition repeatedly accused the government, in its Spanish policy, of ignoring British strategic and political interests, blaming this abandonment of national interests on the government's part to an ideological prejudice against the Spanish Popular Front government. It was difficult for Labour to understand how a Conservative government could ignore the obvious threat to Britain's position in the Mediterranean that Fascist penetration in the Iberian Peninsula would constitute. Convinced that the interests of Britain were dependent upon the victory of the Spanish republic and the defeat of the Fascist powers in the Mediterranean, Labour insisted that the government should restore to the Spanish government its right to buy arms.[6] Although the government was forced to admit that nonintervention had not worked as satisfactorily as had been expected and that

[3] Cf. *Daily Herald*, July 29, 1936, p. 2; July 24, 1936, p. 13; August 14, 1936, p. 2; *Report of the Thirty-sixth Annual Conference of the Labour Party*, 1936, p. 304; 315 *H.C.Deb.*, July 31, 1936, col. 1892.

[4] "Is the Embargo Right?" *Daily Herald*, August 22, 1936, p. 8.

[5] Resolution of National Executive, October 28, 1936, *ibid.*, October 29, 1936, p. 1. For breaches of nonintervention, cf. *Report and Findings of the Committee of Enquiry into Breaches of International Law Relating to Intervention in Spain* (London: Committee of Enquiry, 1936); Hispanicus, *Foreign Intervention in Spain* (London: United Editorial, 1938).

[6] Cf. Philip Noel-Baker, 315 *H.C.Deb.*, July 31, 1936, col. 1892; Hugh Dalton, 317 *H.C.Deb.*, November 5, 1936, col. 292; Ellen Wilkinson, 318 *H.C.Deb.*, December 1, 1936, col. 1115.

there had been infractions, it maintained that its support of that system had prevented the spread of the conflict beyond the borders of Spain. Rather than abandon an admittedly faulty system, the government was determined to improve and to strengthen it by the establishment of a system of control and supervision which would prevent the dispatch of war matériel and "volunteers" to the combatants in Spain.[7]

While the Labour party temporarily resigned itself to the fact that a policy of nonintervention was to be followed by the government, it insisted that the policy at least be made effective. The line which Labour took throughout was that it was inadvisable for the British government to act by itself; for that reason it objected to the measures which "shackled" the government to nonintervention, irrespective of what the Fascist powers might do. The government's entire policy—placing an embargo on the sale or sending of arms to Spain, forbidding its merchant ships to carry arms from foreign ports to Spain, and invoking the Foreign Enlistment Act, which prevented its own nationals from volunteering for service in the Spanish conflict—was not nonintervention, but "one-sided intervention." As a result of this policy, the Spanish government was deprived of all outside assistance while the Fascist powers continued to supply men and munitions to Franco's rebels.[8]

When the Non-Intervention Committee's "control system" providing for the "observation" of the Spanish frontiers broke down as a result of a series of naval incidents culminating in the withdrawal of the Fascist powers from the system, the Labour party demanded the reference of the whole matter to the League of Nations and the restoration of the right of the Spanish government to buy arms.[9] However, the government's aim was to see that international co-operation in the work of the Non-Intervention Committee and the scheme of naval observation was restored as soon as possible. In pursuance of that objective, the British government submitted to the Non-Intervention Committee a "compromise plan" reconstituting the naval patrol and combining the Fascist powers' proposal for the grant of belligerent rights with the Anglo-French scheme for the withdrawal of "volunteers." As soon as the committee's discussion of the plan resulted in a complete deadlock, the Labour party declared that the proposals

[7] Cf. Anthony Eden, 316 *H.C.Deb.*, October 29, 1936, col. 44; Stanley Baldwin, *ibid.*, col. 144; Lord Dartmouth, 103 *H.L.Deb.*, November 3, 1936, cols. 8–9.

[8] Clement Attlee, Limehouse, January 10, 1937, *Daily Herald*, January 11, 1937, p. 2.

[9] Resolution of National Executive, *Report of the Thirty-seventh Annual Conference of the Labour Party*, 1937, p. 12.

could not effect their purpose, that they were "an attempt to bridge the unbridgeable" and that "no agreement was worth having unless there was the will to carry it out."[10] As the government was determined to see its compromise accepted without any major modifications by all of the powers participating in the Non-Intervention Committee, it made one last effort through diplomatic channels to bring the Fascist powers back into the nonintervention system. The chief problem which delayed agreement among the powers on the compromise plan was the relation in time between the withdrawal of "volunteers" and the grant of belligerent rights. However, at the eleventh hour the Italian government accepted the British proposals and the plan was adopted by the Non-Intervention Committee and forwarded to the contestants in Spain for their approval.

Italy's "contribution" to the negotiations in the Non-Intervention Committee was not received with the same enthusiasm by the Labour party as it had been by the government. Labour deplored the "pitiful and dilatory" negotiations on which the Non-Intervention Committee had once more begun and it criticized the government for its willingness to accept Italian assurances with regard to the withdrawal of "volunteers" from Spain. Noel-Baker declared that under the cover of the "much-advertised" negotiations in the Foreign Office Mussolini had been applying nonintervention in his own way, and cited as evidence the instances of Italian intervention in Spain, beginning with the dispatch of 6,500 "volunteers" at the end of 1936 and ending with the Italian "victories" at Málaga, Bilbao, Santander, and Gijon. During this whole time, Noel-Baker said, the British government was negotiating the setting up of "that wonderful control under which not a single shipment of arms has yet been found, although everyone knows the war has been conducted with foreign arms." If the present negotiations which the government was undertaking for the withdrawal of "volunteers" also proved a failure, Labour demanded that the frontiers be opened and the Spanish government be given the opportunity to receive arms.[11]

The government's policy toward Italy not only widened the cleavage that existed between the Conservatives and the Opposition, but succeeded in dividing the "National" government itself. Although it was apparent that the government as a whole was in favor of a general settlement with the Italian government, when the Anglo-Italian conversations were opened in 1938 the Foreign Secretary resigned, explaining that he felt that before opening those conversations the government should have insisted upon further progress in the with-

[10] Clement Attlee, 326 H.C.Deb., July 30, 1937, col. 3533.
[11] Philip Noel-Baker, 328 H.C.Deb., October 28, 1937, cols. 287-90.

drawal of Italian "volunteers" from Spain. Supporting Eden's stand against the Prime Minister and the rest of the cabinet, the Labour party voiced its disapproval of the government's position by moving a vote of censure, deploring the circumstances in which the late Foreign Secretary had been obliged to resign his office and registering its lack of confidence in the government's present advisers in their conduct of foreign affairs. According to the leader of the Opposition, the late Foreign Secretary, who had striven under great difficulties to try to get some kind of performance for the promises made at the last election, was the only one who was conscious of the election pledge on which the "National" government had won a majority. The fact that he had stood alone, Attlee said, showed very plainly that during these past years he had been "used as a cloak" because he was such a good "peace man" and "League of Nations man." To the Opposition, there appeared to be a "deep gulf" between the outlook of the late Foreign Secretary and that of the Prime Minister. The resignation of Eden meant the reorientation of the government's foreign policy and a departure from its 1935 electoral program in which it had declared its support for a system of collective security. However, the Opposition's attempt to make a major political issue, and even a general election, out of the resignation of Eden met with little success. Although a few cabinet supporters had attacked the Prime Minister for coming to terms with Fascist Italy, there was no real break away from the Conservative ranks. When the division was taken, although a considerable number of Conservatives abstained from voting, most of the supporters of the "National" government went into the government lobby to defeat the Labour vote of censure.[12]

Eden's resignation actually had an importance out of all proportion to the differences with his colleagues that brought it about. The government's decision to open negotiations with the Italian government did not involve a real change of policy, for negotiations with Italy had been decided upon the previous year while Eden was still Foreign Secretary. Yet the resignation of Eden was the beginning of a change which intensified the growing opposition to the "National" government's foreign policy. Members of the Opposition who had attacked Eden while he was Foreign Secretary for championing the policy of nonintervention and for not effectively supporting collective security applauded him, after his resignation, as a martyr to the League cause. Labour's protest at the "momentous change" in the direction of British foreign policy was voiced in Parliament and at public meetings

[12] 332 *H.C.Deb.*, February 21, 1938, cols. 65–67; February 22, 1938, col. 317. The Labour censure was defeated, 332–170.

throughout the country. On February 25 the party announced that already over three thousand meetings had been held to protest against the resignation of the Foreign Secretary and that thousands of citizens had signed the petition for the "recall of Eden" organized by the "Council of Action for Peace and Reconstruction." This organization had also conducted a test ballot in certain constituencies which were representative of a wide cross section of opinion and which possessed government majorities of between five and seven thousand. The question which the electors were asked was, "Do you approve of Mr. Anthony Eden's stand for good faith in international affairs, and will you support his demand for the re-establishment of peace and security through the League of Nations?" The results of the ballot showed that an overwhleming majority of those who voted in those constituencies favored Eden's stand in foreign affairs.[13]

After the resignation of Eden the conversations with Italy were resumed and a pact was concluded at Rome. In exchange for a promise by Great Britain to facilitate the recognition of the Italian conquest of Ethiopia, Italy promised to adhere to the British plan for the withdrawal of Italian "volunteers" from Spain.[14] When the Prime Minister submitted the agreement to Parliament, the Labour Opposition declared that it could not approve "an agreement made with a State actively engaged in wanton aggression in Spain." Its main objection was that the agreement conferred on the Italian government the immediate advantage of legitimizing its intervention in Spain and allowed that intervention to continue, in defiance of the Non-Intervention Agreement, until the war in Spain was concluded. On the question of what constituted a Spanish "settlement," which was the prerequisite for bringing the agreement into force, the Opposition differed from the government. According to the Prime Minister, a settlement did not mean that the Spanish conflict was settled, but that the Spanish conflict was unlikely to threaten the peace of Europe; while to the Opposition a settlement meant the complete withdrawal of foreign troops and the end of the Spanish war. The Labour party felt that the "Chamberlain-Mussolini bargain" was a "betrayal" of the Spanish republic, obviously grounded upon a tacit understanding that no ef-

[13] Results of test ballot, *Politics in Review*, V (January–March, 1938), 42:

	Electorate	Votes Cast	Yes	No
Bradford	55,166	16,163	15,552	611
Manchester	46,606	10,610	10,002	608
Cambridge	44,197	12,047	10,930	1,117
Clapham	47,612	9,409	8,743	667

[14] Cf. Agreement Between the United Kingdom and Italy Consisting of a Protocol with Annexes and Exchanges of Notes, *British State Papers*, Cmd. 5726 (1938).

fort would be made to implement the pledge to withdraw Italian forces and equipment from Spain until the war had ended in a rebel victory. It was evident that Britain had become an accessory to the Italian invasion of Spain, in that the pact revealed the eager desire for a Franco victory as a solution of the Spanish question which would gratify Chamberlain as well as Mussolini. In Labour's opinion, there was nothing in the agreement and all of its annexes that was worth the paper on which it was written. As five out of eight parts of the agreement were "reaffirmations made necessary by past bad faith," there was not the slightest guaranty that the new declarations would necessarily be observed. Besides, there was no insistence on the immediate withdrawal of Italian troops and matériel, despite the Prime Minister's statement that no agreement with Italy would be completed until it contained a "settlement" of the Spanish question. The governing fact about the negotiations, Labour insisted, was that Chamberlain undertook them while Mussolini was still engaged upon the conquest of the Iberian Peninsula.[15]

In spite of the protests of the Opposition, and even some dissenting voices from the Conservative ranks, the Anglo-Italian agreement was approved by Parliament. When the division was taken in the House of Commons no cabinet supporter voted against the agreement, although in the Upper House two Conservative peers, Cecil and Lytton, went into the lobby with the Labour peers against the motion. Commenting upon the approval which the agreement received, Noel-Baker said that the Prime Minister had secured the support of the House of Commons for his two motions of May 2 and November 2 only because he had led Parliament to believe that the withdrawal of 10,000 "war-weary Italian volunteers" from Spain was merely the first step in an effort to end intervention altogether in the immediate future. In contradiction, Noel-Baker pointed out, the admission by the new Foreign Secretary, Viscount Halifax, that Mussolini had always made it plain that he was not prepared to see Franco defeated meant that, when the Anglo-Italian negotiations began, the British government was aware that Mussolini insisted upon Franco's victory, that it had accepted Mussolini's condition, and made the agreement on that basis. In the light of these facts, he declared,

If the Prime Minister had told us the truth on those terms on 21st February, on 2nd May, on 26th July, or even on 2nd November, he would not have got his votes in this House.[16]

---

[15] Cf. Herbert Morrison, 335 *H.C.Deb.*, May 2, 1938, cols. 545–53; Lord Snell, 110 *H.L.Deb.*, November 3, 1938, col. 1634; *Daily Herald*, April 18, 1938, pp. 2, 8; *Labour*, V (May 1938), 194.

[16] 342 *H.C.Deb.*, December 21, 1938, cols. 3048–51. For Halifax', statement cf.

The withdrawal of "volunteers" from Spain, as provided in the British plan and reaffirmed in the Anglo-Italian agreement was further delayed by the refusal of the Franco regime to co-operate in effecting the proposals. Consequently, with the advance of the rebels toward Barcelona, the Labour party renewed its efforts to induce the government to abandon the fiction of nonintervention and restore to the hard-pressed Spanish republicans their right to buy arms. At a special meeting of the National Executive, a resolution was adopted, calling the attention of the government to the continued violation of the policy of nonintervention by Italy and Germany and urging upon the government the opening of the Franco-Spanish frontier. At the same time, the National Council of Labour addressed a letter to the Prime Minister expressing the deep concern felt by the Trades Union Congress and the Labour party with the continued adhesion of the British government to the so-called nonintervention policy. The National Council reiterated the view that the position of the British government was indefensible and constituted a "flagrant and one-sided benevolence to the Fascist rebels." The gravity of the situation in Spain prompted the leader of the Opposition to request that the Prime Minister immediately summon Parliament. In his appeal to the Prime Minister, Attlee pointed out that while the Spanish government had already dismissed all its foreign troops, German and Italian troops were still aiding Franco. Nonintervention had therefore become a means of ensuring the defeat of the Spanish government.[17] When the Prime Minister refused to meet Labour's demands, the National Council decided to send a deputation to the Prime Minister to make urgent representations on the necessity for taking prompt action both to remove the embargo on the supply of arms to the Spanish government and to supply food for the starving people of Spain. However, the result of the National Council's efforts was as disappointing as previous appeals on the subject had been. The Prime Minister maintained that if intervention on behalf of the Spanish government were to take place, it would have to be on a very considerable scale to alter the state of affairs in Spain at that moment. Since he was satisfied that the government's policy had been right all along, this was certainly not the mo-

110 *H.L.Deb.*, November 3, 1938, col. 1624. The votes for the agreement were 345–138, 340 *H.C.Deb.*, November 2, 1938, col. 662; and 55–6, 110 *H.L.Deb.*, November 3, 1938, col. 1675.

[17] Cf. *The Times*, January 19, 1939, p. 12. The Spanish Premier Negrin had informed the League of the Spanish government's decision to evacuate all non-Spanish nationals serving in its ranks. *Official Journal*, Special Supplement 183, Records of the Nineteenth Ordinary Session of the Assembly, Plenary Meetings, September 21, 1938, p. 90.

ment to change it. He did not consider the situation in Spain "a menace to the peace of Europe," but if nonintervention were abandoned, that would mean that the Spanish situation would be a menace to Europe.[18]

With the fall of Barcelona, the flight of the republican government into France, and the collapse of resistance in Catalonia, the Spanish conflict drew rapidly to a close and the recognition of Franco suddenly became a matter of immediate possibility. The National Council of Labour held an emergency meeting to record its grave dissatisfaction with the Prime Minister's refusal to give an assurance that any decision to recognize the insurgent authorities as the *de facto* or *de jure* government of Spain would be communicated to Parliament for its consent before any action was taken. It expressed profound opposition to any recognition of the insurgent authorities as long as the legitimate government of Spain continued to function, such recognition being, in the Council's view, contrary to public law and against the wishes of the great mass of British public opinion. At the same time, the National Council, in co-operation with the London Trades Council and the London Labour party, decided to hold a great national demonstration in Trafalgar Square to protest against the recognition of the rebels as the government of Spain. Local Labour organizations were urged to arrange that their meetings be converted into demonstrations against the recognition of Franco, "especially when a considerable part of the country was still in the hands of the Republican Government which was carrying on an heroic struggle against heavy odds."[19]

Although no cabinet decision on recognition was made public following the meeting of Ministers on February 15, the cabinet had decided to empower the Prime Minister "to act whenever he and Halifax thought fit."[20] On February 23, when the Prime Minister was again asked whether the government had come to a decision with respect to the recognition of the rebel authorities, his reply was that he had nothing to add to his previous statement that if and when the government came to a decision the House would be informed as soon as possible.[21] When Chamberlain suddenly announced, on February 27, that the government had decided to inform General Franco of its decision to recognize his government as the government of Spain, he was immediately challenged by the leader of the Opposition. Attlee

[18] 343 *H.C.Deb.*, January 31, 1939, col. 76.

[19] *Daily Herald*, February 15, 1939, p. 1; *Report of the Thirty-eighth Annual Conference of the Labour Party*, 1939, p. 36.

[20] Cf. *Daily Herald*, February 25, 1939, p. 1.

[21] 344 *H.C.Deb.*, February 23, 1939, col. 575. Also cf. 343 *H.C.Deb.*, February 14, 1939, col. 1559.

insisted that a decision had, in fact, been made by the government and
that the Prime Minister had been empowered by the cabinet to take
action at any time; yet the Prime Minister had refused to give any
answer with regard to that decision when questioned in Parliament.
To the Labour party, it was quite evident from French press reports
that the government's decision must have been made before the twenty-
third of February. In fact, the Labour press reported that the French
premier had informed the Chamber of Deputies on February 24 that
he was officially advised by Great Britain to recognize Franco. It was
assumed, therefore, that the Prime Minister had advised Daladier with
regard to recognition the day preceding his refusal to inform Parliament.[22] This refusal, Attlee claimed, enabled the Prime Minister to
get away without a debate in the House; and by such a response, "he
was misleading the House as no Prime Minister had ever done before."
As Attlee reminded Chamberlain, he was, after all, a British Prime
Minister with all the responsibilities that belonged to that office, one
of which was the responsibility of answering for his actions to members of Parliament. It was quite obvious that the Prime Minister had
made up his mind and had notified the premier of another country
of the decision which he had refused to communicate to Parliament.
In addition, Attlee said, the Prime Minister made a statement to the
House to justify his action which was "a tissue of half-truths which
are worse than lies."[23]

In Labour's opinion, the government's decision to grant "unconditional" recognition to Spanish insurgent forces dependent upon foreign intervention constituted "a deliberate affront to the legitimate
Government of a friendly Power," a "gross breach of international
traditions" and a further stage in a policy which was "steadily destroying in all democratic countries confidence in the good faith of
Great Britain." In conceding unconditional recognition, the British
government had thrown away the Spanish government's last chance
of securing acceptance of its peace terms. The two main conditions
upon which the Spanish government had based its peace offer, and
upon which Labour believed the British government ought to have
insisted, were that all foreign troops should be evacuated from Spanish
soil and that there should be assurances of clemency and amnesty to
those who had opposed the Franco regime. However, the government
believed that it was quite impossible for it to exact such conditions
as the Opposition suggested unless it was prepared to go to war to

22 Cf. *Daily Herald*, February 25, 1939, p. 1; February 28, 1939, p. 4; Alexander
Werth, "France and the Recognition," *New Statesman and Nation*, XVII (March 11,
1939), 349–50.
23 344 *H.C.Deb.*, February 27, 1939, col. 874; February 28, 1939, cols. 1100–1101.

enforce them. Besides, it felt that such conditions were wholly unnecessary because it had received assurances from General Franco
himself regarding clemency and the future integrity and independence
of Spain. The hope was expressed that the "annoyance of the Opposition" would not be allowed "to obscure from the world the remarkable clearness and continuity of British policy in Spain."[24]

[24] Attlee quotes from an editorial in *The Times*, February 28, 1939, 344 *H.C.Deb.*,
Feb. 28, 1939, cols. 1099, 1105–6.

IO

THE FINAL STAGE

The Labour party was convinced that the free hand given to Nazi Germany in rearming, in remilitarizing the Rhineland, and in intervening in Spain had paved the way for the Nazi annexation of Austria and Czechoslovakia and the second World War. Since 1933, Labour had repeatedly condemned the Fascist repression and tyranny in Germany and warned of the Fascist danger to European peace and democracy. It had protested against the establishment of the Hitler dictatorship, the destruction of freedom, justice, and parliamentary democracy, the suppression of all opposition and minority groups "by terrorist methods of shameless brutality and unrestrained licence," and the complete demolition of the whole structure of the political and industrial working-class movement in Germany.[1] The party had collaborated with the Trades Union Congress, the co-operative movement and the Labour and Socialist International in carrying out an intensive campaign and mass demonstrations against the dangers of dictatorship, in protesting against "anti-semitic demagogy," in providing relief to the refugees of Fascism, in organizing a moral and material boycott of Hitlerism, and in demanding that the democratic governments bring before the League of Nations all the problems raised by the victory of Hitlerism.[2] In addition, the Labour party had opposed any yielding to Hitler and force by the revision of the peace settlement in favor of Nazi Germany. On that basis, it had condemned the "National" government's policy of supporting the project for a four-power pact to include Germany, of conceding to Hitler the unilateral right of denouncing the disarmament provisions of Versailles by reintroducing conscription, and of recognizing German naval rearmament by concluding the Anglo-German Naval Agreement. Labour believed that there could be no compromise with Fascism, "no

[1] Cf. National Council of Labour, "Democracy v. Dictatorship," March 24, 1933, *Report of the Thirty-third Annual Conference of the Labour Party*, 1933, pp. 222–25, 277; "Fascism and Dictatorship," Reports of the *Sixty-fifth Annual Conference of the T.U.C.*, 1933, p. 340; *Sixty-sixth Annual Conference of the T.U.C.*, 1934, p. 257; "Socialism, Democracy and Fascism," *Report of the Thirty-fourth Annual Conference of the Labour Party*, 1934, p. 142.

[2] Cf. "Strategy and Tactics of International Labour During the Period of Fascist Reaction," *Fifth L.S.I. Congress* (Zurich: L.S.I., 1933), pp. 20–21; "Fascism at Home and Abroad," *Report of the Thirty-fourth Annual Conference of the Labour Party*, 1934, pp. 293–308.

half-way house of accommodation"; and that it was essential to "fight Fascism without fear and without faltering."[3]

With Hitler's "provocation on the Rhine," Labour realized that once again the Nazi dictatorship sought to gain its ends by breaking its pledged word, that once more the world was faced with a grave menace to peace. The National Council of Labour considered that the new and far-reaching demonstration of Nazi foreign policy involved in the unilateral denunciation of the Locarno Treaty was an immediate repercussion of the war between Italy and Abyssinia and fresh evidence of the insecurity created in Europe by Nazi Germany.[4] British Labour supported the Socialist and Trade Union Internationals in denouncing in the strongest terms "this wanton act" and in warning that such a breach of international good faith would, if condoned, destroy all confidence in international agreements and the whole system of collective security. It was clear to Labour that the purpose of this latest violation was a preliminary to the fortification of the demilitarized zone and the establishment of air bases as part of the preparation for an attack upon peaceful states, east and west. The pretext for this breach of a solemn pledge was that the Franco-Soviet Pact conflicted with the Treaty of Locarno, an assumption that disregarded the fact that this disputed question could be settled by submitting it to the Permanent Court of International Justice. Labour insisted that in any discussions with Hitler's emissaries it was the peaceful states within the League of Nations that should determine the agenda and the lines of procedure; Hitler should not be allowed to dictate what proposals should or should not be examined. Hitler now sought to conceal his aggressive intentions under professions of good will by claiming to be a peacemaker. He could prove the sincerity of his proposals only if he was prepared to join with other nations in limiting armaments by international agreement and submitting them to international inspection and supervision. Viewing the military occupation of the Rhineland as a threat to the peace of the world, Labour believed that the only means to safeguard peace was by resolutely organizing collective security. Convinced that peace was indivisible, Labour held that the principle of the Locarno Pact should be strengthened, extended, and applied through the League of Nations as widely as possible. Once again, Labour declared that it was fully prepared to shoulder the risks and responsibilities of such collective organization of peace.[5]

[3] Chairman's address, Joseph Compton, Report of the Thirty-third Annual Conference of the Labour Party, 1933, p. 134.

[4] "The European Situation," Report of the Thirty-sixth Annual Conference of the Labour Party, 1936, p. 34.

[5] Resolution of Joint Conference of Executive of L.S.I. and Bureau of I.F.T.U., London, March 20, 1936, ibid., pp. 302–3.

The Labour party noted with satisfaction that the League of Nations had condemned the breach of treaty on the part of Nazi Germany. It was Labour's conviction that any breach of the peace was the concern of the whole League, not merely of a group of Locarno powers. It therefore criticized the government's method of dealing with this violation of international law by "negotiating in a corner" on the basis of Locarno rather than through the League. The impression created by these proceedings was that the British government was trying to maneuver away from a League of Nations policy and into an Anglo-French alliance. The government's proposal for military consultations with the staffs of France and Italy and a mixed British and Italian force stationed on German soil Labour regarded as "fantastic and absurd" in view of Italy's own violation of the League Covenant. The Labour party regretted the sharp distinction still to be observed in the government's foreign policy between the major obligations of Locarno and the minor obligations which might arise under the Covenant of the League if peace were threatened in any part of the world outside the Locarno area. Believing that if the peace of Europe were disturbed anywhere it was disturbed everywhere, Labour urged that it be made clear that Germany had no free hand in Central and Eastern Europe to attack either Austria, Czechoslovakia, or Soviet Russia.[6]

The Labour party had warned that the greatest danger would follow from the British government's decision on the remilitarization of the Rhineland to stand mainly on Locarno, which was far too narrow a basis, instead of bringing in the whole strength of the League for the preservation of law and order. Hence it viewed the Nazi annexation of Austria as the logical consequence of the government's failure to guarantee the peace of Europe beyond the Rhine. Labour deplored the Nazi march into Austria, although it was not prepared to "weep over the dead body of Dr. Schuschnigg's Government." It felt that the fate of Austria had been sealed when the Social Democratic party of Vienna was destroyed by the Austrian Fatherland Front. Now, Austria, invaded and annexed, had "fallen from a dictatorship of Schuschnigg under the very much more brutal dictatorship of Hitler."[7] The real issue, at present, was the method which had been adopted in the amalgamation of the two countries and the implications which arose as a result of the application of that method. There had been a display of naked force against the will of the Austrian people, causing widespread alarm throughout Europe and unsettling the minds of all

---

[6] Hugh Dalton, 310 *H.C.Deb.*, March 26, 1936, cols. 1450–58.

[7] Manifesto on the International Situation, L.S.I. and I.F.T.U., Paris, March 16, 1938, *Report of the Thirty-eighth Annual Conference of the Labour Party*, 1939, p. 371.

the neighbors of the German Reich. Labour recalled that this action was taken at the very time when the British government was pursuing friendly conversations with the German government, when the Hitler-Halifax conversations were being followed up by a visit of the German Foreign Minister. Action of this kind, Labour held, was destructive of all intercourse between governments and showed the futility of dealing with dictator states on the assumptions that usually prevailed in the intercourse of states. Each successive instance of bad faith, each breach of a treaty, each successful act of aggression had led to another. In Labour's view, the annexation of Austria had shown that peace could not be built upon a false basis by "separate bargainings with separate dictators, separate attempts to buy off aggression." What was needed was a return to League principles and League policy, a collective stand made, not only by Great Britain and France but by the League. The Labour party demanded firmness: it was no use allowing the German government to imagine that if it attacked Czechoslovakia, the British government would do no more than it had in the case of Austria. Now that Czechoslovakia was the next move, the British government would have to decide if it could afford to see Czechoslovakia go down with the others.[8]

The Prime Minister's refusal to give a pledge to Czechoslovakia or to France in respect of Czechoslovakia was regarded by the Labour party as a repudiation of the principles of the League Covenant. The government appeared to be entirely oblivious to the fact that it was already pledged to Czechoslovakia as it was to every other country belonging to the League. All that would happen in the event of a pledge's being given to Czechoslovakia was that it would constitute a specific pledge which would impose no greater obligations on Great Britain than were imposed by her general pledge under the League Covenant. If this pledge were given it would have more of a psychological than a juridical value, but it might emphasize to Germany and other potential aggressors that in the year 1938 the British government had reconsidered the position and was prepared to give this additional pledge to Czechoslovakia. The Labour party ventured to assert that a British lead would bring in not only southeastern Europe, but Turkey and Greece, probably Poland, certainly Holland, Belgium, Scandinavia, Finland, and the Baltic States; and such a combination, founded on the law, would be irresistible indeed. However, the government felt unable to give the prior guaranty suggested in relation to an area where its "vital interests" were not concerned.[9]

[8] Clement Attlee, 333 *H.C.Deb.*, March 14, 1938, cols. 54–55.

[9] Cf. Neville Chamberlain, 333 *H.C.Deb.*, March 24, 1938, col. 1405; and replies of Arthur Henderson, *ibid.*, cols. 1485–88; and Philip Noel-Baker, *Ibid.*, col. 1506.

The Labour party was gravely disturbed by the Prime Minister's failure to disclose any constructive policy for the prevention of war in Europe. The day after Chamberlain's statement in the House of Commons, the National Council of Labour issued a "Peace Manifesto" condemning the government's refusal to make any immediate use of the machinery of the League of Nations and collective security to put a check on the lawless aggression of the Fascist dictators. Labour called for an immediate meeting of the League Assembly and for special consideration by the European members of the League, particularly France, Britain, and Russia, of the steps to be taken to guarantee peace in Central Europe. It was Labour's policy to unite the peace-loving countries in an effort to preserve the peace of Europe by a common stand against aggression, whether it took the form of direct invasion or of stirring up and supporting by arms internal conflict in other states. The adoption of such a policy would reassure the small nations that Britain had taken the initiative, that they would not be sacrificed to the ambitions of the Fascist powers, and that collective security— the most effective means of defense for Great Britain and other states —would be made a reality.[10]

As the pressure mounted against Czechoslovakia, the Labour party asserted that even at this late hour, general war could still be avoided if all the democratic forces were brought into action without delay and with the necessary vigor. Labour warned that although a general European war had been averted in May only by the firm attitude of certain governments, an acute crisis might arise again at any moment. This recent experience of resisting the threat of German invasion had proved that, if peace were to be maintained, a supreme effort would have to be made to organize collective defense on a firm basis under the leadership of the Great Power members of the League. Calling attention to the obligations imposed upon members of the League and their Council, under Article XI of the Covenant, to propose measures for the safeguarding of the peace of Europe, Labour urged a meeting of the League Council with this object as soon as possible.[11]

During the parliamentary recess in the summer of 1938, it became evident that the Runciman mission, which had been sent by the government to seek a solution to the differences between the Czech government and the German minority movement in that state, was not meeting with success. It was clear that German pressure was being exercised within and without the Czech borders. The Nazi technique

[10] Text of Peace Manifesto, *Report of the Thirty-eighth Annual Conference of the Labour Party*, 1939, p. 372.

[11] Manifesto on the International Situation, L.S.I. and I.F.T.U., Paris, March 16, 1938; resolution of Executive of L.S.I., Brussels, May 29–30, 1938, *ibid.*, pp. 28, 371.

usually applied prior to invasion was obviously in operation. The imminent danger of war called for a statement from the National Council of Labour. The Labour movement emphatically repudiated the right of the British or any other government to use diplomatic or other pressure to compel an acceptance of such a humiliation as that of Czechoslovakia's yielding its democracy to force and admitting a totalitarian system within its borders. Since the interests of Britain were too closely involved for this country to be able to stand aside, Labour felt that the British government should leave no doubt in the mind of the German government that it would unite with the French and Soviet governments to resist any attack upon Czechoslovakia. The Labour movement was confident that such a policy would have the solid support of the British people. Whatever the risks involved, Labour believed that Britain should make its stand against aggression; there was "now no room for doubt or hesitation."[12]

The new position created by the joint adoption by the British and French governments of the plan of surrender to Hitler's threat of aggression brought forth a vigorous protest from the Labour party. After considering the proposals submitted by Britain and France to the Czech government with a view to meeting Hitler's demands regarding the transference of Sudeten territory and population, the National Council of Labour declared that this was "a shameful betrayal of a peaceful and democratic people" and constituted "a dangerous precedent for the future."[13] When the Labour party heard of the Godesberg ultimatum, it noted with "profound humiliation" that the Czech government had been "forced under irresistible pressure by both the British and French Governments to accept with pain the proposals elaborated in London." Although the Czech government had gone to the extreme limit of concession under the auspices of Lord Runciman, the British government, setting aside all considerations of freedom, equality, and justice, had consented to the virtual destruction of the Czech state. This "shameful surrender to the threats of Herr Hitler," this "sacrifice of a gallant democratic people," this "sacrifice of vital British interests involved in the sanctity of international law," Labour asserted, would not bring peace.[14] All sections of the Labour movement were urged to use every opportunity for demonstrations and meetings in support of the preservation of Czechoslovakian integrity. At the London demonstration, Attlee warned that the whole fate of

[12] "Labour and the International Situation: On the Brink of War," September 8, 1938, *Report of the Thirty-eighth Annual Conference of the Labour Party*, 1939, pp. 13–14.

[13] London, September 20, 1938, *ibid.*, p. 15.

[14] Statement of National Council of Labor, September 21, 1938, *ibid.*, p. 16.

Western civilization would be decided on the issue of Czechoslovakia. Speaking for the Trades Union Congress, Dukes, of the General and Municipal Workers, stated the challenge: "If the test has to come, let it come now." The meeting closed dramatically with the audience standing in silence, pledged to a demand from the National Council of Labour to the Prime Minister for "no further concessions of the slightest kind to Herr Hitler."[15]

During the Czech crisis, the Labour party had demanded the immediate summoning of Parliament in order that its principles might be reaffirmed "with the utmost energy and determination." When Parliament finally reassembled on September 28, the Prime Minister made a lengthy statement on the developments in the international situation since the adjournment of the previous July. Reporting on the failure of the negotiations up to that point, he indicated that attempts to secure direct discussions between the German and Czech representatives, which he had urged upon Hitler at Godesberg, had also been refused. He had sought to secure a further opportunity for negotiation by addressing communications to Hitler and Mussolini, indicating his own readiness to proceed immediately to discuss with German and Czech representatives, together with representatives of Italy and France, arrangements for the transfer of essential territory and populations. In the course of his speech, the Prime Minister suddenly announced the receipt of a communication from Mussolini that Hitler had postponed mobilization for twenty-four hours and that, in company with Mussolini and Daladier, he, Chamberlain, had been invited to meet Hitler at Munich the following day. The leader of the Labour Opposition welcomed the statement of the Prime Minister that even at this late hour a fresh opportunity had arisen for further discussions which might lead to a prevention of war. Labour was desirous of neglecting no chance of preserving peace, but "*without sacrificing principles*."[16] After the debate, the leader of the Opposition interviewed the Foreign Secretary, Lord Halifax, and impressed upon him the misgivings that he and many of his colleagues shared as to the possibility of further sacrifices' being demanded from the Czech government, their dissatisfaction with the absence of Czech representatives from the forthcoming conference and the lack of any references by the Prime Minister to the governments of the Soviet Union or the United States.

When the results of the Munich discussions were revealed, the Labour party denounced them as "a victory for brute force." The

[15] *Daily Herald*, September 27, 1938, p. 5. Also cf. Attlee, "Stand Fast for Peace and Freedom," *ibid.*, September 23, 1938, p. 10.

[16] 339 *H.C.Deb.*, September 28, 1938, cols. 5–26. Italics mine.

agreement was, in the main, the concession of an extension of the time
limit in which the cession of territory and populations had to be made
by the Czech government from October 1 to October 10. That government had been urged by the British and French governments not to
resist the Nazi invasion, but to accede to the proposals and so avert
the probability of a European war. In view of this agreement, the
National Council of Labour expressed its belief that Czechoslovakia
had "submitted with dignity, fortitude and unbroken unity" to terms
of settlement which were "equivalent to those of a military conquest."
While the statesmen who assembled at Munich were claiming the
credit for preserving peace, it was Czechoslovakia which was paying
the price. British Labour expressed its profound sympathy for the
Czech people and offered to them a solemn assurance of its resolute
support in every effort that could be made to preserve the independence
and integrity of their country. It declared that it was now the inescapable duty of the governments which sanctioned the cession of
territory and allowed it to be occupied by Germany's armed forces
"to protect the Czech people against acts of tyranny, spoliation and
injustice."[17]

After the Munich crisis, the Labour party raised the question of
whether it was "peace now" or "only a short breathing space and a
fatal worsening of strategical and economic conditions for the British
Commonwealth before an inevitable war." As far as Labour was
concerned, Munich was not only a tremendous victory for Herr Hitler,
but also one of the greatest diplomatic defeats that Britain had ever
sustained. Without firing a shot, by the mere display of military force,
Hitler had achieved a dominating position in Europe, overturned the
balance of power, destroyed the last fortress of democracy in eastern
Europe which stood in the way of his ambition, and successfully
defeated and reduced to impotence the forces that might have stood
against the rule of violence. And what did the British government
get in return for its concessions? Labour asked. Two promises, one
from Signor Mussolini and one from Herr Hitler! The Labour party
agreed with the First Lord of the Admiralty, Duff Cooper, who had
resigned from the government over Munich, that a firm declaration
by Britain, France, and the Soviet Union to stand against aggression
would have "stopped this tragedy" and prevented war. Throughout
the whole of these proceedings, however, there had been a "cold-
shouldering" of the Soviet Union which convinced Labour that the
Prime Minister and his supporters would "almost prefer to lose the

[17] "Labour and the Crisis," October 3, 1938, *Report of the Thirty-eighth Annual
Conference of the Labour Party*, 1939, p. 19.

British Empire with Russia neutral than to hold it with Russia as an ally." Russia might well "hold aloof" in the future, Labour warned, when she considered what "little trust" could be placed in the Western democracies. As a result, Britain would be isolated, with France and all her potential allies gone. It did not appear to Labour that anything was ever done to bring this case before the League of Nations, although two years before the Prime Minister had said that if there was any question of a threat to Czechoslovakia, he would at once take it to the League, with assurances that Britain would be prepared to do her "full duty." When the "National" government abandoned the League and collective security, Labour knew that sooner or later a challenge would come to Great Britain.[18]

With the march of German troops into Prague, the "National" government's policy of appeasement was destroyed as completely as the independence of Czechslovakia. However, the end of appeasement did not signify the beginning of a realistic foreign policy so far as Labour was concerned, and the party renewed its struggle for a policy of collective defense against aggression. Labour demanded that the government take action even at this late stage to assemble together and to amalgamate all the scattered forces desirous of peace. There was not much time to save Europe, Labour warned; and as a result of what happened to the Czechs, Poland would be placed at an immense military disadvantage, Hungary could be overwhelmed in hours, and Rumania was "on the way."[19] When the Prime Minister finally announced a British guaranty of Polish independence, Labour insisted that the government "take immediate, active and energetic steps to bring into this arrangement other Powers, large and small, with the wider object of obtaining the maximum amount of co-operation in the defence of peace." The guaranty to Poland, however satisfactory and as a very valuable nucleus of a much wider understanding, was clearly not enough to meet the needs of the present situation. Labour demanded a clearly defined system of mutual aid with the understanding that an attack upon one was an attack upon all. In these times, Labour held, it was important to mobilize in the cause of peace all states prepared to stand against aggression.[20]

The Labour party expressed a similar satisfaction with the guaranty to Greece and Rumania, but had some misgivings regarding the

[18] Clement Attlee, 339 *H.C.Deb.*, October 3, 1938, cols. 52–66; Hugh Dalton, *ibid.*, col. 136. Also cf. Personal Explanation by Duff Cooper, *ibid.*, cols. 29–40. Labour's censure motion was defeated 369–150 and the Conservative motion of confidence carried 366–144.

[19] David Grenfell, 345 *H.C.Deb.*, March 15, 1939, cols. 447–48.

[20] Arthur Greenwood, *ibid.*, April 3, 1939, cols. 2476–80.

slowness in the government's negotiations with other "Peace Powers," particularly the apparent reluctance to get into touch with the Soviet Union. Believing that Russia could not be ignored in this connection, the party pointed out that since her entry into the League of Nations, Russia had been more loyal to its principles and decisions than the British government and had declared her willingness to stand by any kind of undertaking which would keep the peace through the establishment of collective security. There could be no question, in Labour's opinion, that Russia "might well prove to be the final, decisive and smashing factor on the side of keeping the peace in the world." Pressure upon the government to conclude a pact of mutual assistance with Russia was progressively maintained, and the government was urged day after day at "question time" in the House of Commons to report progress. Now that Britain was pledged to the principle of collective defense against aggression, Labour demanded to know why negotiations with Russia had not been pushed. Four and a half months had elapsed since the "swoop upon Prague," and still the government had not succeeded in building up a "Peace Front strong enough to prevent a repetition of these intolerable aggressions." The Labour party attacked the government for its "diplomatic dawdling" over the negotiations with Russia, criticized the dispatch to Moscow of a Foreign Office official, William Strang—who lacked the power to make decisions regarding the formation of an alliance between the two countries —and urged that the Foreign Secretary should go to Moscow or that Molotov should be invited to London. Labour believed that the government would be "guilty of an intolerable betrayal of the cause of peace" if it refused immediately to consolidate the peace front by a triple pact concluded by France, Great Britain, and Soviet Russia on the basis of reciprocal obligations to resist aggression.[21]

In the midst of Labour's campaign for a peace front against Fascism, the conclusion of the Nazi-Soviet Nonaggression Pact was revealed. When the House of Commons was recalled in consequence of the increased tension, Labour spokesmen pointed out that the situation had arisen largely from the mistaken policies of the government in the past. While Labour did not propose, in this time of crisis, to "rake over the embers" of the past, it did recall that there were, in the early days, "criminal hesitations" on the part of the British and French governments in their relations with Russia and in the negotiations to bring her into a firm peace alliance. That there should have been irrita-

[21] Hugh Dalton, 350 H.C.Deb., July 31, 1939, cols. 2006–15; Chairman's address, George Dallas, Report of the Thirty-eighth Annual Conference of the Labour Party, 1939, pp. 215–16.

tion on Russia's part at these hesitations, that there should have been serious distrust on her part of both the British and French governments, was understandable. But it could provide no excuse for what was considered "a bigger betrayal of peace and of European freedom even than Munich."[22] Now, however, Labour had to look to the immediate future. Obligations had been undertaken with regard to Poland which would have to be honored. The National Council repeated the determination of the Labour movement that there should be no weakening in its declared policy of collective resistance to any further act of aggression by the German government. In view of the growing gravity of the situation, the Council reaffirmed its steadfast resolve that the obligations undertaken by Britain in defense of the independence of Poland should be honored to the full.[23] In Parliament, the Labour Opposition admitted that the peace front had been "gravely impaired" by Russia's defection. However, Britain and France remained firmly in alliance and close friendship and they had "other friends." British Labour was "unshaken in its attitude of resistance to aggression" and made it clear to the aggressor that in its view "liberty, like peace, was indivisible."[24]

At the beginning of September, the National Executive Committee and the Executive Committee of the parliamentary Labour party met to consider the situation arising from the German invasion of Poland and the implications of the British Treaty of Guarantee. It was agreed that Arthur Greenwood would make immediate representations to the Prime Minister indicating that the two executives were prepared to support the fulfilling of the treaty with Poland and that the government would be expected to announce to the House of Commons as to when, in company with the French government, the two countries were prepared to take action to honor the treaty obligations to which they were committed. As soon as Parliament convened, Greenwood expressed the necessity of the government's definitely announcing its attitude to the German aggression against Poland. As for the Labour party, it was determined, "at whatever cost, in the interests of the liberty of the world in the future," to use all its resources in men and material to defend Britain and others against aggression. There could "now be no withdrawal" and in any event, Britain was "honour bound."[25]

On September 3, the Prime Minister announced to the House of

[22] *Daily Herald*, editorial, August 22, 1939, p. 8.

[23] Press Statement, August 23, 1939, *Report of the Thirty-ninth Annual Conference of the Labour Party*, 1940, p. 8.

[24] Arthur Greenwood, 351 *H.C.Deb.*, August 24, 1939, cols. 11–14.

[25] *Ibid.*, September 1, 1939, col. 133.

Commons that as a result of Hitler's declining to observe the integrity and independence of Poland, a state of war had been declared between Great Britain and Germany. In the course of the discussion which ensued, Arthur Greenwood, on behalf of the Labour Opposition, pledged support "for the fulfilling of Britain's pledged word and unbreakable intention to defend Poland, and so to defend the liberties of Europe." The "intolerable agony of suspense" was over, Greenwood stated, and "the hated word 'war' had been spoken." Labour would utilize all its forces to co-operate in the war effort; but "should there be confused councils, inefficiency and wavering, then other men must be called to take their places."[26] The Trades Union Congress, meeting at Bridlington, arrived at similar decisions and adopted a declaration of its support for the war. The Congress was "convinced that the Nazi Government made Danzig and the Polish Corridor, as it made the seizure of Austria, the destruction of Czechoslovakia, and the annexation of Memel, another pretext to carry out its purposeful policy of violence and aggression"; that "no concessions that Poland could have made would have saved her people from the dismemberment that befell the brave Czech nation"; and that compliance with these demands would not have "satisfied the insane ambition of Germany's rulers," or "saved the Peace of Europe." The Congress believed that the Nazi government, "having chosen for its people the way of war, must be resisted to the utmost" and opposed by all the forces that the civilized nations could concentrate for its defeat and overthrow. Since the defeat of ruthless aggression was essential if liberty and order were to be re-established in the world, the Congress, "with a united and resolute nation," entered the struggle "with a clear conscience and steadfast purpose."[27]

[26] Arthur Greenwood, 351 *H.C.Deb.*, September 3, 1939, col. 293.

[27] Declaration of the Trades Union Congress, Bridlington, September 4, 1939, submitted by the General Council and adopted with only two dissentients. *Report of the Thirty-ninth Annual Conference of the Labour Party*, 1940, p. 11.

II

THE OLD WORLD AND THE NEW SOCIETY

While the Labour party pledged its support to the war effort, it refused to take part in the Chamberlain government. During the early stages of the conflict, Labour was critical but not obstructive of the government's conduct of the war. Pursuing a course of "constructive" opposition, it pressed for effective control over prices and the equitable sharing of war burdens, for more effective mobilization of the nation's economic resources, and especially for the setting up of proper machinery for economic co-ordination under an economic general staff. It raised many issues connected with service pay and allowances, the hardships attendant on the call for the armed forces, the effective maintenance and supplementation of the social services to meet the needs of war, the improvement of air-raid precautions, and the evacuation of mothers and children from the threatened areas. In addition, it drew attention to the continuance of unemployment in the distressed areas, despite the evident need for the full use of the services of every available worker.[1] Labour's criticism was continuous and progressively sharpened in the light of the government's "futile efforts" to win the war. Then at the "frightful tragedy" in Denmark and in Norway, Labour decided to challenge the government in accordance with its warning that in the event of "confused councils, inefficiency and wavering," the cabinet should be replaced. It felt that "the sooner there was a change in the direction of policy, and more vigour and foresight, and more stiffness of action" were shown, the more certainly a great disaster might be averted. Labour therefore made the challenge that resulted in the fall of the Chamberlain government. In supporting the Conservative revolt against Chamberlain's leadership, Labour realized that under existing circumstances there was no possibility of an appeal to the electorate. Since any change in the government would have to be made in the existing Parliament, any government to take the place of the existing one would have to work in that Parliament. Believing that the country wanted a new administration, the National Executives of the Labour movement made their decision and asked the party conference for its endorsement.

The unanimous decision of the National Executive Committee that the Labour party should take its share of responsibility as a full

[1] Cf. G. D. H. Cole, *A History of the Labour Party Since 1914* (London: Routledge & Kegan Paul, 1948), p. 377.

161

partner in a new cabinet which, under a new Prime Minister, would command the confidence of the nation received the approval of a preponderant majority of the party conference. In reply to the dissenting minority opposing the support of "a War to ensure the survival and dominance of Anglo-French Finance-Capitalism," the leader of the parliamentary party insisted that when Labour took its stand against aggression, "it could have done none other than it did, in view of its declarations of policy, in view of its whole history and principles." Labour had done its utmost to try to avert the calamity of war, to try to check aggression in its early stages. When aggression was finally challenged and war broke out, Labour took its stand because it knew that "should Nazism win there would be an end to freedom of thought, an end to freedom of conscience, an end to the rights of the workers to combine." Attlee had the "greatest sympathy and respect" for those who took the absolute pacifist position, but he had "little patience" with those who talked "claptrap about an imperialist war." They had to face the issue that Hitler would not care whether one were an imperialist or a pacifist or anything else. Whatever might be the conditions in capitalist democracies, there was always hope and opportunity for the labor movement; but where Nazism reigned all hope was gone.[2]

The deputy leader of the party, Arthur Greenwood, reinforced Attlee's plea for full support to the new administration in its effort to secure a swift victory and a just peace. Greenwood maintained that it would have been "an act of treachery and cowardice," at this critical hour, when "three poor little States" were being "ground under heel," when others might follow, and when the war was coming nearer and nearer to Britain's shores, for the Labour movement to stand aside and not bring into play all the enormous forces which it commanded. Labour was faced with a situation which meant one of two things: either not accepting responsibility and remaining aloof, or taking its courage into its hands. If it had shirked its responsibility, "the brand of cowardice" would have been upon it, its prestige, "higher than it was in the history of the past, would have dwindled to nothing," and people would say that Labour was a movement with no sense of responsibility. In addition, if Labour stood apart from the effective prosecution of the war and remained out of this new government, it would "go into the stony wilderness of barren criticism" and have no choice in the making of the peace. The deeper Labour got its foot in now, the more certain it was that it could impose on the other elements in the government the kind of peace which it believed in and which it

[2] *Report of the Thirty-ninth Annual Conference of the Labour Party*, 1940, pp. 123-26. The critical resolution was moved by P. R. D. Shufeldt (Chelsea D.L.P.).

knew would be the only basis for a settled peace in the future. When Labour had played its part fully, it would have won in the country "an even greater respect" than it now had. On the home front, with the power that it would then possess, it could build a socialist state. Abroad it could "bring the most powerful factor in the world to get that kind of just and eternal peace" which it desired. Labour was not prepared to run away from the risks, dangers, and disputes that it might have to face. It was not going to run away from them and not take a noble part in the establishment of a permanent edifice of peace after the war.[3]

Throughout the duration of the war, the Labour party regarded as its supreme aim the winning of complete victory. After the resignation of the Chamberlain government, the entry of Labour into the Coalition, and the Nazi invasion of the Soviet Union, there was virtually no opposition within the party to the prosecution of the war to a victorious conclusion. With the entry of Russia and the United States into the war, and the world-wide extension of the conflict, Labour reaffirmed its belief in the necessity for achieving a final triumph over its enemies and "welcomed with pride the Grand Alliance of the United Nations fighting for the liberties of the world." It extended to the peoples of the U.S.S.R. "a declaration of its profound confidence in their unflinching purpose and ability to withstand at all costs the renewed assaults of their powerful, implacable and barbarous enemy." It called upon all British workers "to produce and transport as much material and equipment as possible for the use of the heroic Soviet armies." It was confident that at the first opportunity battle would be joined by British forces against the enemy in Europe and that the burdens and sacrifices falling upon the Soviet armies and peoples would be lightened as Britain shared with them "the struggle and the glory of the final and crushing defeat" of their enemy. Labour also "rejoiced in a renewed fellowship of arms with the great American people," whose mighty resources were "now being flung decisively and unhesitatingly into the great cause of freedom and civilisation." In addition, it "saluted the gallant and untiring struggle of the Chinese people against the ruthless might of Japan" and declared its "solidarity with the oppressed peoples of Europe in their bitter struggle against the German Nazi and Italian Fascist tyrants." Labour was convinced that "all the Governments and peoples now joined in an unbreakable alliance against the rapacious and aggressive tyrannies in the East and West must continue in a new, closer and enduring association after victory."[4]

[3] *Ibid.*, pp. 131–33. The vote for the resolution supporting Labour's part in the new government was 2,413,000–170,000.

[4] National Executive resolutions on "Victory" and the "International Situation," *Report of the Forty-first Annual Conference of the Labour Party*, 1942, pp. 99, 151–52.

Although the Labour party admitted that victory was the immediate task, it believed that before the peoples were "still further estranged by hatred and suffering," a lasting and just peace might be brought nearer by stating clearly at once what the immediate war purpose was and what should be the principles and methods of the final settlement. Moreover, Labour felt that if the German people realized that they could have an honorable peace under fair conditions, this might contribute to a shortening of the war. Labour's first pronouncement on peace aims was made by Clement Attlee, two months after the declaration of war, in an address to a meeting of Labour candidates and members of Parliament. Attlee's program called for nothing less than the establishment of a new world order. In the first place, there would be no dictated peace at the conclusion of this war. There would be restitution to the victims of aggression, but all ideas of revenge and punishment would be excluded. There would be recognition of the right of all nations, great and small, of whatever color or creed, to live and develop their own characteristic civilization, provided they did not thereby infringe the rights of others. There would be a complete abandonment of imperialism, aggression, and the use of armed force as an instrument of national policy. Finally, there would be acceptance of the principle that international anarchy was incompatible with peace, and that in the common interest there would be recognition of an international authority superior to the individual states and endowed not only with rights over them but with power to make them effective, operating not only in the political but in the economic sphere. It was Attlee's conviction that "Europe must federate or perish."[5]

Attlee's peace statement was followed in February of 1940 by a declaration of the National Executive—*Labour, the War and the Peace*—which was circulated throughout the movement and endorsed by the annual party conference. The party "unreservedly" supported the Allied war of resistance to Nazi tyranny and Nazi aggression and "a fight to a finish against Hitler and his gang." It proposed that the present close co-operation between the British Commonwealth, France, and their Allies in the political and economic spheres should be the nucleus of a wider association or commonwealth of states, membership of which should be "open and advantageous to all nations." It repeated Attlee's demand for a new association, the collective authority of which would transcend over a proper sphere the sovereign rights of separate states. In the traditional pattern of Labour's foreign policy, it called for an authority which would control such military and eco-

[5] "Labour's Six Principles for a New World Order," *Manchester Guardian,* November 9, 1939, p. 8.

nomic power as would enable it to enforce peaceful behavior as between its members, secure the all-round reduction of national armaments to the level required for the preservation of internal order, and ensure that all international disputes, wherever arising and of whatever sort, would be settled by peaceful means, through predetermined procedures of arbitration and conciliation.[6]

In order that it might be "ready for peace" and be sure that its immense opportunities would not be wasted, the National Executive set up the Central Committee on Reconstruction to prepare an "Interim Report on the Problems of War and Peace Reconstruction." The report—*The Old World and the New Society*—contained a restatement of Labour's foreign policy and applied its principles to the international situation arising out of the war and the approaching peace settlement. Labour's "new society" would be built upon the foundations of international co-operation, replacing the "old world" of prewar international anarchy. The principle of collective security against aggression would be given its appropriate methods and institutions by the rebuilding of an international organization. This organization would have the necessary instruments, judicial, executive, and legislative: (*a*) to complete the peaceful solution of international disputes, (*b*) to impose sanctions, both economic and military, against any nation-state rejecting such a peaceful solution, (*c*) to promote common action upon matters of common concern, and especially in this realm, to protect the interests of minorities, both racial and religious and of those people not yet able to stand alone, and (*d*) to organize positive and continuous co-operation between states for the purpose of raising the international standard of economic life, particularly, of assisting, materially and technically, the less developed nations to a higher level of well-being. The Labour party was convinced that no experiment in peace which did not recognize the due rights of nations to security and independence could have the prospect of success. It denied, however, that this recognition could imply any nation's right to sovereignty in the sense claimed and exercised by states in the interwar years. It believed that all the authority the nations, great and small alike, required for their self-respect and freedom was fully compatible with their full participation in, and acceptance of, the making of international standards in matters of international concern. Finally, Labour was bound to emphasize that the future power of democracy to maintain international peace was, in the long run, inseparable from the growth, in each country, of the common ownership

[6] London, February 9, 1940, *Report of the Thirty-ninth Annual Conference of the Labour Party*, 1940, pp. 188–90.

of the main instruments of production and their co-ordinated planning for common ends. This was "no doctrinaire affirmation"; it was "the inescapable lessons both of the inter-War years on the one hand and of the War itself on the other." Only the rapid socialization of these instruments of production would provide that plane of common action where co-operation for abundance instead of division through scarcity was the chief motive in international effort.[7]

The Old World and the New Society was merely a general statement reflecting the continuity of the principles of Labour's foreign policy. During the concluding stages of the war, the application of those principles was made in the form of a series of reports on the specific problems of postwar reconstruction. The report on *The International Post-War Settlement* provided the most detailed plan, thus far, of Labour's international policy for the postwar world. The purposes of the settlement were to prevent future war, both by removing its causes and by organizing in advance collective and preventive action against all forms of aggression; to make sure, none the less, that if aggression should occur, it would be crushed quickly and completely; to achieve a high and ever rising level of economic well-being in all lands, the ending of mass unemployment, poverty, and malnutrition and an effective system of social security everywhere; and to promote the spread of democracy and political freedom throughout the world. To each of these purposes socialism was a "fundamental necessity." Each could be achieved only by international co-operation as well as by national action.

Labour's first aim, according to *The International Post-War Settlement*, was to continue the closest possible Anglo-American-Russian co-operation. If these three powers held together, all would be well; if they fell apart, all would be "dark and uncertain." But Anglo-American-Russian co-operation should not lead to an exclusive group nor be an instrument of domination over the rest of the world. Rather, it should be the solid nucleus of a world organization. On the question of arms and defense, Labour held that pacifism was an unworkable basis of policy. There should be sufficient armed forces, readily available and properly organized and pooled under international agreements, to protect, not to destroy, the essential freedoms of mankind and to enforce the rule of law among the nations. Britain should seek to create the beginnings of a single international force and try to persuade as many other nations as possible to agree to the prohibition of private manufacture in arms. In accordance with the Atlantic Charter and the Moscow Declaration, Labour was resolved that British foreign

[7] *The Old World and the New Society* (London: Labour Party, 1942), pp. 24–27.

policy should be directed to ensuring the success of a general international organization which would promote the common interests of all and secure all nations against aggression, with the least practicable diversion of the world's resources to armaments and preparation for war. The organization should be world wide and, in due course, should include all nations in every continent. It should establish the binding force of international law through a new world court of international justice. This system of law, and indeed the whole international political organization, should depend upon the consent and upon the active support of the peoples of the world. In the economic sphere, many new forms of international organization would be needed: not only a strengthened and developed International Labor Office, but new international institutions and agreements to plan relief and rehabilitation, to organize abundant world-wide food supplies, to regulate international trading and transport and monetary relationships. Just as the armies of occupation might grow into an international force, so—and much more easily—might the civilian agencies set up to supervise relief, repatriation, and resettlement, including transfers of population and the rebuilding and revival of economic life in Europe and Asia, grow into an international civil service with great future possibilities. Expansion, not restriction, should henceforth be the watchword and the aim of all economic planning. As to the "further future," Labour worked for a "Socialist future" because war was "inherent in the nature of capitalist society." It was convinced that only as the framework of civilization were socialist, could it hope both for the assurance of economic plenty and a peace which it was in the interest of all states to preserve.[8]

The International Post-War Settlement was accepted by the annual party conference as the basis for an enduring peace. On the whole, the report was well received by the conference and its criticism was a matter of emphasis rather than content.[9] The chief criticism of the statement was that it revealed a "lack of solidarity, of collective understanding, of united will, and indeed of Socialist purpose." It was alleged that Labour would, "under the shackles of this Statement, be able to make no Labour or Socialist contribution to the Peace Treaty." The "Parliamentary Peace Aims Group," including Rhys Davies, W. G. Cove, and R. R. Stokes, insisted that "Socialists must feel the dynamic pulse of a co-operative world, and respond to the great ideal of international brotherhood." It was their belief that it was "the

[8] *The International Post-War Settlement* (London: Labour Party, 1944), pp. 2–7.

[9] Cf. resolutions proposed, *Report of the Forty-third Annual Conference of the Labour Party,* 1944, pp. 133–40.

first duty of all Socialists to strive to bring into reality what the international spirit of brotherhood dictates, and world economy demands."[10]

The Fabian Society agreed that Labour's policy for the international postwar settlement should be founded uncompromisingly on socialist principles. It felt that it was necessary to insist upon this "supremely important point" because it was not consistently recognized in the statement. The result was that the policy proposed was "contradictory and inconsistent, speaking with two contradictory voices, one that of international socialism, and the other of an apologetic socialism which assures the world that it is just as 'realist' and 'strong' as Tory nationalism and really not very different from it." It was absolutely essential, according to Fabian spokesman Leonard Woolf, that the labor and socialist forces, which had proved their faith in the resistance movements throughout Europe, should be organized as the nucleus of a new Labour and Socialist International which would work out a common policy for achieving peace and prosperity. Woolf recognized that after the war the economic system of some states would be socialist and of others capitalist, and that this of itself made it impossible to move straight from economic anarchy to a fully developed system of international government of the world's production and consumption. Nevertheless, it was essential that the international authority should from the start have powers enabling it to encourage and direct the planning of production and consumption on a world scale, to remove uneconomic barriers against international trade, to make rules or regulations which would promote international economic co-operation and prevent economic aggression by, e.g., the restriction of supplies, the depreciation of the exchange rates, or the abuse of monopoly powers. The planning of full employment, the development of social security, and the raising of labor standards were dependent upon international organization. None of this was possible without the abandonment by the national state of its claim to complete economic sovereignty.[11] It was the conviction of the Fabian Society that what Labour could offer, and what the Tories could not, was an agreement to create and support institutions in Europe which would plan reconstruction on socialist principles. Given an agreement of this sort, a political agreement to give joint backing to the working-class movements inside Europe would follow. The Labour party was

[10] *Labour and the Post-War Settlement* (London: Parliamentary Peace Aims Group, 1944), pp. 7–8.

[11] Leonard Woolf, *The International Post-War Settlement* (London: Fabian Research Series No. 85, 1944), pp. 3–6, 21.

urged to act as a cohesive and dynamic force which would take energetic economic and political action in Europe.[12]

Toward the end of the war, British Labour co-operated with the international labor and socialist movements in preparing a program of peace for the postwar world. The representatives of the Labour parties of the British Commonwealth of Nations, assembled in conference at the end of 1944, expressed "the determination of the common people to march beyond military victory to economic abundance and international order." They were convinced that at no time in the history of labor movements had the opportunity for advance been so great. It remained for the Labour parties of the British Commonwealth "to take advantage of it and to march in the forefront of the world movement towards Socialism." Labour would plan for peace as it had planned to win the war, "with foresight and determination and without regard to vested interests or crusted prejudices." Labour's new democratic world order would be based upon a program of full employment, higher standards of living, and the retention of the principal wartime financial controls. The new world organization would be open to membership of all peace-loving states, large and small, for the maintenance of international peace and security, and would provide for the renunciation of war as an instrument of national policy, the settlement of all disputes by peaceful means, and the prevention of aggression through the imposition of economic and military sanctions, the international control of armaments, and the creation of an international police force. The conference was particularly conscious of the grave responsibility resting on the Labour and Socialist parties of the Commonwealth. Through unity in ideas and in action, the Labour movements of the Commonwealth could not only strengthen the bonds of co-operation between their own peoples, but give new strength and encouragement to the popular forces everywhere. The Labour movement had a major responsibility to ensure that governments pursued an international policy which would encourage the emergence and victory everywhere of democratic and socialist forces, deny aid and comfort to discredited monarchies, spokesmen of unrepresentative governments, and other past ruling classes, and lay solid foundations for lasting peace through collective security against aggression and through positive measures for economic and social development in all lands.[13]

[12] Fabian Society, *Labour and Europe* (London: Fabian Research Series No. 71, 1943), pp. 8, 27.

[13] "From a People's War to a People's Peace," London, September 12–27, 1944, *Report of the Forty-third Annual Conference of the Labour Party*, 1944, pp. 212–14.

British Labour looked forward to the rapid revival of the Trade Union and Socialist Internationals in which it, and the Commonwealth Labour parties, would seek to play their full part. It collaborated with the representatives to the World Trade Union Conference for the purpose of uniting the labor movements of the freedom-loving nations to work together for: "speedy and uncompromising victory" over the enemy; an enduring peace; the eradication of Fascism in all its forms; international co-operation in the economic sphere which would utilize the rich resources of the world for the benefit of its peoples, yielding employment with rising standards of living and real security to the men and women of all nations; and a democratic society which would assure political and civil equality and full cultural opportunity for all the peoples of the earth. The World Trade Union Conference welcomed the binding guaranty of the Allied governments to establish a general international organization to maintain peace and security, to give effect to the principles of the Atlantic Charter, and to summon a conference of the United Nations at San Francisco. It also attached "supreme importance" to the removal of the economic causes of war and urged the use of the proposed Economic and Social Council for the initiation of great schemes of international economic reconstruction, embodying the principle of public control and administration. The conference, therefore, called upon all governments to co-operate for the purpose of establishing an international monetary system and institutions of international economic co-ordination capable of promoting a steady expansion of foreign trade; of regulating international trade and tariffs; of reaching international agreement to regulate the conditions and prices of staple commodities entering into international trade; of making long-term loans for the economic and industrial development of colonial territories and backward countries.[14]

British Labour also co-operated with European socialists in preparing a program for "a people's peace." The Conference of European Socialist Parties, reaffirming its faith in the "trinity of arbitration, security and disarmament," asserted that the Dumbarton Oaks proposals, as modified at Yalta, constituted a considerable achievement in this matter. It welcomed the agreement ultimately reached which brought together, in the search for collective security, all the nations engaged in the struggle for freedom, and in particular the Soviet Union and the United States, whose presence was essential to the building of peace. Although it believed that the proposals as a whole could form the basis of a new security organization, it felt, nevertheless, that the structure and the procedure of the new organiza-

[14] *Labour*, VII (March 1945), 196–37, 207.

tion might be capable of improvement. As to the structure, it was essential that the Assembly should constitute the final court of appeal in all economic and social questions, should be able to take majority decisions, and should become the international forum through which all important matters could be submitted to the judgment of public opinion. The composition of the Security Council, in particular the provision for election for only two years of the representatives of the small nations, carried with it the risk of some instability. This could be remedied either by prolonging the period of office or by making it possible for states belonging to particular regions to form groups nominating joint representatives who should be re-eligible. Regarding procedure, the Socialists rejoiced that at Yalta the participating countries were able to agree on the principle of majority decision in the case of demands for arbitration; recognized that in matters calling for sanctions it might be inevitable in the initial stage that the great military powers bearing special responsibilities should be unanimous in their decisions; but remained convinced that peace would be finally and solidly established only when all states, great and small, submitted to decisions taken by an adequate majority. Nor could they remain satisfied with the provisions whereby the application of military sanctions was made to depend upon special agreements for the placing of armed forces at the disposal of the international organization; such agreements should be specifically provided for in the document establishing the organization. It was important to make provision both for the immediate setting up of machinery for the international control of the private and public production of armaments and for the rapid constitution of the first nucleus of an international police force. The Socialists held that as peace and prosperity were "one and indivisible," peace would not become real and permanent unless the peoples of the world succeeded in getting rid of the many causes of economic conflicts which led to war. This could be achieved only "by correcting the inequalities resulting from the geographical distribution of natural resources; by guaranteeing the full employment of our ever-increasing means of production; and by putting an end to the machinations of international trusts and cartels and private capitalism in all its forms." The common goal of all socialist parties was "a new world social structure with planned production and economic co-operation to meet all economic needs. To their traditional defence of the rights of man and their demand for political democracy Socialists have always added the claim for an economic democracy, national and international."[15]

[15] London, March 3–5, 1945, *Report of the Forty-fourth Annual Conference of the Labour Party*, 1945, pp. 163–70.

As the European war drew to a close, the Policy Committee of the National Executive, in preparation for the forthcoming General Election, drew up a manifesto outlining the specific policies which a Labour government would pursue if called to office. In *Let Us Face the Future*, the Labour party looked forward to a world of progress and peace. It felt that all its planning for a finer and nobler world, all its discussion on the reorganization of industry, on housing, on health, on standards of life, on education and leisure would be utterly vain unless it could deal with the problem of peace. Recalling its record of support for collective security, it reaffirmed the necessity of joining with those who had contributed to the common victory in forming an international organization capable of keeping the peace in years to come. Labour would consolidate in peace the great wartime association of the British Commonwealth with the United States and the Soviet Union. However, the alliance would not be limited to the prevention of war. As the economic well-being of each nation largely depended upon world-wide prosperity, Labour would build a new United Nations — "allies in a new war on hunger, ignorance and want."[16] The Labour party was convinced that the problem of peace could be solved only by building up an international organization for its maintenance. It realized that if it advocated a world organization, if it advocated the rule of law in the world, if it advocated enforcement of the rule of law, it must be prepared to make its own contribution. As Ernest Bevin reminded the party conference, collective security involved commitments; it was "no use talking about an international police force unless you supply policemen, and decide the means by which you will supply them." As that was "inescapable," Labour must not "bury its head in the sand."[17] After the party conference had endorsed the Executive's Election Manifesto, the Executive promised to "take the greatest notice" of the request from the rank and file to "apply the Socialist analysis to the world situation; to oppose the crystallisation of power politics into a so-called League of Nations consisting only of the victorious Powers; and to struggle for the establishment of the United Socialist States of Europe as being the only means of ensuring a just and lasting peace."[18]

Labour's conviction that a socialist civilization was the only foundation for a lasting peace became the basis for the party's electoral

16 *Let Us Face the Future* (London: Labour Party, 1945), p. 11.

17 *Report of the Forty-fourth Annual Conference of the Labour Party*, 1945, p. 117.

18 Resolution on "War Aims," moved by Leigh Davis (Willesden D.L.P.), *ibid.*, p. 112.

pronouncements on foreign policy in the General Election held at the conclusion of the European war. Explaining why the electorate should vote Labour, the party stated that

The British Labour Movement comes to the task of international organization with one asset; it has a common bond with the working peoples of all countries, who have achieved a new dignity and influence through their long struggles against Nazi tyranny.[19]

Emphasizing the advantages of a socialist foreign policy, Labour claimed that the Tories had lost the peace last time because they put the defense of capitalism before everything else. Today, when the need for fundamental social change was more urgent than ever, the Tories, by making preservation of the present social order their first care, would go on backing reactionaries everywhere, as they had already done in Greece and Italy and tried to do in France, Belgium, and Yugoslavia. Since the Tories were still the "last-ditch defenders of capitalism," they would lose the peace again if returned to office. On the other hand, Labour's policies and instincts in international affairs had been proved right by the test of twenty-five years' experience. With a sound foreign policy, Labour stood for reconstruction on the basis of socialism. Labour was trusted abroad by the masses and resistance movements and all who believed in international co-operation and justice. "A Labour Government could and would win the peace."[20]

[19] *Let Us Face the Future*, p. 11.
[20] Diplomaticus, *Can the Tories Win the Peace?* (London: Gollancz, 1945), p. 103.

12

A SOCIALIST FOREIGN POLICY: THE FIRST
FIVE YEARS*

Although the 1945 General Election was fought mainly on domestic issues, it was felt that so momentous an event as the return of a Labour government to power with a full majority[1] for the first time in the history of British politics was "bound to have enormous consequences" as far as issues of foreign policy were concerned. Those who had "bitter memories" of the "shameful record of Toryism" in foreign policy were hopeful that that long era had come to a total end. Great Britain, it was expected, would have a "socialist" foreign policy that would give a lead to all democratic forces throughout the world. From back-bench members of the Labour party the hope was expressed that the Foreign Secretary and the other members of the government would not insist "too eagerly" upon continuity in foreign policy.[2]

In spite of the Labour government's assurance that it was endeavoring to carry out the principles of foreign policy held faithfully by the Labour party for so many years, in the Foreign Secretary's first statement to Parliament there appeared to be no noticeable departure from the foreign policy inherited from the Coalition government. With regard to Party Chairman Harold Laski's declaration that a Labour government would give all possible support to the liberation of the Spanish people from their "Fascist prison" and would aid Greece in her search for an "ordered and democratic freedom," Mr. Bevin took exception. Considering Greece, the Foreign Secretary announced that the government would adhere to the policy which it had publicly supported when Greece had been liberated. As to Spain, the regime in Spain was one for the Spanish people to decide. Britain did not propose to take any measures which might promote or encourage civil war in that country.[3]

The charge that the Labour government was following not a "socialist" foreign policy but a "Tory" foreign policy was repeatedly

---

* Most of this chapter first appeared in two articles by Elaine Windrich in *World Affairs Interpreter*: "The British Labour Government and Franco Spain," XIX (April 1948), 41–55; and "British Labour's Foreign Policy," XXI (July 1950), 155–70.

[1] The Labour party received 11,992,292 votes and 393 seats.

[2] Michael Foot, 413 *H.C.Deb.*, August 20, 1945, cols. 336–40; Lieutenant Peart, *ibid.*, col. 358.

[3] *Ibid.*, cols. 289, 296.

made by certain groups within the British Labour movement. These critics felt that there was, unfortunately, a wide discrepancy between the theoretical basis and the practical application of Labour's international policy and that in spite of the "brave words" of official Labour spokesmen, the government had thrown overboard the party's traditional policy and was continuing in national unity with the Tories the foreign policy inherited from the Coalition government.[4] In their opinion, the policy toward Franco Spain constituted a "test case" for the application of the principles of Labour's foreign policy. Observing the government's Spanish policy, they found a strange paradox indeed —a Labour government, ideologically in sympathy with socialist governments throughout the world, tolerating a regime which it had originally condemned as a Fascist dictatorship and refusing to co-operate with or to encourage an alternative Spanish regime. In every instance when action against the Spanish dictator seemed to be opportune, the Labour government not only hesitated to act itself but refused to co-operate with other powers who expressed a willingness to undertake concerted measures to restore a democratic government in Spain. On three occasions—the Labour victory in the British General Election, the end of the European war, and the consideration of the Spanish issue by the United Nations—the Labour government was presented with the opportunity to fulfill its pledges to the Spanish republicans and yet failed to implement these promises. When it was recalled that throughout the Spanish Civil War the British Labour party, then in the Opposition, consistently attacked a Conservative government for following a policy of nonintervention and for refusing to supply the Spanish government with the means necessary to defend its authority against the Fascist rebellion, it was difficult for these critics to reconcile the Labour government's policy toward the Franco regime with the party's previous commitments to the Spanish republicans. Thus it appeared to them that the Labour government had reversed its previous stand on the Spanish question and was continuing a policy conceived by a Tory government. While the Labour government's Spanish policy might be received with approval, if not acclamation, by the Conservative Opposition, it was a continual source of disturbance and dissatisfaction within the Labour movement.[5]

During the General Election campaign of 1945, the Labour party warned the electorate that only by voting Labour to power could they

[4] Cf. K. Zilliacus, "Mr. Bevin and British Foreign Policy," *Labour Monthly,* XXVIII (February 1946), 71, for an extreme left-wing attack.

[5] For an analysis of the groups opposing the Labour government's foreign policy cf. "Bevin's Parliamentary Critics," *Socialist World,* I (June–August 1947).

be sure of having a government which would give no encouragement
to the Spanish Fascists. At the same time, they were advised to put
to every Tory candidate the question, "Do you endorse the friendly
attitude of Mr. Churchill toward the Franco government of Spain?"
Much to the embarrassment of the Conservative party, General Franco
became an important figure in the campaign when he chose to announce that he and his cabinet desired to co-operate to the limit with
Britain and the United States. What disturbed the Tory party or-
ganizers was that the Franco appeal made a topical issue of an address
made by Churchill in May of 1944 concerning Franco Spain. At that
time, Churchill praised the policy of "neutrality" pursued by the
Franco government throughout the war, denied any intention of the
British government to take forcible action against a government whose
internal form of administration did not come up to its own ideas, proclaimed that the internal arrangements in Spain were a matter for the
Spanish government to decide, and expressed an eagerness to improve
the "good relations and extremely fertile trade" with Franco Spain.
The most remarkable feature of Churchill's address, according to the
Labour party, was the "flattering, almost fulsome, tone of his references to the rulers of Spain." Franco's "blatant gestures of sympathy"
with Hitler and Mussolini, the "subtle tyranny of Franco's Fascism,"
and the fact that Franco had imported Italian and German armies to
help him win the Civil War had somehow become irrelevant and now
seemed to rouse in the former Prime Minister no animosity. Not only
were Churchill's views subjected to the attack of the Labour party
during the election campaign. Other influences—"the banks, the bondholders and the concessionaries of the men with investments in the Rio
Tinto copper mines in Franco's Spain"—were also held responsible for
determining the Spanish policy of the Tory party. In the seven years
preceding the war, Labour charged, the Tory government had "kow-
towed" to Hitler, Mussolini, and Franco and had betrayed in succes-
sion China, Abyssinia, Spain, Czechoslovakia, and the League of Nations. And in the former "National" government, Labour pointed out,
there were many supporters of the "pro-Fascist policy": Lord Croft,
who described General Franco as "a great Christian gentleman," Lord
Dunglass, Butler, Lennox-Boyd, and Petherick, all defenders of the
policy of "appeasement."[6]

In the light of the Labour party's electoral pronouncements, as
well as its policy throughout the Spanish Civil War, the Labour victory
in the General Election was expected to bring a positive policy toward

[6] F. Seymour Cocks, "Tory Foreign Policy? A Sinister Rabble Decides It,"
Daily Herald, July 4, 1945, p. 2.

the Franco regime. Professor Laski's declaration that "at long last we are going to be in a position to do full justice to our Spanish comrades" was but a further indication of the unabated concern of Labour with the Spanish problem. Speaking at the National Congress of the French Socialist party, the chairman of the British Labour party proclaimed,

In no circumstances would a Labour Government help to uphold royalist or other regimes that did not enjoy the support of the people. Spain, in her turn, must be free from the Franco regime or any imitation of it.

Suggesting a course of action, Laski stated that the government would, if necessary, bring economic pressure to bear to allow a republican government to organize the election of a parliament.[7]

Following its victory in the General Election, the Labour government co-operated with the governments of Soviet Russia and the United States, in a Three-Power Declaration from Potsdam, debarring from membership in the United Nations the Spanish government, which, "having been founded with the support of the Axis Powers, does not, in view of its origins, its nature, its record and its close association with the aggressor States, possess the qualifications necessary to justify such membership." According to the Labour press, the "first fruits" of Potsdam were gathered when Franco protested against the "unprecedented allusion" to Spain and asserted the hope that the attitude of the powers would alter, once the passions excited by war and propaganda had calmed down. The very fact that this public statement had been extorted from the Spanish government was considered to be a gain, for hitherto Franco had sought to hide from his people the hostility which his regime had provoked in the outside world. The proclamation from Potsdam was hailed by the Labour party as a "death sentence" to the Franco regime and the General was warned that the days of his dictatorship were numbered. British Labour was committed to the restoration of democracy in Spain.[8]

The question of how far the new Labour government would go in the direction of restoring Spanish democracy was answered by the Foreign Secretary upon his return from the Potsdam conference. Mr. Bevin made it clear that the British government did not intend to intervene in Spain when he said that further civil war and bloodshed were too high a price to pay for the disappearance of General Franco.

[7] *The Times*, August 13, 1945, p. 3; interview in *La Tribune Économique*, quoted in *Daily Herald*, August 18, 1945, p. 4.

[8] Editorial, "Down to Business," *Daily Herald*, August 3, 1945, p. 2; "Spain," *ibid.*, August 7, 1945, p. 2; "Spain, What Next?" *New Statesman and Nation*, XXX (August 18, 1945), 102.

In his opinion, intervention by foreign powers in the internal affairs of Spain would have the opposite effect to that desired and would probably strengthen the position of General Franco. Although Mr. Bevin stated that his government would not go further than the declaration issued at Potsdam and was not prepared to take any steps which would promote civil war in Spain, he declared it to be obvious that the Labour government would "take a favourable view" if steps were taken by the Spanish people to change their own regime.[9]

It was evident that Bevin's statement of policy did not please many of his supporters and that most members of the Labour party would agree with Laski in advocating strong action to get rid of the Spanish dictator. Nevertheless, approval of the policy announced by the Foreign Secretary was voiced from two unexpected quarters. Churchill, denying that he or his party were "supporters, admirers or partisans of the present regime in Spain," agreed that it would be wrong to intervene in Spain in a forcible manner or to attempt to relight the civil war in that country, and indicated his approval of the terms of "that wounding, and deliberately calculated wounding," Potsdam Declaration against the Franco regime.[10] And from Madrid it was reported that official Spain had been "set agog" by Bevin's statement in Parliament. A slightly edited version of the Foreign Secretary's speech was received with "much joy," which included a good deal of "undisguised relief" that the "black fears" of what a Labour government might do had not materialized. However, in Mexico, where the Spanish republicans had formed a government in exile, Bevin and the Labour government were subjected to severe criticism for not taking a more positive policy in regard to the Spanish situation. Señor Giral, the liberal premier, went so far as to say that the Falangist regime would have fallen but for Bevin's statement, which permitted the regime to consolidate itself for a further period.

While the National Executive Committee of the Labour party, the General Council of the Trades Union Congress, and the External Affairs Group of the parliamentary party recorded their strong approval of Bevin's forthright condemnation of the Franco regime, they expressed the hope that the government would, in conjunction with its Allies, seek to restore in Spain the democratic government destroyed by Mussolini and Hitler.[11] It was the French government, however, that took the initiative in raising the question of relations with the Franco regime. The French cabinet made a decision which was equiva-

[9] 413 *H.C.Deb.*, Aug. 20, 1945, col. 296.
[10] *Ibid.*, August 16, 1945, cols. 88–90.
[11] Reports of the *Forty-fifth Annual Conference of the Labour Party*, 1946, p. 26; *Seventy-eighth Annual Conference of the T.U.C.*, 1946, pp. 139–41.

lent in all but name to breaking off relations with Spain, including, among other things, the closing of the Spanish frontier. At the same time, the French government informed Britain and the United States that the situation in Spain constituted a danger to international peace and security.[12] Following up the French *démarche*, the United States sent a memorandum to Britain and France suggesting that the three governments join in expressing their desire to see the end of the Franco regime and declaring their readiness to support an interim Spanish government which would administer the country until the people could choose their own form of government.[13] From Paris it was reported that the American note would doubtless confirm the impression deeply rooted in all sections of French public opinion that Franco's only reliable supporter was Great Britain.[14]

Contrary to this impression, the Labour government responded favorably to the American suggestion and agreed to participate in the framing of a joint statement on relations with Spain. Stating that so long as General Franco continued in control of Spain the Spanish people could not expect "full and cordial association" with those nations which had defeated the Nazi and Fascist regimes, the three powers made it clear that they had no intention of interfering in the internal affairs of Spain and that the Spanish people must in the long run work out their own destiny. However, "patriotic and liberal-minded" Spaniards were encouraged to find means of setting up an interim government by an offer of "full diplomatic relations" and "practicable measures to assist in the solution of Spain's economic problems."[15] The cautious phrasing of the joint declaration raised the question of how far the principle of no interference in Spain's internal affairs would be upheld in practice if means could not be found to make Franco withdraw peacefully. At any rate, not much satisfaction was given to those Labour members who were pressing Bevin to break off diplomatic relations with Franco. Consequently, the parliamentary Labour party's External Affairs Group passed a resolution in this sense, and on the publication of the joint declaration, its chairman, Seymour Cocks, told the House of Commons that there was a very strong feeling in the Labour party and the Trades Union Congress that the British ambassador in Madrid should be withdrawn.[16]

[12] *The Times*, December 27, 1945, p. 3.
[13] *Ibid.*, March 1, 1946, p. 4.
[14] Cf. "Spanish Coup d'État," *New Statesman and Nation*, XXXL (February 9, 1946), 93–94.
[15] Text, *The Times*, March 5, 1946, p. 4.
[16] 423 *H.C.Deb.*, June 5, 1946, cols. 2050–51.

Nor was the French government convinced that a joint declaration on future relations with Spain was a satisfactory solution to the Spanish problem. It had, therefore, in its note to the British and American governments, also suggested that the Security Council be asked to pronounce the Franco regime a danger to international peace and to recommend appropriate action, beginning with oil sanctions, by the members of the United Nations. The British reply, presented by Duff Cooper, ambassador in Paris, said that the Spanish government was a Spanish affair, dismissed any question of danger to the peace, expressed doubts as to the efficacy of France's proposed economic sanctions, and declared that Spain had not been alone in helping the Axis. In view of this reply, it was said that the British were so unsure of the reactions of Moscow that they had joined with the Americans in repressing a French desire to raise the Spanish question in the United Nations Security Council. Nevertheless, it was expected that France or the Soviet Union would raise the Spanish issue at New York, even in the face of Anglo-American disapproval.[17]

It was the Polish government, however, that brought the question of Spain before the Security Council. Supported by the Soviet Union, the Polish delegate, Oscar Lange, asked that the Security Council, in accordance with Articles 39 and 41 of the Charter, call upon all members of the United Nations who maintained diplomatic relations with the Franco government to sever such relations at once. In contending that a Fascist dictatorship in Spain constituted a threat to world peace, Poland, France, Mexico, and the Soviet Union were opposed by Britain and the United States. Attempting to prove that the Polish communication to the Security Council was ill-founded and that the situation in Spain did not constitute danger to peace and security in the world, the British delegate, Sir Alexander Cadogan, declared:

I cannot admit that the case so far made against the Spanish Government has established such a threat to the peace, breach of the peace or act of aggression, and I do not therefore consider that it is appropriate to ask now for a collective severence of diplomatic relations.[18]

In view of the attitude taken by the British and the American delegations, there seemed little prospect of the Security Council's reaching any agreement. However, the Australian delegate reconciled the two schools of thought by proposing that the Security Council appoint a subcommittee of five of its members to examine the statements before

[17] Cf. "The Security Council and Franco," *New Statesman and Nation*, XXXI (April 20, 1946), 274.
[18] *Official Records of the Security Council, First Year*, Thirty-fifth Meeting, April 18, 1946, p. 185.

the Council concerning Spain, receive further statements, and report to the Council before the end of May (1946). This compromise, it was believed, would enable the supporters of the Polish resolution to keep the question of Franco Spain before the United Nations, while allowing Britain and the United States to avoid the necessity of voting against any anti-Franco action, thereby opening themselves to the charge of protecting the remnants of Fascism. Nevertheless, charges were leveled against the British government for refusing to agree to any resolution with teeth in it and for preferring the Australian resolution, which was disagreeably reminiscent of the devices whereby the old Non-Intervention Committee avoided taking any positive action in support of the republican government of Spain.[19]

Actually, the only suggestion for positive action in the report of the Security Council subcommittee was the proposal that the Spanish case be referred to the General Assembly in September, with a recommendation that unless the Franco regime were withdrawn and other conditions of political freedom met, the Assembly should call upon the member states to break off diplomatic relations with Madrid. Since the subcommittee had produced a unanimous report, there appeared to be no practical alternative to breaking off diplomatic relations with Franco Spain. Nevertheless, the British delegate proposed that the recommendation to sever relations with the Spanish government be deleted from the Security Council resolution. Pointing out that the British government had declared on several occasions its "detestation" of the Franco regime, Sir Alexander Cadogan said that the form of government in any country was a matter for domestic jurisdiction and expressed the hope that the British amendment would not be misrepresented or distorted for propaganda purposes.[20] Although the British amendment was rejected, when the Security Council was ready to vote overwhelmingly in favor of giving Franco until September to abdicate or face a diplomatic break with the members of the United Nations, the Soviet delegate for the first time used the veto. Since the Soviet Union had vetoed the recommendations of the Security Council subcommittee, the Polish delegate suggested a drafting committee to see whether an agreed form of resolution could be placed before the Council. However, it proved impossible for the drafting committee to agree upon a text to be submitted to the Security Council. As a compromise measure, Dr. Evatt proposed, on behalf of the Australian

[19] "Compromise on Franco," *New Statesman and Nation*, XXXI (May 4, 1946), 310.

[20] *Official Records of the Security Council, First Year*, Forty-sixth Meeting, June 17, 1946, pp. 344–49.

and British delegations, the Polish representative dissenting, that without prejudice to the rights of the General Assembly under the Charter, the Council "keep the situation in Spain under continuous observation and maintain it upon the list of matters of which it is seized."[21]

In the General Assembly, Britain and the other members of the United Nations once again registered their unwillingness to do more than record their disapproval of Fascism in Spain. The American proposal that Franco should be "invited" to hand over his power to a provisional government was not endorsed, twenty-two delegates in the Political Committee voting for it and twenty-two against. The Polish resolution that there should be a general breaking-off of relations with Spain met with a similar fate, and a French motion that members of the United Nations refuse to import foodstuffs from Spain until they were assured that these were no longer needed for the Spanish people was rejected by a vote of thirty-two to ten. In the end, the only positive recommendation which was carried, and this secured a two-thirds majority only because of the large number of abstentions, was that member states should recall the head of diplomatic missions now in Madrid.[22] "The tragic consequence of this victory for the non-interventionists," according to the Labour party critics, was that Franco could now argue that, since the United Nations clearly had no intention of taking effective steps to oust him, he could be deposed only at the cost of another civil war, from which many Spaniards, who might welcome United Nations intervention, would shrink.[23]

Dissatisfaction with the government's policy toward Spain, and with its international policy in general, was expressed at the annual Labour party conference in the form of five critical resolutions. The Spanish resolution, moved by Henry Solomons of the South Hammersmith D.L.P., called upon the government to break diplomatic relations with the Franco government and to appoint a representative to the provisional Spanish republican government. Supporting the resolution, Francis Noel-Baker reminded the conference that British Labour had put itself under a very special obligation to the Spanish republicans ten years ago and had renewed that pledge during the General Election. He was very deeply ashamed that after eleven months in power Labour had done nothing more to help the Spanish republicans than to make a number of strong pronouncements against Franco in the House of Commons. In reply to the resolution on Spain, Bevin

[21] Cf. *Official Records of the Security Council, First Year,* Forty-ninth Meeting, June 26, 1947, p. 401, for resolution.

[22] *Official Records of the General Assembly, First Session,* Fifty-ninth Plenary Meeting, December 12, 1946, pp. 1221–22.

[23] "Non-Intervention Wins," *New Statesman and Nation,* XXXII (December 14, 1946), 434.

remarked that if other countries had not intervened in the internal affairs of Spain the Franco regime would have disappeared without civil war. In his opinion, the resolution would get the resentment, not the support, of the Spaniards because they were anxious not to be thrown into civil conflict again. Following Bevin's speech, the resolution was put to a vote and lost, although one hundred hands were raised for breaking off diplomatic relations with Franco. Since no card vote was taken, it was difficult to determine what strength these hands represented; but since no trade-union delegate had spoken in favor of the resolution, it was probable that they were almost entirely from divisional Labour parties.[24]

Although the Labour government had received a resounding endorsement for its foreign policy, the fact that criticism still existed—ranging from uneasiness over the Spanish situation to a complete rejection of its whole conception of foreign affairs—was apparent at the annual meeting of the Trades Union Congress. At Brighton, a resolution was proposed by F. Foulkes of the Electrical Trades Union condemning certain aspects of the government's foreign policy, including its relations with Spain. Although this resolution was defeated by a majority of over a million, the minority vote of 2,444,000 was considerably larger than most delegates expected in view of the strong wording of the resolution. In spite of the fact that the majority of the Congress refused to endorse what amounted to a blanket condemnation of the government's international policy, there was overwhelming support for a separate resolution on Spain, moved by R. J. Silverthorne of the Association of Engineering and Shipbuilding Draughtsmen, calling upon the government to sever economic and diplomatic relations with Franco Spain. Although Arthur Deakin, for the General Council, asked that this matter be left with the Council in accordance with its policy of supporting the World Federation of Trade Unions in approaching the United Nations concerning the Spanish question, a card vote of 4,534,000 against 1,391,000 showed that the Congress was determined to press the government for action against the Franco regime.[25]

The remarkably large Trades Union Congress vote against the government's foreign policy, and in particular its policy toward Franco Spain, encouraged a considerable number of Labour critics to express

[24] Report of the Forty-fifth Annual Conference of the Labour Party, 1946, pp. 155–67.

[25] Report of the Seventy-eighth Annual Conference of the T.U.C., 1946, pp. 469–73. Also cf. resolution on Spain, moved by E. J. Hicks of Civil Service Clerical Association, and defeated by 4,083,000–3,025,000. Ibid., Seventy-ninth Annual Conference of the T.U.C., 1947, pp. 501–8.

their concern in a letter to the Prime Minister condemning the policy. With regard to Spain, they stated that the government's continued recognition of the Franco regime and its "apparent inertia" in pursuing the matter through the United Nations had given the impression that its "detestation" of General Franco was more than counterbalanced by its fear that a communist regime might succeed the Falange. From Spelthorne came a further attack upon the government's international policy in the form of a statement marked "Private and Confidential" and circulated to divisional Labour parties, trade-unions, and Labour members of Parliament. The authors of the Spelthorne protest set out to prove that the government opposed any policy which threatened Fascism in Spain and that its foreign policy in general was a gross betrayal of the Labour cause and of democracy throughout the world. In defense of the government's foreign policy, the new secretary of the Labour party, Morgan Phillips, sent to all divisional parties a strongly worded reply in which he refuted every accusation. Concerning the Spanish situation, he declared that Britain was the only power in the world continuously working both inside and outside Spain for a means of removing Franco. He added, however, that the government would not support "gestures" which could have no positive results.[26]

The Labour government's decision to conclude a monetary agreement with Franco Spain and its reluctance, at the United Nations General Assembly, to support a positive course of action to rid Spain of the Franco regime convinced its foreign-policy critics that the party secretary's assurances did not correspond with the government's policies. The Monetary Agreement, which was to come into effect on April 8, 1947, and remain in force for two years, provided that each side would hold currency of the other up to a maximum of £2,000,000 to cover the needs of current trade. The new agreement, the government claimed, did not represent any change of British policy toward Spain nor any deviation from British obligations under the United Nations resolution of the previous year. From an economic point of view, Labour critics admitted, the agreement, by preparing the way for brisk Anglo-Spanish trade, would be a great benefit to both countries. But from a political point of view, it made nonsense of the Labour government's whole Spanish policy; for almost the only way in which it could effectively help an alternative Spanish government was by withholding trade from Franco while offering it to a democratic Spanish government. In simultaneously "detesting" and trading with

[26] Morgan Phillips' reply, *Daily Herald,* December 17, 1946, pp. 1, 4; editorial, "Spelthorne," *ibid.,* p. 2.

Franco, the Labour government was charged with confusing its opponents and appearing "at best muddle-headed, at worst perfidious."[27]

When the United Nations General Assembly reopened the discussion of relations with Spain, in 1947, it was confronted with a concerted attempt on the part of Britain and the United States to block full debate on the issue. Both powers had taken the view that the resolution of the previous December, calling upon members to sever diplomatic relations with Madrid, had had little effect upon the Spanish regime and that any further action by the Assembly would not succeed in removing Franco. They were, therefore, sympathetic with the El Salvador resolution requesting that the topic be dropped from the Assembly's agenda. To this proposal, however, most of the other members refused consent. Many of the Latin-American states insisted that the item be discussed and that the Assembly at least reaffirm its previous denunciation. The Soviet bloc, not content with a mere reaffirmation, demanded that a more determined stand be taken on the Spanish issue; and Poland, with the endorsement of the Soviet Union, called upon the Security Council to take measures short of armed force against the Franco regime.

Despite opposition from the British and American delegations, the Political and Security Committee of the General Assembly voted to set up a drafting subcommittee to produce an agreed version of the various proposals submitted for Assembly action. After surveying the three sets of proposals submitted by the Latin-American, Slav, and Benelux delegations, the drafting committee succeeded in reaching agreement on the text of a compromise resolution reaffirming the Assembly's resolution of the previous December (1946) and expressing its confidence that the Security Council would exercise its responsibilities under the Charter as soon as it considered that the situation in Spain required action.[28] In the plenary session, however, the General Assembly voted to eliminate the paragraph of the compromise resolution reaffirming the 1946 resolution barring the Franco regime from all agencies and conferences under United Nations auspices and requesting all members to recall their diplomatic representatives from Madrid. Commenting on this decision, the British delegate, Sir Hartley Shawcross, reminded the Assembly that his delegation had voted against the paragraph of the 1946 resolution referring to Security

[27] Cf. "Trading with Franco," *New Statesman and Nation*, XXXIII (April 12, 1947), 246. The terms of the agreement are given in *The Times*, April 5, 1947, p. 9; April 24, 1947, p. 8; April 25, 1947, p. 8.

[28] *Official Records of the General Assembly, Second Session, First Committee*, One Hundred and Fifth Meeting, November 11, 1947, p. 419.

Council action, although it had voted for the resolution as a whole.[29] This time, he added, the British government had voted both to reaffirm the previous resolution and in favor of the paragraph mentioned, because Britain made no secret of the fact that she disapproved of certain aspects of the Franco regime and would like to see that regime replaced. The British delegate failed to explain, however, just how the new resolution would operate to "replace" the Franco regime in Spain.[30]

Criticism of the Labour government's foreign policy was not, however, limited to the policy toward Spain. As the rift between East and West grew wider, the anxiety within the Labour movement was increased by the fact that the government had not repudiated Mr. Churchill's Fulton speech and had apparently accepted the doctrine of continuity in foreign policy proclaimed by the Conservative party, as shown by its attitude toward Spain. Those who opposed Mr. Bevin's policies regretted the government's apparent continuance of a traditionally Conservative party policy. They urged the government to return to the Labour party's policy of supporting socialist forces throughout the world and to consolidate in peace the wartime association of the British Commonwealth of Nations with the United States and the Soviet Union, as set forth in *The International Post-War Settlement*. From various sections of the movement—the workshops, the trade-union branches, the local Labour parties—two questions were constantly being asked: Is there a difference between the foreign policy of the Labour government and of former governments? and is the policy sufficiently "socialist"?[31]

The government's reaction to the attack upon its foreign policy was to deny the charge of betraying its electoral pronouncements in the field of foreign affairs. The Foreign Secretary could not conceive of any circumstances in which Britain and the Soviet Union could go to war, and he regarded the United States with this same spirit. The great task of Britain was to weld those forces together to keep the peace. As to the charge of setting up a Western bloc, the government believed in the closest co-operation with all the Western countries, not an exclusive friendship but an all-inclusive friendship. The government had not pressed unduly for an alliance with the Western powers

[29] Cf. *Official Records of the General Assembly, First Session*, Fifty-ninth Plenary Meeting, December 12, 1946, p. 1198.

[30] *Ibid., Second Session*, One Hundred and Eighteenth Plenary Meeting, November 17, 1947, pp. 1096–97.

[31] J. W. Kagan, South Hendon D.L.P., *Report of the Forty-fifth Annual Conference of the Labour Party*, 1946, p. 151.

because it had been actuated all the time by the wish not to divide Europe. As the Foreign Secretary explained,

I am not going to be a party, as long as I hold this office, to any design, any strategy, any alignment of forces, any arrangements of defence to attack Russia.[32]

Mr. Bevin's assurances, however, did not dispel the doubts and misgivings of those Labour "rebels" who expressed their disappointment with the government's alleged departure from the central thesis upon which the Labour party had fought the General Election by censuring the government in Parliament in the form of an amendment to the Address from the Throne. The main concern of these critics was that during the election the party had affirmed that if a Tory government were elected it would drift into close association with the United States, thereby rendering inevitable a division of the world into two ideological blocs. On the other hand, only a Labour government could stop the drift into two world blocs; only a Labour government could mediate fairly between Russia and the United States; only a Labour government could seek genuine friendship with Russia as well as the United States. Accusing the government of "drifting away from that central piece of policy," R. H. S. Crossman, spokesman for the Labour "rebels," moved an amendment expressing the urgent hope that the Labour government would

so review and recast its conduct of International Affairs as to afford the utmost encouragement to, and collaboration with, all Nations and Groups striving to secure full Socialist planning and control of the world's resources and thus provide a democratic and constructible Socialist alternative to an otherwise inevitable conflict between American capitalism and Soviet Communism in which all hope of World Government would be destroyed.[33]

Before the vote on the amendment was taken, the Prime Minister rose to the government's defense by stating emphatically that the government did not believe in the forming of groups—east, west, or center. It believed, rather, in the United Nations and worked for international organization in the interests of peace and prosperity for the whole of the peoples of the world. To achieve that goal, Mr. Attlee explained, it was necessary to deal with the underlying causes of war by positive, constructive world planning. By co-operating in social and economic organizations and by encouraging the socialist move-

[32] *Ibid.*, p. 168.
[33] 430 *H.C.Deb.*, November 18, 1946, col. 526. Among those signing the amendment were Crossman, Silverman, Reeves, Stokes, Hewitson, Perkins, and Lee.

ments in Austria, in Germany, and in Italy, the government was, in fact, carrying out socialist policy. Following the Prime Minister's defense of the government's foreign policy, an unsuccessful attempt was made by the Labour "rebels" to withdraw the amendment. However, when the vote was taken, the "rebels" abstained, and the government's policy was endorsed by 353 to 0, the Tories voting with the government.[34]

Criticism of the government's foreign policy was not, however, entirely of a destructive nature. The alternative presented was that British policy in international affairs ought to be such as to strengthen the forces of liberal socialism all over the world, particularly in the countries that shared a common tradition of West European culture. Britain, confronted with two great powers, neither of whom could be contended with in terms of power, must become the spokesman of the militarily weaker nations with whom British contacts were closest for reasons of culture or history, and must build up positive forms of intimate collaboration in both political and economic affairs. As a world state was, for the immediate present, out of the question, the only practical equivalent to the two great-power units of the United States and Russia was a West European group within the framework of the United Nations. Such a Western group, based upon the principles of democratic socialism could not possibly be aggressive, or act as a satellite of the United States or the Soviet Union. Socialist policy had affirmed and reaffirmed these ideals for nearly half a century; they were the climate of socialist opinion. Now, when for the first time there were socialist governments all over Europe, British Labour must work for their closest association.[35]

The realization of such a plan was, at the outset, countered by the creation, under the leadership of Mr. Churchill, of an all-party committee to further the cause of a united Europe, which included six Labourites, five Conservatives, and five Liberals. The aim of the United Europe Committee was to unite all the peoples of Europe "to secure their mutual peace and common prosperity, and to preserve and enrich their heritage of civilisation and freedom." This United Europe would have the status of a regional group under the United Nations and would "naturally seek the close friendship and co-operation of the Soviet Union and the United States of America."[36] The appeal of the United Europe Committee, according to the Labour

---

[34] 430 H.C.Deb., November 18, 1946, col. 580. Cf. Michael Foot, "Rebellion with a Difference," Tribune, 517 (November 22, 1946), 2.

[35] Cf. G. D. H. Cole, Labour's Foreign Policy (London: New Statesman and Nation, 1946), pp. 8–9, 16.

[36] Daily Herald, January 17, 1949, p. 2.

party, was sectional and exclusive and would arouse suspicion and opposition in Russia, tending to create deeper divisions between Britain and the Soviet Union. Consequently, the Executive of the party advised members not to support the committee launched by Mr. Churchill; and those alleged to have "collaborationist tendencies" received from Party Secretary Morgan Phillips a letter with the following statement:

The Labour Party is firmly committed to the belief that the future of Europe depends on the success of the United Nations and on the strengthening of friendly collaboration between Russia, America and Britain. Mr. Churchill's Committee explicitly excludes Russia from Europe, and, in view of his personal record and his known opinions, it is likely to be interpreted, rightly or wrongly, as aiming essentially at the elimination of Russian influence in Europe.[37]

In spite of the government's assurances, it was clearly evident—in Parliament, in the Labour press, and at the Labour and Trade Union Conferences—that a minority of Labour's own supporters were sincerely disturbed about the government's activities abroad. Many loyal members of the party were genuinely concerned about the general line of Labour's foreign policy, considering it to be a continuation of Tory foreign policy and an exclusive line-up with capitalist America against Soviet Russia.[38] The government's reply to these consistent attacks upon its international policy appeared in the form of a statement—*Cards on the Table*—which was presented to the party conference at Margate in May of 1947. With regard to the charge of continuity, the government pointed out that the policy of the Conservatives was to seek a permanent and exclusive Anglo-American alliance expressly directed against the Soviet Union, while the policy of Labour was to accept common action with the United States only where there was a common interest, rather than be drawn into commitments excluding the possibility of similar collaboration with Russia. The Labour government had put the attainment of a united, independent Europe in the forefront of its aims and had fought steadily to prevent the crystallization of the wartime divisions of Europe into spheres of influence. While Labour would continue to strengthen its ties in Western Europe, its interests were too widespread, its principles too international, for it to restrict itself to the idea of regional blocs, however construed. On the whole, the Executive's statement of policy was favorably received by the party confer-

[37] *Ibid.*, May 27, 1947, p. 1.
[38] Cf. *Keep Left*, by fifteen Labour M.P.'s (London: *New Statesman and Nation*, 1947).

ence. Even those who charged that *Cards on the Table* was a departure from the foreign policy set out in *The International Post-War Settlement* agreed that the Labour party's answer to the United States of Europe propaganda of Mr. Churchill was a United States of Europe policy of its own, providing for close co-operation with Russia and taking the form of a regional agreement within the United Nations.[39]

In spite of the fact that the party was virtually in accord with the idea of European unity, the government did not press Western Union in the hope that the conclusion of the peace-settlements agreement between the four powers would close the breach between East and West, thus avoiding the necessity of crystallizing Europe into two separate blocs. However, the government found that it could not agree to four-power co-operation when one of those four powers proceeded to impose its political and economic system on the small states. Although it had always accepted the view that the friendliest relations should exist between Russia and her neighbors, the government felt that this should not involve cutting off Eastern Europe from the rest of the world and turning it into an exclusively self-contained bloc under the control of Moscow and the Communist party. These developments, in the opinion of the Foreign Secretary, pointed to the conclusion that the free nations of Western Europe must draw closely together to organize the "kindred souls of the West" just as the Russians had organized their "kindred souls." The time was ripe for a consolidation of Western Europe designed upon a regional basis to fit in with the Charter of the United Nations. Since the Labour government had consistently striven for the closer consolidation, economic development, and spiritual unity of Europe as a whole, the continuation of the present division of Europe would be "by the act and will of the Soviet Government."[40]

The fact that the Foreign Secretary's plea for Western Union was welcomed by both sides of Parliament caused some Labourites to wonder just how Mr. Bevin's plan for a united Europe differed from Mr. Churchill's project, heretofore officially boycotted by the Executive Committee of the Labour party. The two main questions directed to the government from the back benches of the Labour party were whether European unity was to be based upon essentially socialist principles and whether the Union was to be an exclusive bloc directed against the Soviet Union. Regarding the former, the Prime Minister explained that the government naturally desired to see all countries

[39] Cf. *Report of the Forty-sixth Annual Conference of the Labour Party*, 1947, p. 161.

[40] 446 *H.C.Deb.*, January 22, 1948, cols. 383–408.

embracing the principles of democratic socialism as "a dynamic counter to Russian Communism"; but it was not a part of Labour's policy to force socialism upon other nations.[41] As to the charge of exclusiveness or aggressiveness, the Foreign Secretary insisted that there was nothing aggressive whatever in these regional agreements. Removing the fear of attack on the part of some small powers might eventually diminish the threatened division of the world into two hostile blocs. The government, however, could not wait to overcome opposition; it had to proceed to develop and unite with those with whom it could unite, hoping that in the end others would join them.

The government's project for Western Union had the general effect of unifying the dissident elements in the Labour party. Subsequently, a number of prominent Labourites who had once opposed the creation of regional blocs endorsed the organization of a Western European Union to counter communist expansion. One of these Labourites, Sir Hartley Shawcross, admitting that he had once been "violently pro-Russian," called for a union of the democratic powers to avoid "falling into the pit which the totalitarians are preparing for democracy."[42] Other converts, such as R. H. S. Crossman and R. W. G. Mackay, who had once urged the government "to prevent the division of the world into hostile blocs" and "to repudiate President Truman's proposal for collective security against communism,"[43] now supported a parliamentary motion emphasizing the necessity for creating in Western Europe "a political union strong enough to save European democracy and the values of Western civilisation."[44] In addition, overwhelming approval of the government's declaration that "a policy of democratic socialism, combining human freedom and economic planning, is British Labour's alternative to both Communist dictatorship and American capitalism" was granted by the party conference. The conference accepted a resolution moved by Fenner Brockway, former secretary of the pacifist Independent Labour party, urging the government "to co-operate with the European Socialist Parties in taking practical steps to achieve the United Socialist States of Europe." Party unity was virtually complete when the conference, by a card vote of 4,097,000 to 224,000, rejected a foreign-policy manifesto from the remains of the "rebel" clique in the Labour movement.[45]

[41] *Ibid.*, col. 619.

[42] Address at Stourbridge, March 12, 1948, *The Times*, March 13, 1948, p. 4.

[43] Cf. *Keep Left* (London: *New Statesman and Nation*, 1947), p. 46.

[44] 448 *H.C.Deb.*, March 18, 1948, cols. 2302–3.

[45] *Report of the Forty-seventh Annual Conference of the Labour Party*, 1948, pp. 172, 184–85.

Thus assured of party support, the Labour government proceeded to implement the concept of Western Union. However, six months were to elapse before the government acted to widen the scope and membership of the Brussels Pact—providing for mutual defense and economic collaboration—concluded by the five Western European powers in March of 1948. During this interval the government participated in the sixteen-nation European Economic Conference in Paris which moved closer toward the unity of Western Europe by adopting a convention for the collective handling of the European Recovery Program, establishing an Organization for European Economic Co-operation, and integrating the economic phases of the Paris Convention with the defense provisions of the Brussels Accord. Following the Paris meeting, machinery was set in motion by the Brussels powers to implement the provisions of the Pact by the creation of a Permanent Organ of the Consultative Council of the Western Union —composed of representatives of the foreign ministers—and a Permanent Military Committee—responsible to the defense ministers of the respective governments. This, however, was as far as the government intended to go without first consulting the Commonwealth and receiving assurances of support from the United States. Consequently, the government refused to recognize the deliberations of the unofficial Congress of Europe, rejecting as premature the projected Western European Assembly advocated by Mr. Churchill before The Hague Congress.

Progressing cautiously, the Labour government continued to work for "an increasing degree of union between all the countries of Western Europe" in the hope that Western Europe would ultimately constitute "an area of peace and prosperity and ordered progress" in association with the peoples of the Commonwealth overseas and with the United States of America. Accordingly, the foreign ministers of the Brussels powers, meeting in Paris at the end of October, decided to propose to the United States negotiations for a North Atlantic Security Pact embracing North America and Western Europe. In addition, they decided to set up a Committee for the Study of European Unity to examine the Franco-Belgian suggestion for the convening of a European assembly and the British suggestion for the establishment of a European council appointed by and responsible to the governments for the purpose of dealing with matters of common concern. After considering the preparatory work of the Unity Committee, the foreign ministers agreed that there should be established a Council of Europe consisting of a ministerial committee meeting in private and a consultative body meeting in public, and they decided to invite other European countries to take part in the negotiations for the creation of the Council of Europe. As a result, Italy, Eire, and the Scandinavian powers joined the Brussels powers to draft a statute establishing a Council of Europe "to achieve a greater unity between its members for the purpose of safeguarding and realising the ideals and principles which are their common heritage, and facilitating their economic and social progress."[46] Thus, Western Union and the Organization for European Economic Co-operation had been expanded into the Council of Europe which would in turn be integrated into the United Nations as a regional arrangement. As to the defensive aspect, Western Union would merge into the projected North Atlantic Security Pact.

The Labour government's participation in the North Atlantic Pact was given a resounding endorsement in Parliament by a vote of 333 to 6. The only opposition came from the Communists and the left-wing Independents who had been expelled from the Labour party. The Foreign Secretary asserted that the Pact had been made necessary by the failure of the United Nations Security Council to guarantee peace. As such a situation, allowed to continue, would inevitably lead to war, the Western nations were driven together in sheer self-defense. The Pact was not, however, contradictory to the United Nations or to the Anglo-Soviet Alliance. It was hoped that the Security Council might yet be made an effective instrument for the maintenance of peace. The members of the North Atlantic Pact could no longer be treated as weak nations, Mr. Bevin declared, and the recognition of that fact might well lead to a final settlement with the Soviet Union. With an unmistakable mandate from his party to renew the struggle for an agreement with Soviet Russia, Mr. Bevin told the party conference that if the Western powers and the Soviet Union were unable to agree "how we shall live," at least they might agree "to live together."[47]

After five years of Labour rule, the party claimed that under its leadership Britain had "regained her moral position in the Western world" and "won the confidence of many millions in Africa and Asia." By applying the moral principles of socialism to its relations with other peoples, the Labour government had made Britain a "symbol of justice and social advance." Labour would continue, if retained in power, to work realistically for peace. While recognizing that it was not possible to lay down the details of a policy to be pursued for five years

[46] Text of Statute, *The Times*, May 6, 1949, p. 5.

[47] *Report of the Forty-eighth Annual Conference of the Labour Party*, 1949, p. 189.

ahead, the Labour party stated its aims and principles in world affairs and produced the achievements of its first postwar government "as proof that its ideals are both sincere and realistic." In world affairs Labour had pursued, and would continue to pursue, three supreme objectives: The first, and incomparably the greatest, was peace and the establishment of the United Nations as a body capable of fulfilling the high purposes for which it was created. Lasting world peace could be secured only by the rule of law among the nations. The Labour movement had always been dedicated to that ideal and the Labour government had sought by every means in its power to strengthen the United Nations as an effective instrument for the achievement of that purpose. It was not the fault of the Labour government that the United Nations had thus far failed to command the authority which the cause of peace required. But in the next five years, despite all setbacks, Labour would "seek to enhance that authority, strenuously, patiently and tirelessly." While a Labour Britain would stand firm against any attempt to intimidate her or to undermine her position in the world, she would remain ready at any moment to co-operate fully with Soviet Russia as with any country prepared to work with her for peace and friendship. Believing that the purposes of the United Nations were best served by still closer associations between friendly countries within the Charter, Labour had put particular energy into strengthening the associations of the British Commonwealth of Nations, the Atlantic community, and Western Europe.

Labour's second aim was that Britain should stand upon her own feet, dependent upon extraordinary economic aid from no other country, but playing her full part in leading other nations who would join with her "in building rising standards of life and bolder and freer opportunities of social development." Britain's achievement of economic independence, like her common interest in building defensive security with those nations which would join in such a system, depended in large part on the movement for closer co-operation between the nations of Europe in a so-called Western European Union. This "great project" was the culmination of a policy which Britain had pursued since the first days of peace, through the European Recovery Program, the Treaty of Dunkirk, the Brussels Pact, and the Council of Europe. Without a steady march toward closer European unity, none of the states in Western Europe could hope to make its economy strong and prosperous. No country had given more leadership in this great movement than Labour Britain. She had given material support, persistent leadership in the delicate work of negotiation, and the assurance of strength which derived from the "spectacular development of her own resources at home." She had, moreover, helped forward this work without jeopardizing other relationships which were indispensable to the creation of a true Western Union. The realization that an important part of Great Britain's value to Western Union depended upon Commonwealth support made the British government "careful to accept no over-hasty formula for a United Europe. Without that care the foundations of a Western Union closely linked with the Commonwealth could never have been laid." Britain would continue her support and leadership in the years to come, always remembering that she was "the heart of a great Commonwealth extending far beyond the boundaries of Europe."

Neither peace nor British independence could be secured in a world tormented by fears of slump, unemployment, near-starvation, and poverty. The war against these evils was the final aim of Labour's foreign policy. It was this consideration which had provided one of the chief motives behind Britain's activities in Europe and which made her welcome President Truman's declaration of aid to the underdeveloped areas of the world. Despite all her own difficulties, Britain had proved in the past five years the practicality of her recognition that world recovery, like peace, was indivisible. Next to the United States, she had made by far the greatest contribution to European recovery, through UNRRA, in gifts and credits, and later through the European Recovery Program. Britain was planning new forms of aid in the development of the Middle Eastern area, "that the desert may bloom again and the age-old scourge of poverty and disease be lifted." In Southeast Asia, Britain aimed to help in re-establishing stability and raising standards of life; it was Britain's statesmanship which produced the Special Committee to tackle the acute spread of famine and which supported the United Nations effort to bring peace to Indonesia. All over the world, great sacrifices had been made to help the people of less fortunate lands. Labour Britain was proud of the part which she had played, "while she was fighting for her very economic existence, to hold back famine, disease and collapse over so wide an area of this stricken planet." The British people, under a Labour government, would continue "to do their duty as good citizens of the world."

The common base from which Labour would launch its campaign in pursuit of these objectives was a successful policy of recovery at home. "Perhaps the greatest of all the manifold contributions of Labour Britain to the cause of peace and world recovery" was "the example of economic and political rebirth in these islands." During these five years, the British people had used their hard-won political rights to gain economic rights; they had shown that a parliamentary system could move swiftly to change the power relationships in society; they had given real content and fresh meaning to the ideals of social democracy; they had "made this dramatic social advance while retaining and enhancing all the cherished practices of free speech, free association and the protection of the claims of the heretic." Foreign affairs and domestic affairs could not be separated. It was Labour's home policy, and the deeds with which it had fulfilled its words, which had enabled Britain to command a leading role in world affairs.[48]

[48] Cf. *Labour Believes in Britain* (London: Labour Party, 1949), pp. 24–27; *Let Us Win Through Together* (London: Labour Party, 1950), p. 11; *Labour and the New Society* (London: Labour Party, 1950), pp. 6–10. The latter was not issued until August 1950, for presentation to the party conference of October 1950.

13

A SOCIALIST FOREIGN POLICY: THE
SECOND TERM

In the 1950 General Election the Labour party's international program was endorsed by over thirteen and a quarter million votes, the highest vote ever polled by any single party in the history of British politics.[1] In terms of representation, however, the party suffered severe losses, with its parliamentary membership reduced to 315 and its parliamentary majority over the combined Conservative and Liberal Opposition reduced to eight. The effect of this parliamentary alignment was that the Labour government was utterly dependent upon solidarity within its own ranks. The slightest deviation, even if expressed as silent opposition or abstention, could bring about the defeat of a government whose continued existence would be determined by its retention of the approval of practically all of its parliamentary supporters. In the field of foreign policy, Labour could no longer afford the luxury of rebels within its ranks. As party division was tantamount to government defeat, the rank and file of the movement would, of necessity, have to accede to the will of the party majority. In spite of this precariously balanced parliamentary alignment, the Labour party succeeded in retaining the reins of government for over eighteen months—a period terminated only by the decision of the Prime Minister to appeal to the nation, at a time deemed favorable to electoral success, for a renewed lease of power.

In its first foreign-policy pronouncement after the General Election, the Labour government renewed its electoral pledges "to give full support to the United Nations," to do its "utmost to ensure the success of the Council of Europe," to maintain "whole-hearted support of the Organization for European Economic Co-operation" and "the closest relations with the other Powers signatory to the North Atlantic and Brussels Treaties," to play its "due part, in collaboration with the other Powers, in strengthening common means of defence," to take all necessary steps to ensure that its armed forces were "ready to meet their responsibilities in all parts of the world," and "to co-operate with other Commonwealth Governments in matters of common interest in South and South-East Asia."[2] In the course of applying these princi-

[1] The Labour party received 13,266,592 popular votes.
[2] King's Speech, 472 *H.C.Deb.*, March 6, 1950, cols. 37–38.

ples, the Labour government was confronted with a series of international crises, beginning in Europe, with the issues of European unity, German rearmament, East-West rivalry, and culminating in the Far East with the Korean conflict and in the Middle East with the Egyptian and Persian disputes. Each of these international episodes, occurring during Labour's second term of office, constituted a "test case" for the application of the Labour party's foreign policy. As the future Foreign Secretary, Herbert Morrison, explained, during the General Election:

. . . they test something more than our good sense and level-headedness. They test our understanding of the causes of our trouble. In the old-fashioned history books, wars and revolution seemed to happen suddenly between one page and the next. But they didn't really come without causes, and they don't today. The difficulties and dangers of the twentieth century are not acts of fate, like a thunderstorm or an earthquake; they are the results of what your grandfathers and other people's grandfathers did in the past. If you forget that, you go badly wrong. For we can't cure the ills of the world if we don't understand them.[3]

The first test of the Labour party's policy of "still closer associations between friendly countries within the Charter" came with the proposal from the French Foreign Minister, M. Schuman, for the pooling of the French, German, and other European coal and steel production. Prior to the French initiative, it had been the declared policy of the Labour government to promote the entry of Germany as a free member into the comity of nations. Since the French proposals were designed to facilitate that process, they were regarded by the British as "a notable contribution towards the solution of a major European problem."[4] The Labour government welcomed the French suggestion, "fully alive to its bold character and far-reaching importance for future relations between France and Germany" and earnestly hoping that the international discussions upon it might lead to "a new era in Franco-German relations, with beneficial effects for Western Europe as a whole." However, it soon became perfectly clear, in the course of informal discussions between M. Monnet, the chief planning officer of the French government, and British officials that while the French had not worked out how their proposals would be applied in practice, their views on the procedure for negotiations were definite. They thought that the governments should accept at the outset the principles of the pooling of resources and of a high authority whose decisions would be binding on governments, and that the next step

[3] Electoral broadcast, October 17, 1951, *The Times*, October 18, 1951, p. 2.
[4] Prime Minister Attlee, 475 *H.C.Deb.*, May 11, 1950, col. 589.

should be the conclusion of a treaty in which these principles would be embodied. Shortly thereafter, the French government secured the agreement of the German government to the proposed basis on which the negotiations should proceed. This fact naturally determined the course of the subsequent exchanges of view between the two governments and made difficult the achievement of the British government's desire to play an active part in the discussion of the French proposal without commitments to the acceptance of its principles in advance. The British government did not feel able to accept in advance, nor did it wish to reject in advance, the principles underlying the French proposal. It considered that a detailed discussion, which would throw light upon the nature of the scheme and its full political and economic consequences, was a normal, and indeed essential, preliminary to the conclusion of a treaty. It felt that there was a substantial difference of approach between the two governments as to the basis on which the negotiations should be opened and that an unhappy situation would arise if, having bound itself to certain principles without knowing how they would work out in practice, it was to find itself, as a result of the discussions, compelled to withdraw from its undertakings. The British government found it impossible, therefore, in view of its responsibilities to Parliament and people, to associate itself with the negotiations on the terms proposed by the French government.[5]

The Labour party's publication of the statement *European Unity*, simultaneous with the government's reply to the Schuman proposals, brought forth a storm of protest from the Opposition parties. The chief criticism of the party statement was that it was doctrinaire, sectarian, and isolationist. The passages particularly subjected to attack were those which claimed that the Labour party's attitude toward problems of European unity was "determined by the principles of democratic Socialism"; that it "could never accept any commitments which limited its own or others' freedom to pursue democratic socialism and to apply the economic controls necessary to achieve it"; that its socialist principles demanded "that the movement towards European unity should be such as to permit the continuation of full employment and social justice in Britain and the extension of those benefits over the rest of Western Europe"; and that "no Socialist Party with the prospect of forming a Government could accept a system by which important fields of national policy were surrendered to a supra-national European representative authority, since such an authority would have a permanent anti-Socialist majority and would

[5] Government communiqué of June 3, 1950, *British State Papers*, Cmd. 7970 (1950).

arouse the hostility of European workers."[6] The Opposition's criticism of the Labour party's attitude toward European unity did not, however, extend to a condemnation of the government's assertion that Britain could not "hand over essential details of national policy to be decided by an external authority or by the vote of a majority in some European council or assembly." There was general agreement with the view that co-operation between governments, without compulsion, was the only way and that a complete economic union of Europe was "impracticable because of the disturbances and tensions which the attempt would at once produce." The passages in *European Unity* which set out, on practical not political grounds, why Britain must always hold its connections with Europe in balance with its connections with the Commonwealth and the United States reflected "both British opinion and the facts of British life in the world."[7] Consequently, the censure of the Opposition was limited to a motion requesting the government, "in the interests of peace and full employment, to accept the invitation to take part in the discussions on the Schuman Plan, subject to the same condition as that made by the Netherlands Government, namely, that if the discussions show the plan not to be practicable, freedom of action is reserved."[8]

The Labour government refused any compromise or withdrawal in face of the Opposition challenge to its foreign policy. Instead, it decided to defend its rejection of the invitation to participate in the preliminary talks on the Schuman plan for pooling European heavy industry under conditions proposed by the French, and to make it an issue of confidence. Sir Stafford Cripps accordingly moved an amendment to the Opposition motion of censure stating that Parliament

welcomes the initiative of the French Foreign Minister on 9th May and, while recognising that it was not possible for His Majesty's Government to take part in the international consideration of his proposals on terms which committed them in advance of such consideration to pool the production of coal and steel and to institute a new high authority whose decisions would bind the Governments concerned, approves the declared readiness of His Majesty's Government to take a constructive part in the conversations with the hope that they may be able to join in or associate themselves with this common effort.[9]

It was obvious, from the attitude of the rank and file of the party, the trade-unions and the Labour press, that on this issue the movement was virtually in accord. As evidence of this solidarity of view, a fur-

---

[6] *European Unity* (London: Labour Party, 1950), pp. 3–8.
[7] Editorial, *The Times*, June 13, 1950, p. 5; June 16, 1950, p. 7.
[8] 476 *H.C.Deb.*, June 26, 1950, col. 1907.   [9] *Ibid.*, col. 1933.

ther amendment was tabled by a group of Labour members of Parliament, which recognized the significance of the endeavor to unify Europe's coal and steel industries but fully supported the government in its refusal to enter undefined commitments and stressed "the importance of relating its responsibilities in the Commonwealth and Sterling Area to any further proposals or discussions."[10] The back-bench government supporters and the divisional Labour parties were clearly not prepared to accept the federal solution implied in the French proposals. The reasons for this rejection were repeatedly made clear: A Britain which became part of a federal Europe would no longer be able to deal with the sovereign dominions on equal terms; nor would the colonies of the British Empire, which were moving toward self-government, be willing to submit to a European authority. In addition, the Labour party was not prepared to place its planning powers at the mercy of a European parliament. No one had yet explained how a federal authority for Europe could be made truly democratic. But the rejection of this idea did not mean that Labour was opposed to planning Europe's basic industries. That could be done by governments which retained their responsibility to their own parliaments and their own people. No planning body for Europe's basic industries could work unless the individual governments had direction over their own basic industries. For its own part, Labour believed in the Commonwealth; it believed in full employment; it believed in democratic responsibility.[11]

As for the trade-unions' attitude, Sir William Lawther of the Mineworkers' Federation declared that, "we Britons are living in a free, democratic country and we do not want to be ordered about by an authority not responsible to anyone." Lawther presumed that trade-unions would be summoned to help the delegates drawing up a scheme only when their advice was needed; that was clearly not enough. It was essential that British Labour should know what part the workers would be called upon to play. How would the proposal work out in practice? he asked. How would the new authority be constituted and what precisely would be its powers? Was there to be a fixed annual target for coal and steel production? Was the British standard of wages and hours to be adopted and that of other countries accordingly increased or decreased?[12] Lincoln Evans of the Iron and Steel Trades

10 *Daily Herald*, June 23, 1950, p. 1. The amendment was signed by Richard Adams, Jack Jones, Arthur Allen, J. P. W. Mallalieu, Tom Reid, and Walter Padley, and supported by twenty-five others.

11 Cf. Michael Foot, "Tories on the Spot," *Daily Herald*, June 23, 1950, p. 4; editorial, *ibid.*, June 13, 1950, p. 2; June 14, 1950, p. 2; "Britain's Place in Europe," *New Statesman and Nation*, XL (July 8, 1950), 33.

12 *Daily Herald*, June 22, 1950, p. 2.

Confederation agreed with the suggestion that there should be an equalization of conditions of the workers in coal and steel in Western Europe but admitted that the way in which this was going to be achieved under the Schuman plan was "somewhat vague." Nor was it clear to him how this scheme could be confined in any country to the particular industries concerned. The standard of living involved more than trade-union organization and activities; it was also dependent upon the social and investment policies of the government. Given Britain's present precarious balance-of-payments position, any scheme to control and pool exports was "bound to be subject to the closest scrutiny." Until clearer assurances were given to such questions British Labour could do no other than refuse to commit itself in advance, for a most unhappy situation would arise if it gave a pledge now and had to withdraw it later. While it was possible, and even essential, that some agreement should be made to harmonize the development plans of the coal and steel industries and the extent to which capacity should be expanded to meet European home and export requirements, there was a better chance of this being done in a limited field, thereby creating the "climate of confidence" necessary for the more ambitious aims of the French plan to become realities.[13]

In the government's opinion, the real issue in the "great debate" on the Schuman plan was not whether Britain was in favor of cooperating with Europe and working out their economic problems, but whether Britain ought to have accepted certain principles which were to be embodied in a treaty prior to going into the discussion. Replying to the Opposition's demand that Britain should have adopted the same attitude as that of the Netherlands government, the Chancellor of the Exchequer maintained that the two cases were not comparable. The reservation attached by the Netherlands government to its acceptance of the Schuman plan was a reservation upon the feasibility of translating the accepted principles into practice. It did not entitle the Netherlands government to do what the British government insisted it must be able to do, namely, to discuss whether in principle a new, high, supranational authority could be made acceptable to Parliament and the people. Could the British have persuaded the French to admit them to the negotiations and to allow them to discuss the very questions of principle which they could not accept without discussion and which the French thought it vital not to discuss? It was by no means certain, Cripps said, that the French would have been content with a similar reservation from Great Britain. It was one thing to contemplate the possibility of the withdrawal of a government, such as the Nether-

[13] Lincoln Evans, *Man and Metal*, XXVII (June 1950), 81.

lands, responsible for only one-fortieth of the coal production and one one-hundred-fiftieth of the steel production and quite another to risk the withdrawal, on this basis, of a country such as Britain, with one-half of the coal and one-third of the steel production. The government felt that it would have been most undesirable to try to evade the declaration of unity of objective which the French desired by some sort of acceptance with a reservation when, whatever it might have said, it meant that it could not accept the principle of the supranational authority without very full discussions as to its implications. Cripps was convinced that the "sensible and candid agreement" with the French government that Britain should not participate for the time being was at least a better solution and less liable to damage future relations than if the government had put itself into a position in which it might well have been accused, at a later date, of either going back on its promises or of wrecking the negotiations by its refusal to agree to the principle upon which they had been launched.

The Labour government felt that the Opposition was not fully aware of the complexity of the matter which must come under review before a decision could be arrived at in this vitally important field. Britain could not enter lightheartedly upon any scheme or plan which might affect profoundly the two basic sections of its industrial and economic life. There were many aspects of the problem which arose directly or indirectly out of these proposals that any responsible British government must examine and decide upon before agreeing to the principles underlying the Schuman plan. First, there was the question of access to raw materials, many of which were now imported from other European countries. What effect would supranational control have upon that? Then there was the question of access to markets as affected by tariffs, quantitative restrictions, subsidies, and the effect upon export trade to the Commonwealth and Empire where Britain enjoyed preferences in exchange for those given. The whole price structure of the two industries was vital to the standard of living of the workers and to the other industries which depended on them for their fuel and raw material. Another important matter was that of capital expenditure and its bearing upon the efficiency of the industry. Britain was today, for instance, shutting down uneconomic pits and opening others. Was the question to be left to the direction or recommendation of this supranational authority which could cause a whole coal field or steel center to go out of production without any social or political responsibility for its action? These two sections of British industry were so extensive that whatever happened or was done with regard to them would have an effect upon the whole of British industrial life.

If, for example, Britain's share of the extra-European markets for coal and steel was to be seriously reduced through the action of the supranational authority, how could Britain continue to get her essential imports? What concerned the Labour government was whether the members of the Opposition were telling the country that they were satisfied that Britain could safely and honestly have accepted the principles underlying the French memorandum. To accept them would have bound Britain to remove from the control of Parliament not only all matters concerning the production of coal and steel but in fact a great range of other matters that would inevitably be affected by decisions in these large sections of British industry. The government believed, therefore, that it had adopted the only honest and sensible course that was open to it.

As to the criticism that the government was less concerned with matters of European co-operation than was the Opposition, the Prime Minister was careful to point out that it had never been the position of the Labour government, or indeed of the Labour party, that it should deal solely with socialist governments. The Labour party held certain very definite economic beliefs; and it had expressed the view that no full and final integration of European economy could take place except on the basis of common economic policies and that such policies should be those of a planned social democracy. This it had stated in its pamphlet *European Unity*; and it was no more surprising to find such a statement than it would be to find the Conservative party stating that such an integration should be on the basis of the sort of unplanned economy in which it believed. But that had no relation whatever to present government policy which dealt with the factual situation that there was not an identity of view in economic matters between the principal governments of Europe. Consequently, the Labour government approached its problems on the basis of this known fact and attempted to get agreement on practical action, leaving aside unnecessary theoretical discussion. Thus the history of the advance in European unity since the war was largely the history of a series of practical steps—the Organization for European Economic Co-operation, the European Payments Union, the Brussels and North Atlantic Treaty Organizations—which had gradually extended the mutual trust and confidence in political and economic co-operation so that it might one day grow into something even closer. This record of five years' work toward European solidarity in all fields proved beyond any shadow of doubt that the Labour government had taken a leading part in all of the work. Throughout this period of intense intra-European activity, it had been able to carry the Commonwealth with it and had not in any way sacrificed the interests of the Commonwealth to those of Europe. However, in the government's opinion, participation in a political federation, limited to Western Europe, was not compatible either with its Commonwealth ties or its obligations as a member of the wider Atlantic community or as a world power; and it challenged the Opposition to deny this fact.[14]

Although the national debate on the Schuman plan evoked bitter partisan rivalries, there was virtual agreement between the government and the Opposition on the two main conclusions reached. Both sides accepted the proposition that Britain could not contemplate, by reason of her world position and the views of her people, the kind of economic union which implied political union. In spite of his unique position as leader of the European Unity movement, with its majority of Continental federalists, Mr. Churchill did not support British participation in a federation of Europe. To the challenge of whether he would himself assent to a supranational authority with power over British coal and steel, he said, "Without hesitation the answer is No." In addition, both sides regarded the French objective of the elimination of the agelong feud between France and Germany as a further, and a desirable, step in the strengthening of European peace. The government was, therefore, prepared to do its utmost either to join in or to associate itself with any scheme that met with the approval of the six countries meeting in Paris. It would, however, await the results of that meeting before taking any initiative, for it did not wish, any more than did the French, that by any suggestions it might make the chance of agreement among those powers on the basis of the principles laid down in the Schuman plan should be diminished. Even *The Times* was willing to concede that the government had every right to defend itself stoutly against the double charge that the federal form of the Schuman proposals was only an act of French defense against British intransigence and that better British diplomacy could readily have turned aside the French and their Continental friends from their federal goal.[15]

The Labour party's attitude toward the Schuman plan was not, however, entirely a negative one. Although the government had stated its reluctance to propose an alternative scheme while the French negotiations were in progress, the trade-unions and the party had been devoting considerable attention to the problem of integrating the coal and steel industries of Western Europe. As early as March of 1950,

[14] Sir Stafford Cripps, 476 *H.C.Deb.*, June 26, 1950, cols. 1933–48; Prime Minister Attlee, *ibid.*, June 27, 1950, cols. 2163–72. The Conservative motion was defeated, 309–289, the amendment carried, 309–296.

[15] Editorial, June 28, 1950, p. 7.

British Labour had participated in a Conference of Socialist Experts on International Control of Basic Industries held in Witten in the Ruhr. The discussions of this study group, convened by the International Socialist Conference, on the structure, control, and organization of Europe's basic industries actually foreshadowed the proposals later introduced by the French Foreign Minister. The report adopted by the socialist experts considered that the remote ideal was complete international ownership and control and that the next best solution—also remote—was international control of nationalized industries. The immediate solution proposed by the conference was international control of nationalized and privately owned industries through modified committees of the Organization for European Economic Co-operation, which would also send full reports to the Council of Europe for debate. This plan, the experts felt, might serve as an immediate possibility until the time when "all countries in Western Europe accept at least the principles of full employment planning, the planned economy and national control of basic industries."[16]

The British trade-unions, participating in the Conference of Trade Unions of E.R.P. countries, held in Rome in April of 1950, were also unanimous in recognizing the importance of European unity; they felt problems such as the co-ordination of investment, liberalization of trade, establishment of a payments union, and mobility of manpower would only find a full and satisfactory solution within a united Europe. The democratic trade-unions were convinced that "the importance of unity was so vital that risks must be taken"; but they warned that unless certain policies, particularly the full employment of available resources and a more equitable distribution of national incomes, were followed from the beginning, unity would not be built upon firm foundations and would in the long run be undermined by political and social instability. While the difficulties to be overcome were very great in view of the diversity of economic interests, governmental systems, and political philosophies in Western Europe, all sincere democratic forces were at one on the need for the energetic pursuit of solutions for these difficulties; for it was certain that without unity the economic revival of Europe could not in the long run be fully accomplished.[17]

Shortly after the Schuman plan had been announced, British trade-unions conferred with the International Confederation of Free Trade Unions at Dusseldorf to consider plans for the reorganization of European heavy industry. The resolution unanimously adopted by the

[16] Cf. Wilfred Fienburgh, *International Control of Basic Industries* (London: Labour Party, 1950).

[17] "E. R. P. Unions Chart the Road to Unity," *Labour*, XII (May 1950), 728.

conference affirmed the interest of the free trade-unions in the re-organization of the Ruhr industries and in a rational organization of the heavy industries of Western Europe, demanded that the interests of trade-unions be fully recognized in the administration of the International Ruhr Authority, or any future organization which might take over its powers, and called upon the governments of Western Europe to enter into negotiations with a view to the formation of an inter-European authority for the coal, iron ore, iron, and steel industries which would be open to the participation of other countries. During the discussions on the Schuman proposals, the British T.U.C. representatives, in the absence of information and clarification on a number of points and pending a decision of their General Council, were unable to agree to any commitment with regard to the proposals. Eventually, however, the conference was able to adopt unanimously a resolution which stressed "the vital interest of Free Trade Unions in a rational organization of the heavy industry of Western Europe" and declared that the success of any such plan depended upon the co-operation of the workers and their trade-unions. The conference accordingly recommended that the Executive Board of the I.C.F.T.U. should try to secure adequate trade-union representation in any discussion to be held on the national or international level for the purpose of determining the principles and working of the plan.[18] However, at a subsequent meeting, the I.C.F.T.U. Committee on the Schuman Plan considered that direct trade-union representation at the Schuman plan discussions was inadequate and expressed its disappointment at the failure of the I.C.F.T.U. efforts to secure satisfactory representation at these discussions. The committee decided that the following principles were essential to the operation of the Schuman plan: (1) democratic public control of the proposed high authority, (2) appointment of personalities enjoying the confidence of the free trade-unions both in the high authority itself and at all levels in the proposed system, (3) granting to the high authority of far-reaching powers of control, especially over production investments and prices with a view to achieving an expanded economy and full employment, (4) safeguarding and improving the wages, working conditions, and social security provisions for the free trade-unions of Western Europe.[19]

Within the British Labour movement the opinion had been frequently expressed that the government, by failing to instruct the Bri-

[18] *I.C.F.T.U. Information Bulletin*, V (June 1, 1950), 7. The Dusseldorf resolution was subsequently supported by the Executive Committee of the Miners' International Federation at Brussels, June 9–10, 1950. *Ibid.*, VI (June 14, 1950), 3.

[19] *Ibid.*, VII (July 5, 1950), 3.

tish Labour delegates at Strasbourg to outline a socialist plan for European integration and to state clearly the conditions on which Britain would be prepared to participate in common industrial planning, had forfeited the initiative. Many of the socialist intellectuals believed that a European administration of steel and coal, in which Britain participated, might become the nucleus of an independent Western Union—provided always that the Labour government was successful in obtaining the "proper socialist safeguards."[20] The Independent Labour party took the view that the future of Europe was "bound up in the economic integration of European economic resources to be utilised in the interests of the people of Europe and to be owned and fully developed by the European people on the basis of democratic workers' control." While considering that the Schuman plan might have the effect of ending the age-old rivalry between France and Germany, it felt that this policy should not be restricted to these two countries alone but should include all the European iron and steel resources and should be followed by the gradual elimination of national sovereignty and purely national interests in the exploitation of the mineral wealth of Europe, so that its vital energies might be used along the path of peace rather than of war as in the past. The National Administrative Council of the I.L.P. raised its voice against the danger of this merger's developing into a mere Franco-German cartel forming part of a Western Power bloc, pointing out that the ultimate and abiding success of the plan depended upon the degree of genuine public ownership and workers' control which would be exercised by the free peoples of Europe "as the first step towards the complete socialisation of all European land, basic industry and mineral resources." The deadlock in European affairs could still be broken, the I.L.P. declared, by the acceptance throughout the Continent of the policy for a federal pact which was adopted at the 1949 Paris Congress of the Socialist Movement for the United States of Europe.[21] The "federal unionists" within the British Labour movement were also insistent upon an alternative to the Schuman plan which would have the effect of "coordinating the basic industry of Europe in the interests of Europe as a whole." This group, "disappointed by the little value placed on the internationalism of socialist policy," felt that the Labour government's stand on European unity held out little hope for a foreign policy which would progressively lead toward world socialism. Why was it assumed, the federalists asked, that a European parliament would have a permanent antisocialist majority? Indeed, united in its endeavors,

[20] *New Statesman and Nation*, XXXIV (May 13, 1950), 533.
[21] Resolution of May 21, 1950, *Socialism, European Unity and the Labour Party* (London: I.L.P., *Socialist Leader*, 1950), pp. 9–11.

British Labour should have a good chance of winning Europe for socialism. Socialists on the Continent had already declared in favor of a European federation and the International Socialist Conference, held in Holland in 1949, had agreed that the Council of Europe should be regarded as a step on the road to a permanent European union. As to the Schuman proposals, the federalists argued that production could be planned to meet both the demands for export and the needs of Europe. Because this production would be cheaper and more efficient, industries would be able to afford a rise in the standard of living of workers whose wages were below those prevailing in other countries participating in the plan. Finally, only a democratically controlled supranational authority could afford protection for workers against the unemployment which under present conditions inevitably followed trade recessions. The only way that the federalists could see of ensuring the full observance of the pledges of full employment and social justice by every country in the Council of Europe was by granting legislative and administrative powers to an elected assembly. The Council of Europe provided a proper authority to which the organization for the coal and steel industries of Europe under the Schuman plan could be responsible. In the Council, there was the Assembly which was deemed the "proper place for the Schuman Plan to be brought up"; there was also the Committee of Ministers on which the governments would have the final say. It was thus possible to combine in one political organization the supranational authority with the inter-governmental level.[22]

The Labour party's response to these repeated demands for an alternative to the Schuman proposals was the preparation of a "European Socialist plan" for the integration of Western Europe's basic industries. At the International Socialist Conference in London, the British proposed an international board to govern the coal and steel industries of Western Europe which would be controlled by a commission representing the West European governments, instead of being independent of all governments as under the French scheme. The British socialists insisted that "political control of any international organization to plan Europe's basic industries must be vested in Governments. The job of the international organisation would thus be confined to the most efficient production of Europe's coal and steel." They felt that only governments could decide to pursue the necessary financial and investment policies to make expansionist plans work and to secure international planning for full employment and workers'

[22] *Let the Argument Proceed* (London: Federal Union, 1950) ; R. W. G. Mackay, *Heads in the Sand* (Oxford: Basil Blackwell, 1950).

participation in the administration of industries under international control.[23] The declaration issued at the conclusion of the conference reconciled the British view that the controlling international authority should be intergovernmental, appointed by and responsible to the participating governments, and the French view that the authority should be supranational by conceding that the necessary international organization would have to be worked out by the governments concerned. The conference agreed, however, that "in any form of international organisation the essential principle of democratic control and democratic procedure must be fully safeguarded. This control would involve participation by the trade unions and representatives of the consumers." Restating the socialist principles in favor of international planning of European basic resources, as elaborated at Witten (March 1950) and Copenhagen (June 1950), the conference welcomed the Schuman proposals as "a bold example of European initiative" and declared itself in agreement with the general purposes as expressed in the French communiqué of May 9. Such international planning would be a major step toward European unity and toward securing economic stability and full employment, the socialists declared, if the following general principles were observed:

1. Labour standards within Europe's basic industries must be progressively raised so as to meet the possibilities set by the more progressive countries.

2. The only safe guarantee that labour standards will be set by the more progressive countries is the fullest participation of the trade unions both at the national and international levels.

3. Within the general programme of expansion and full employment the production of European coal and steel must be organised efficiently so that the potential demand is met as economically as possible.

4. In order to ensure the expansion of demand there must be a recognition of the need for new investment both in Europe and the underdeveloped regions overseas. These projects must be co-ordinated and the Governments must introduce the financial and technical policies to support such investments.

5. Individual Governments which join in any effective plan must accept the responsibility for implementing within their own countries decisions made under any international arrangement. This will require new legislation in many European countries.

6. Where essential international planning involves national sacrifices, the burden of these sacrifices should be shared by all countries participating in the plan.

[23] *Daily Mirror,* June 17, 1950, p. 1.

The conference warned, however, that any organization for planning European coal and steel, if not based on expanding demand and maintaining full employment, would quickly develop all the characteristics of a restrictive private cartel. It would produce mass unemployment and derelict areas in many parts of Europe and would rightly provoke the opposition of all European socialists and trade-unionists. On the other hand, with the proper safeguards, as outlined in the conference declaration, the Schuman proposals would then be "worthy of the enthusiastic support of European Socialists."[24]

The Labour party's conviction that "without public ownership and a policy of full employment, the unification of European heavy industry will inevitably lead to a restrictive monopoly, the destruction of full employment and of the workers' standard of living" and the government's refusal "to commit the country in advance to the pooling of European coal and steel without these safeguards" received the overwhelming approval of the annual conferences of the party and the Trades Union Congress. At Brighton, the T.U.C. rejected a critical resolution, moved by Bob Edwards of the Chemical Workers' Union, proposing the establishment of a "European Council for Industry and Labour" as an advisory and consultative body to the Council of Europe and urging the government to participate in the Schuman plan discussions on the understanding that the plan would not be a restrictive cartel, that there would be progressive improvement in the workers' living standard and that trade-union consultation would be guaranteed on a national and international level. Replying for the General Council, Arthur Deakin suggested that it would be premature to establish an industrial consultative body to the Council of Europe, since the Council did not yet exercise any executive functions either politically or economically. The time for that would be when political and economic organs with precise functions had themselves been established, whether under the auspices of the Council of Europe or on a North Atlantic basis, using and developing the Organization for European Economic Co-operation. As for participation in the Schuman plan discussions, the conditions laid down in the resolution were essential and would, in fact, be insisted upon by any Labour government. Most of these conditions had already been recognized in statements by the originators of the proposal. The position of the government was "well set out in *European Unity*," and Congress policy, Deakin suggested, was "to support the Government in the declara-

---

[24] Text of Declaration on the Co-ordination of Europe's Basic Industries by the Conference of West European Socialist Parties, London, June 17, 1950, *Report of the Forty-ninth Annual Conference of the Labour Party*, 1950, p. 200.

tion made on behalf of the Party."[25] At Margate, the Labour party conference concurred with the decision reached by the T.U.C. on the question of European unity. The resolution moved by Mrs. I. Chaplin of Holborn and St. Pancras South C.L.P. and adopted by the conference, supported the policy statement on the Schuman plan issued by the National Executive Committee of the party on June 11. In addition, the conference approved the government's decision "to base its own constructive approach to the unification of European heavy industry on a policy of public ownership and full employment within the socialist declarations of the Party."[26]

The partisan debate on the Schuman proposals and the preparation of a socialist alternative plan were suddenly overshadowed by the turn of events in the Far East. On June 27, the day on which the government received parliamentary endorsement of its European unity policy, the Prime Minister announced that the authorities of North Korea had invaded the territory of the government of the Republic of Korea. This, Mr. Attlee asserted, was "naked aggression and it must be checked." The government, in accordance with its pledge "to give full support to the United Nations," had authorized the United Kingdom representative on the Security Council to support a resolution introduced by the United States recommending "that the Members of the United Nations furnish such assistance to the Republic of Korea as may be necessary to repel the armed attack." The Prime Minister was certain that there would be no disagreement, after the bitter experience of the past thirty-five years, that the salvation of all was dependent upon prompt and effective measures to arrest aggression wherever it might occur, using for this purpose the international machinery which the peace-loving nations had established.[27]

In support of the Prime Minister's statement, the National Council of Labour declared that the invasion of South Korea by the communist armed forces of North Korea constituted "a flagrant act of aggression in violation not only of the principles of the United Nations but in defiance of the Security Council and of the United Nations Commission on the spot." Believing that it was "imperative for the United Nations to take action to bring to an end this alarming departure from cold war to hot war and so avoid the grave danger of a third world conflagration," the National Council gave its "full support

[25] Report of the Eighty-second Annual Conference of the T.U.C., 1950, pp. 397–402.

[26] Report of the Forty-ninth Annual Conference of the Labour Party, 1950, pp. 164–69.

[27] 476 H.C.Deb., June 27, 1950, cols. 2160–61.

to the Security Council and to the action of the Prime Minister in informing the President of the United States that the British Government approves the measures being taken to support Southern Korea against Communist aggression."[28] The General Council of the T.U.C., associating itself "unreservedly" with the declaration of the National Council of Labour, maintained that such faith in collective security and firm action was not new to the British trade-union movement, but was consistent with the policy that it had steadfastly maintained since the League of Nations was founded as an instrument of collective security and for the establishment of peace and justice throughout the world. In conformity with this policy, it had sought, in the years between the two World Wars, to make its influence felt when the League was confronted with acts of lawless aggression. At the end of the second World War, it had once more ranged itself solidly in support of a charter which promised stronger and firmer action against all aggressors and enemies of peace in the future. The full-scale armed attack launched upon the Republic of Korea by the North Korean forces was undeniably, in the Council's view, "a clear act of aggression. It was unmistakably a threat to international peace. As such it was manifestly the responsibility of the Security Council of the United Nations to take decisive action for immediate cessation of hostilities." The General Council maintained that its attitude on the question of Korea revealed the "continuity of trade union policy over many troubled years of international lawlessness and aggression." Echoing the words of the International Confederation of Free Trade Unions, the T.U.C. expressed its conviction that this United Nations action would secure "the whole-hearted support of all free and democratic trade unions."[29]

Thus assured of party approval, the government decided to request the full support of the House of Commons for the action taken in conformity with its obligations under the United Nations Charter and to make its policy of "helping to resist the unprovoked aggression against the Republic of Korea" a matter of confidence, thereby demonstrating British solidarity behind the United Nations' armed assistance to the Korean Republic. According to the Prime Minister, the issue before Parliament was a simple one:

The world was faced with an act of naked aggression committed against a sovereign State established by the United Nations and recognised as the

[28] Text of Declaration, *Report of the Forty-ninth Annual Conference of the Labour Party*, 1950, p. 11.

[29] "Unions Back the United Nations," *Labour*, XII (August 1950), 827; "British Unions Will Back United Nations," *ibid.*, N.S. I (September 1950), 3.

lawful Government of South Korea. There could not be a greater affront
to the United Nations, and any suggestion of condoning such an action
would have struck at the whole basis of the United Nations.

This was immediately recognized by an emergency meeting of the
Security Council, Attlee explained, and embodied in its resolution of
June 25, adopted by nine votes to nil, calling upon the North Korean
authorities to cease hostilities and to withdraw their armed forces.
The Prime Minister felt that it was important to establish the validity
of this resolution and of the second resolution, passed on June 27 by
seven votes to nil, authorizing United Nations action to halt the North
Korean aggression, as a reply to the Soviet charge that the Security
Council had not been properly constituted when it had adopted these
resolutions. He pointed out that the procedure had grown up in the
United Nations, with the support of the U.S.S.R. itself, that if a
permanent member present at a meeting chose to abstain from voting,
the resolution of the Security Council should be regarded as legally
effective and that if a permanent member chose to refrain from voting
by failing to be present at all, that member should be regarded as having deliberately abstained from voting. In view of the fact that the
absence of a permanent member had twice in the past been accepted as
not invalidating a Security Council resolution, the absence of the
Russian representative did not invalidate the resolution on the Korean
dispute. Furthermore, the Charter did not permit a permanent member
to be deliberately absent and to impose a blanketing veto on all the Security Council's proceedings. Answering the second Soviet complaint—
the representation of China on the Security Council—the Prime Minister asserted that up to the present time Dr. Tsiang's right to continue
as a representative of the Chinese Nationalist government had been
approved by a majority of the members of the Security Council. Thus,
by the rules and practices of the Security Council, the Nationalist representative was entitled to occupy a seat and cast a vote for China.
Consequently, the U.S.S.R. had no right to impose its own view on the
question of Chinese representation on other members of the Security
Council and no justification to maintain that the Security Council was
not properly constituted. As to the question whether the United States
was justified in taking action under the United Nations Charter, Attlee
cited the right of collective self-defense referred to in Article 51 of the
Charter and expressly recognized by the members of the North Atlantic Pact. The broad principle was that all states might be endangered
if the aggressor was allowed to get away with the fruits of aggression
in any part of the world. It was "abundantly clear" to him that there
was this right of self-defense and, after the passing of the resolution

of June 27, justification for the continued action of the United States, the United Kingdom, and of other members was to be found in that resolution. If the United Nations was not to go the way of the League of Nations, the members had to be prepared to act when the need arose. This matter had to be carried through and settled to show that "aggression does not pay"; to preserve peace, the rule of law had to be upheld. "We are all in this," the Prime Minister warned; "we cannot leave it to someone else to do."[30]

The government's decision to support United Nations intervention in Korea and to place United Kingdom forces at the disposal of the United States Command in the Far East was endorsed by the House of Commons without a division. The only dissent came from a few Labour members who expressed their "deep concern at the alarming situation in Korea" and "the possibility of another world conflict arising therefrom." The spokesmen for this group, S. O. Davies and Emrys Hughes, called upon the government

to withdraw all British naval forces from the affected area; to give, in accordance with the decisions of the Cairo Conference in 1943 and the Moscow Conference in 1945, full recognition to the claim of the Korean people for the unification and independence of their country; to repudiate all British commitments which involve on our part any obligation to maintain the present division of the nations of the world into two powerful and dangerously poised hostile groups; and to declare in conformity with the Government's socialist principles our determination to give every encouragement to all peoples aspiring for freedom and self-government.

In presenting this amendment, Mr. Davies charged that the government had aligned itself on the side of what was very well known to be the corrupt regime of Syngman Rhee, an alliance of black marketeers and collaborators. That was the crowd—not the people and not the nation—with which the British government was asked to identify itself and "to plunge this country into war, to sustain and maintain a rotten regime of that kind." The government, in so doing, invoked the United Nations Charter; but "was North Korea invited, in accordance with the Charter, to appear before the Council of the United Nations before the warlike intervention of the United States?" Davies asked. And did the government consider the full significance of Mr. Truman's declaration regarding Formosa and the subsequent steps taken by the United States with repect to that area? Davies claimed that had it not been for the "unprovoked aggression" of the United States, the Korean conflict would have been finished in a week. If

[30] 477 H.C.Deb., July 5, 1950, cols. 485–94.

Russia behaved with the same "criminal irresponsibility" as the United States, he added, Britain would soon be involved in a third world war and, as an "annex to the United States," Britain would be the first to be obliterated.[31]

The critical amendment was overwhelmingly rejected by both sides of the House and only one or two "ayes" were heard when the vote was taken upon it. It was evident that Davies' charges and the pacifist appeal of Emrys Hughes to consider the consequences of a third world war before "signing a blank cheque for action by the United Nations at the instigation of the United States" had fallen on completely barren ground. With the government's conclusions, that there was no question of the facts, established by the United Nations Commission report of June 24, that there was an aggression, that the aggressor was North Korea, that the aggression was not justified, and that aggression once started and not checked tended to repeat incident after incident, the House was virtually unanimous in agreement. At the same time, however, the government was asked for assurances from the back benches of the Labour party that Britain would not get "entangled in any adventure" with regard to Formosa, that the conflict in Korea would be limited and localized, military action ceasing when the aggressors had been driven over the thirty-eighth parallel, and that every means of negotiation, mediation, and arbitration of this dispute would be sought at the earliest possible moment. In expressing this concern, Tom Driberg warned that even if the localized police action in the Far East were successful, if the Western powers did not carry out the necessary reforms in such backward areas of the world as they were responsible for, then he "should not be in the least surprised if the whole of Asia were Communist anyway within five or ten years."[32]

In accordance with the suggestions from the rank and file, the Labour government sought every means of negotiation and mediation of the Korean dispute at the earliest possible moment. In view of the fact that the U.S.S.R. had not been represented at the meetings of the Security Council which had discussed the Korean issue, it decided to establish direct contact with the Soviet government in an effort to secure its co-operation in effecting a peaceful settlement of the Korean conflict. The British ambassador in Moscow, Sir David Kelly, was, therefore, directed to express to the Soviet authorities the urgent hope of his government that they would co-operate to this end by using their influence with the North Koreans to stop the bloodshed and to return

[31] 477 H.C.Deb., July 5, 1950, cols. 545–52. Hughes seconded the amendment, ibid., col. 558.

[32] Ibid., cols. 570–77. The government's conclusions were presented by Lord President, Herbert Morrison, ibid., cols. 589–95.

to the status quo. The British government's "preliminary suggestion" was that the forces working for peace should join together to stop the war without concerning themselves for the moment with other causes of difference which had arisen in the past in connection with the Korean question. During the course of the Kelly-Gromyko talks, the Soviet government stated its position that the best means for peaceful settlement was the convening of the Security Council with the indispensable participation of the Chinese People's government and representatives of the Korean people. In reply to this proposition, Kelly explained that the general attitude of the British government to the representations of the Chinese People's government was already well known, but that the question was separate from that of the actual situation, which was that forces representing fifty-three nations were being attacked in South Korea. Was it the view of the Soviet government, he asked, that this situation should be referred to the Security Council with the Chinese People's government participating and that, meanwhile, hostilities should continue? Since the British government was not prepared to make a deal for seating the Chinese Communist regime on the Security Council in exchange for the opening of peace talks on Korea, the ambassador submitted to the Soviet authorities an *aide memoire* confirming and summarizing the views of his government. These were, in brief, that the immediate issue was to stop hostilities in Korea, in regard to which the British government reaffirmed its support for the resolutions of the Security Council, and that the restoration of peace in Korea could not be made conditional on the settlement of other issues. Noting the express desire of the Soviet government for a peaceful settlement, the British government reiterated the hope that it would use its influence with the North Koreans "to bring about the immediate end of hostilities and the withdrawal of North Korean forces to northward of the 38th Parallel." Although its firm adherence to the Security Council resolutions of June 25 and 27 seemed to rule out the possibility of a settlement on the basis of the proposal suggested by Indian Prime Minister Nehru and endorsed by the U.S.S.R. for seating the Chinese Communists in the Security Council before discussing the Korean settlement, the Labour government was determined to continue its efforts to negotiate a peaceful settlement of the Korean conflict.[33]

During the course of its mediation efforts, the Labour government was obliged to clarify its position on two outstanding issues which had thus far impeded its objective of a Far Eastern settlement. With

[33] Prime Minister Attlee's account of the Kelly-Gromyko talks, 477 *H.C.Deb.*, July 20, 1950, cols. 2479–83.

regard to Formosa, the government was asked for reassurance, this time from Fenner Brockway, back-bench Labour member, that it would make it clear that British support in Korea could not be extended to an action unauthorized by the United Nations against China. Brockway warned that war between Communist China, which Britain had recognized, and the United States was "a grave possibility." In reply to Brockway's letter, the Prime Minister admitted that the government was well aware of the "dangerous possibilities" in the situation caused by the decision of the United States government to defend Formosa against any Chinese Communist assault. The government had made it quite clear, however, that its action in opposing Communist aggression in Korea was in accordance with the Security Council resolution and was not concerned with Formosa. That, Mr. Attlee presumed, was well understood in Peking.[34] The Labour government did not feel that the problem of Formosa was "insoluble" nor that it need be "the subject of any bitter debate or ill-feeling." It was convinced that the members of the United Nations could settle it together, just as they would have to settle the Korean problem, and in so doing show the world that they were competent to solve such problems in a manner that would contribute to world peace.[35]

As to the second issue—the representation of Communist China —the government made it clear that it did not intend to break its "long-established friendship with China." It felt that its recognition of the Chinese People's government, which had in fact gained complete and, as far as anyone could judge for any length of time, irrevocable control of the vast area and population of China, was really no more than the recognition of a fact which it could not help and that it was the only way in which it could avoid creating a complete barrier around China. It was not for the British government to inject into the problem of recognition the question of the political color of the government concerned. The case for recognition, in the government's opinion, was overwhelming: In China, the People's government had won the civil war; Britain had large interests there; it had a large number of British personnel in China; it had problems ahead of it which might have led to very serious problems indeed. In addition, the Indian government had decided to recognize the People's government much earlier. Britain had not been able to reconcile what members of the Commonwealth wanted to do with the "very aloof attitude of the United States." The government was convinced that it had been right at that time to recog-

[34] Text of reply to Brockway, *The Times*, August 16, 1950, p. 4.

[35] Foreign Secretary Bevin, *Official Records of the General Assembly, Fifth Session*, Two Hundred and Eighty-third Plenary Meeting, September 25, 1950, p. 88.

nize the People's government and not to leave the Russians to assume that, although the new Chinese regime was a government based on communist principles, they were the only country which would do anything at all for China. Since the granting of recognition, the British government had been trying to get support in the relevant bodies of the United Nations for a course that would bring the People's government into the United Nations. It felt, however, that Communist China's admission ought to be dealt with in the Security Council according to the rules. It could not in a transition period come to the conclusion to throw out one representative and to take on another. In the Foreign Secretary's opinion, the sponsors of the new China had really created the present difficulty, for the first thing that happened was that Russia walked out because at the immediate moment of recognition Britain was not ready to admit a new Chinese representative and had not completed her negotiations for the establishment of diplomatic relations with the new government of China. Britain had simply announced that she was ready to negotiate the establishment of diplomatic relations when the members of the Soviet group sought to force the British to implement the exercise of what they regarded as the consequences, before those negotiations were completed. While the legal position was being examined and the United Nations members were discussing how this change was to come about, the Russians walked out. "The onus of keeping China out of the United Nations," Mr. Bevin declared, was, therefore, with the Russians; they were not present and taking their part. The British, believing that it was better for the new China to be inside the United Nations, had tried quite frankly to get this settled by collecting the seven affirmative votes necessary for her admission. Britain did not want to ostracize anyone on political grounds; feeling that the future association for these countries which were emerging was a good thing, she had proceeded on that basis. The government would continue its efforts, within the United Nations, to settle the question of the representation of China. Mr. Bevin assured the Chinese people that the British government looked forward to the day when they would again take their proper place as one of the great powers and was ready to help them to fulfill their destiny. Britain refused to accept the conception that the world was divided into East and West, Bevin said; she was determined to follow the conception of the United Nations, "a conception of one-world unity."[36]

The Labour government resumed the initiative in the Korean peace

[36] *Ibid.* The British government had supported the Indian resolution for the admission of Communist China, which was defeated in the Assembly, 33–16, with 10 abstentions. Cf. *ibid.*, Two Hundred and Seventy-seventh Plenary Meeting, September 19, 1950, p. 15.

negotiations by submitting to the United Nations General Assembly a proposal for the unification and rehabilitation of Korea. The British plan, adopted in the Assembly's Political Committee as an eight-power resolution, reaffirmed the declaration of the 1948 General Assembly that the Republic of Korea was the only legal government in Korea and recalled that United Nations forces were at present operating in Korea under the Security Council resolution of June 27, recommending that United Nations members furnish such assistance to the Republic of Korea "as may be necessary to repel the armed attack and to restore international peace and security in the area." It proposed that all appropriate steps be taken to ensure conditions of stability throughout the whole of Korea; that all constituent acts be taken, including the holding of elections under the auspices of the United Nations for the establishment of a unified, independent, and democratic government in the sovereign state of Korea; that all necessary steps be taken to accomplish the economic rehabilitation of Korea; that United Nations forces should not remain in any part of Korea otherwise than as was necessary for achieving such specified objectives. The plan also called for the creation of a new and enlarged "United Nations Commission for the Unification and Rehabilitation of Korea," dominated by the Asian countries, to supervise the voting and to work toward the goal of a democratic and unified Korea. Pending the commission's arrival in Korea, the governments represented on it would immediately form an interim committee at Lake Success to consult with and advise the unified command on the proposed measures. In defending the British plan before the General Assembly, the Minister of State assured the members that United Nations military operations would not go beyond the objectives contained in the eight-power resolution. If Peking or the other neighbors of Korea still feared that United Nations forces might carry hostilities further or remain in Korea longer than their limited objectives demanded, such fears were unfounded. The responsibility of political settlement and economic restoration could not be escaped, Younger insisted. The immediate aftermath of slaughter and fratricidal strife was not a favorable setting for the operation of democratic processes, but the United Nations forces would remain no longer than necessary. It would be a "cynical renunciation of collective responsibility," the British delegate concluded, if they were allowed to go before their task was done."[37]

[37] *Official Records of the General Assembly, Fifth Session,* Two Hundred and Ninety-second Plenary Meeting, October 6, 1950, pp. 197–98. The eight-power resolution was adopted by the Political Committee, 47–5, with 5 abstentions. *Ibid., First Committee,* Three Hundred and Fifty-third Meeting, October 4, 1950, pp. 55–61.

The General Assembly's endorsement of the eight-power plan for the creation of a unified Korean state implicitly sanctioned the employment by General MacArthur of United Nations forces on both sides of the parallel until peace was restored. Disregarding the assurances to the Asian powers that United Nations forces did not intend permanently to occupy North as well as South Korea, the Peking government chose to enter the conflict in support of the North Korean forces. For the Labour government, Chinese intervention in Korea produced "a new and most serious situation" which jeopardized the attainment of its objectives in Korea and threatened the success of its efforts "to confine the conflict to Korea and to reach a stable position in the Far East." The danger to United Nations forces and to world peace involved in an extension of the Korean conflict prompted a considerable number of Labour members of Parliament to express their general anxiety that no effort to prevent a worsening of the international situation should be neglected. A group of twenty-nine Labour members, led by Michael Foot, submitted to the House of Commons two motions seeking British initiative to end fighting in Korea and to put forward alternative proposals for a big four conference. The first motion, dealing specifically with the Korean war, asked the government:

to instruct its representatives on the United Nations Interim Committee to seek immediate agreement on the line beyond which the United Nations forces will not advance, with a view to bringing the fighting to an end as quickly as possible.[38]

An additional group of forty Labour members, mainly trade-unionists led by Ellis Smith, while recording appreciation of the government's efforts to strengthen the authority of the United Nations "in a time of growing international tension and misunderstanding," called for an early meeting of the Council of Foreign Ministers to implement the United Nations General Assembly resolution urging all members to co-operate in finding a basis of lasting peace. The members urged the government, in co-operation with the other powers, to prepare a policy for a lasting peace, including

proposals for resolving the fundamental differences between those Great Powers which formed the war-time grand alliance, a world plan for mutual aid, particularly to the under-developed areas of the world, enhanced economic development, increased trade between all countries and a scheme for gradual world disarmament.[39]

[38] *Daily Herald*, November 18, 1950, p. 1.
[39] Motion on the Order Paper: "The International Situation," 481 *H.C.Deb.*, November 29, 1950, cols. 1196–97.

The objective of both these groups was the same: to show that the parliamentary Labour party did not accept the inevitability of a third world war and to urge upon the government the necessity for a British "peace initiative." The demand for steps to limit the advance in Korea and for a new effort to end the drift to war expressed the sentiment of not only the usual Labour "rebels" but of some of the most loyal supporters of the government, members who had never before criticized the government's foreign policy. According to Ellis Smith, whose resolution was backed by a number of the most influential trade-unionists in the House of Commons:

Our resolution has had an electrifying effect. Those of us who have signed the motion have been amazed by the support we have received from all sections of the Labour and Trade Union Movement.[40]

Defending the government's Far Eastern policy, the Foreign Secretary asserted that United Nations objectives in Korea, reaffirmed by the United States government to the British government, remained the same, namely, "to resist aggression, to localise the hostilities and to settle the Korean problem on a basis satisfactory to the United Nations." The advance of United Nations forces, he said, had followed the appeal of the U.N. commander to the North Koreans to lay down their arms. When they did not respond, it became necessary for the United Nations forces to restore peace and order in all parts of Korea in order that "the great and pacific and humanitarian task of unifying the country and restoring its economy could be undertaken." The Foreign Secretary admitted, however, that it would have been better if the members of the United Nations had helped to shepherd China into the organization rather than to oppose her entry. He believed that some of the difficulties with which the United Nations were now faced in the Far East "would have been avoided if there had been those opportunities for mutual discussion of problems which membership of international bodies affords." As to the wider dangers provoked by the Chinese intervention, Mr. Bevin did not "pretend to know the Chinese motives or intentions." Neither he nor anyone else could tell for certain whether the Chinese government's first motive for action arose out of its fear for its frontiers or whether it was acting as "part of a grand strategy for a bigger purpose—a Russian-Chinese conspiracy on a world-wide scale." But even now, the Foreign Secretary was ready, while taking all precautions and joining to the full in resisting acts of aggression, to give the Chinese government some benefit of the doubt. In the desire to seek a settlement and to localize

40 *Reynolds News*, November 26, 1950, p. 1.

the fighting, he recognized that the first essential was to stabilize the military situation and then to explore a political settlement. If the Chinese wanted to avoid a general war, if they showed the slightest sign of willingness to co-operate in exploring solutions by peaceful means, he was satisfied that solutions could be found.[41]

Despite the Foreign Secretary's repeated assurances that the United Nations had no aggressive intentions against the territory of China, there was a general feeling among the Labour party members, shared by many of the Opposition members including the leadership, that the United Nations should not have gone so far north toward the Manchurian frontier but should have consolidated their forces at the "waist" of the Korean peninsula. What profoundly disturbed members on both sides of the House was the thought that the Western powers, leading the United Nations effort in Korea, had lost both their military and their political initiative at this time of test. They were asking in particular "how it was that, at the moment when the British Government and others were suggesting that the Allied forces should not advance right up to the Chinese frontier, General MacArthur ordered the advance which gave the Chinese the opportunity, or the pretext, for the counter-attack." There was in fact "a persistent belief —however well- or ill-founded—that if the United Nations commander had taken the Chinese fears for the frontier at their face value and drawn a new defensive line beyond which his forces would not advance, the prospects for localising the conflict and for bringing about an eventual settlement by negotiation might have been far better than now."[42] What were the Chinese to think of United Nations assurances, the Labour critics demanded, when they saw action in Korea which they found hard to reconcile with them? The gravamen of their charge was not that General MacArthur did not photograph the Chinese troops and did not know they were there, but that he did know they were there and still launched his attack. It was "sheer folly, a fantastic folly," they asserted, to suppose that the United Nations could advance in that way right up to the Manchurian frontier without risking any violent intervention by the Chinese in defense of the frontier and of the power stations. They claimed that what had been "a complete triumph and a complete vindication of the principle of collective security" was itself in jeopardy and had "brought the world to the very brink of ultimate catastrophe." Had the United Nations stopped on the thirty-eighth parallel, they should have had "an incon-

[41] 481 *H.C.Deb.*, November 29, 1950, cols. 1162–67.

[42] Editorial, *The Times*, November 30, 1950, p. 7. Cf. Anthony Eden's plan for consolidation at the "waist" of Korea, 481 *H.C.Deb.*, November 29, 1950, col. 1177.

trovertible answer to all those who told the Chinese and Koreans that this was not an act of collective security at all, but merely an attempt by the Western bloc to provide itself with new bases in contemplation of an Asian war." The obvious conclusion drawn by the Labour critics was that if the United Nations started from the basis of "no war with China," they must then agree to negotiate; that was "the only alternative." At the same time, they should not contemplate leaving Korea. They should stand firm, "but be sensible about it and give China a chance to extricate herself." The United Nations could surely negotiate more persuasively and with more chance of success if China was within the Security Council and if, meanwhile, United Nations forces refrained from "unnecessary provocation."[43]

The Labour government shared the desire of its supporters to bring the war in Korea to an end; but it was determined to get a settlement of the whole Korean problem and a settlement of its relations and the relations of the rest of the world with China. The government also sympathized with the apprehensions expressed by more than one hundred Labour members of Parliament, including several members of the National Executive Committee of the party, as a result of the report from the United States that "the use of the atomic bomb in Korea was under active consideration" and that "the choice of weapons was a matter for the military commander in the field." Following the receipt of an urgent letter from the Labour members urging the government to "dissociate Britain from the use of the atom bomb, emphasise that this country cannot be committed to any action outside the decisions of the United Nations and warn that any unilateral action would be followed by the withdrawal of British forces from Korea,"[44] the Prime Minister decided to take action. After reassuring the members that a decision of such grave import as that of the use of the atomic bomb could not be taken on behalf of the United Nations without the fullest prior consultation with those states who were at present participating in international police action in Korea, he proposed immediate consultations with the President of the United States. The Prime Minister believed that such an interchange of views on "the problems which face us today" might be of advantage to both countries and to the cause of world peace. Judging from the cheers from both sides of the House, Mr. Attlee's decision to confer with the American Presi-

[43] Cf. speeches of Ellis Smith, 481 *H.C.Deb.*, November 29, 1950, cols. 1198–1201; Ian Mikardo, *ibid.*, cols. 1257–60; Sydney Silverman, *ibid.*, cols. 1275–76; Woodrow Wyatt, *ibid.*, November 30, 1950, cols. 1341–42; Tom Driberg, *ibid.*, cols. 1386–87.

[44] Text of letter, *Daily Herald*, December 1, 1950, p. 1. Among the signers were Ian Mikardo, Tom Driberg, and Alice Bacon of the National Executive Committee of the party.

dent gave the greatest satisfaction to his own supporters and conformed with "the earnest wish of all Members for the most intimate consultation in this crisis" between Great Britain and the United States.[45]

As a result of his "full, frank and friendly" talks with President Truman, the Prime Minister was satisfied that "the fullest weight" would be given to the views of the British government before instructions which had political implications were issued to the United Nations commander in the field. On Korea and the Far East the two governments were agreed that aggression must be halted, but they were equally certain that every effort should be made to prevent the extension of the conflict, their ultimate objective being "to reach a stable position in the Far East." While fully appreciating the American view, the Prime Minister defended Britain's "realistic" attitude toward the Peking government. He did not expect that the differences between the attitude of the two governments on the recognition of China could be resolved in talks lasting a few days, although he felt that it would be a mistake to overemphasize the differences. The British government believed that it was right that the Chinese representative in the United Nations should belong to the present government of China and that but for the Korean episode this end would have been achieved. In its attitude toward the longer-term problems, the government's objectives rested on the Cairo Declaration, agreed upon by all of Korea's neighbors, providing for a free and independent Korea living on terms of peace and friendship with the rest of the world. It was for the Chinese Communists to make it clear that they accepted these principles; their recent action had thrown doubt upon this. The question of Formosa, also dealt with in the Cairo Declaration, was one of the most difficult of all problems in the Far East. There were mutual fears and suspicions to be got rid of before a solution could be found, and it was right, the Prime Minister believed, that everyone should try to understand the point of view of both China and the United States. This was not the appropriate moment, however, to settle the matter. Until China showed by actions that she was not obstructing the fulfillment of the Cairo Declaration in respect to Korea, it would be difficult to reach a satisfactory solution. If the parties concerned could be got together, as intended by the Iraqi-Syrian resolution in the United Nations General Assembly, and if they could really get back to the position of the five powers surveying all these difficult questions, it might then be possible to solve this one among others. The British government could see no reason for going

[45] Editorial, *The Times*, December 1, 1950, p. 7.

back on the Cairo Declaration and on the question of Formosa it had, therefore, obtained the agreement of the American President that "consideration of this difficult problem by the United Nations would be helpful." In the Far East as in other parts of the world, the Prime Minister said, there were two courses in dealing with disputes and difficulties which might arise:

Either we must try to negotiate a settlement based on the acceptance of normal standards of international practice and on the principles and obligations of the Charter of the United Nations or, on the other hand, we shall find ourselves drifting inevitably toward war.

If the Chinese accepted the former course a solution could be found compatible with the principles of the United Nations Charter.[46]

In applying this basic principle to the fact of Chinese intervention in Korea, the Labour government concluded that a solution must be sought by means of peaceful negotiation. Consequently, the British delegate in the Security Council secured the adoption of a proposal to invite the Peking government to participate in the discussion of the United Nations commander's report on the intervention of Chinese Communist forces in Korea. In the course of the Security Council discussions, the British government approved a six-power draft resolution calling for withdrawal of Chinese Communist troops and holding out to Peking full assurances on the Manchurian frontier. British policy, according to Sir Gladwyn Jebb, was "directed to bringing military operations to a close" and "to give effect to the purposes of the United Nations." Nothing would give Britain greater satisfaction, he said, than to withdraw from Korea and see a really independent government in that country. Jebb hoped that the Peking government would heed the directives in the six-power proposals and agree to settle the problem of Formosa in accordance with the principles of the United Nations Charter.[47] Further progress in the Security Council negotiations was precluded, however, by the Soviet exercise of the veto. The Labour government then renewed its peace efforts in the General Assembly by supporting the adoption of a "cease-fire" proposal initiated by a number of Asian and Middle Eastern states. The government felt that there must be a cease-fire in Korea first and then

---

[46] 482 H.C.Deb., December 14, 1950, cols. 1354–56. Also cf. Bevin's statement that "anybody who is fool enough to attack Manchuria is bound to produce a world war almost immediately." Ibid., cols. 1459–62.

[47] Official Records of the Security Council, Fifth Year, Five Hundred and Nineteenth Meeting, November 8, 1950, pp. 15–16; Five Hundred and Twentieth Meeting, November 8, 1950, pp. 8–9; Five Hundred and Twenty-first Meeting, November 10, 1950, pp. 19–20.

a settlement by negotiation, there being no interference with Chinese territory, but equally no interference by China with Korean territory. British policy, while making clear that "there must be no reward for aggression," was "to meet the just claims of the Asiatic nations to be dealt with on terms of full equality." The Asian-Arab proposals were a practical step that could end the fighting and if successful would increase the possibilities of subsequently laying the foundation of a settlement of the Korean problem on lines acceptable to the United Nations. Britain appealed to the Chinese and the North Koreans to respond to this initiative and thus bring the conflict to an end.[48]

Despite Peking's rejection of the original proposals of the United Nations Cease-Fire Committee, the Labour government did not lose hope of a negotiated settlement of the Korean war. It felt that the Chinese reply to the committee's second efforts—a set of general principles for a settlement of outstanding issues in the Far East—"though most disappointing, did not finally close the door to negotiations." Before deciding on the interpretation to place on the Peking response, the government found it necessary to elucidate it by putting to the Chinese Communists certain points in their reply and requesting an explanation. The most important issue was reference to a cease-fire and on this point the British chargé d'affaires was informed that, as the Chinese government saw it, there should be two steps in regard to concluding the war in Korea and reaching a peaceful settlement of the Korean problem: The first step should be a cease-fire for a limited period, which could be agreed upon at the first meeting of a conference of powers and immediately put into effect so that negotiations might proceed. The second step, in the Chinese view, was to discuss a number of problems, among them the withdrawal of all foreign troops from Korea, proposals for the future of Korea itself, withdrawal of American forces from Formosa, and inclusion of the Central People's government of China in the United Nations. Although the wording of the Chinese reply, even with further elucidations, was not altogether clear, Britain shared the general feeling of the Commonwealth and Asian countries that the United Nations should patiently pursue every possibility of a peaceful settlement with China so that the new emerging China might be given an opportunity to play her part in a community of nations on equal terms with other members.[49]

In view of these considerations, the Labour government felt that the United Nations should not at this stage take a new and important

[48] Kenneth Younger, *Official Records of the General Assembly, Fifth Session, First Committee*, Four Hundred and Tenth Meeting, December 8, 1950, p. 406.

[49] Prime Minister Attlee, 483 *H.C.Deb.*, January 23, 1951, cols. 38–42.

decision regarding Chinese intervention in Korea. While the government welcomed the American proposal to set up a committee of "Good Offices" which would provide the machinery for exploring every possibility of a negotiated settlement and, recognizing the stark facts of the situation in Korea, likewise agreed in condemning Chinese intervention in support of an aggressor which had thwarted and frustrated the purposes of the United Nations, it did not believe that the time had yet come to consider further measures. To do so implied the abandonment of any hope of reaching a peaceful settlement, and this it had not done. The rejection of the American resolution in its original form did not mean, however, that there was the slightest attempt to condone aggression. Britain's primary purpose was to uphold the principles of the United Nations Charter and to maintain a strong system of collective security. While it was indeed incumbent upon all members of the United Nations to uphold the rule of law, it was on the question of methods that there was room for dispute and on which there seemed to be two clearly defined schools of thought. In contrast to those who thought that because a crime had been committed and the culprit was apparent there was no alternative but to proceed to condemnation and punishment, the British still thought it possible that the culprit might see the light and that a process of persuasion might prove fruitful. The application of such measures as those intended by the American resolution might well result in further crises with consequences none could foresee. So far, the measures taken by the United Nations had been of a military nature, strictly confined to the limited field of Korea. Once they went beyond that field, the British delegate interjected, might not the punishment cause wider havoc than the crime, might not the cure be even worse than the disease? It would indeed be a poor return for the sacrifices of the United Nations, Jebb said, if they involved themselves in a course which led to still further sacrifices, without their having any clear conception of the objective at which they were aiming and without the assurance that all possible means of peaceful negotiation had been tested in order to limit these sacrifices and to enable the bloodshed to come to an end.

In regard to the American proposals, the British delegate in the Political Committee insisted that the members of the General Assembly must above all maintain the position of the United Nations: first, by standing firm in Korea and doing their utmost to repel armed aggression by armed force and, second, by accepting no settlement which would be contrary to the principles laid down as a basis for negotiation. In this way, they would demonstrate clearly that "aggression does not pay." At the same time, however, they must continue to explore to the limit the possibility of a peaceful settlement of the Korean problem. As to what constituted a "peaceful settlement," British views had already been expressed, on the issue of Chinese representation in the United Nations and on the question of the independence of Korea, in a series of resolutions supported in the General Assembly. How then did British policy apply to the American resolution before the Political Committee? The British government had made it sufficiently clear that it deplored the action taken by the Peking government in Korea and felt that it was only right that the United Nations should take full cognizance of it. For that reason, it could express itself in broad agreement with the first five paragraphs of the American resolution, while noting that the wording might well require some modification. But when it came to the consideration of further measures, before the intentions of the Peking government had been fully and exhaustively explored, it expressed "the gravest doubt about the wisdom of such action." The British delegate urged the members of the committee to reflect many times before they took a step that might carry them all much farther along a road on which none of them was yet prepared to proceed in practice. As for the British government, it still would favor a further effort at clarification before deciding that the Korean question was in fact "insoluble except as the result of some general extension of a warlike situation."[50]

After considerable exchanges of views with the United States, the Commonwealth, and other governments, the British succeeded in securing the amendment of the original American proposals. To meet the British objection that it was not correct to say that the Chinese government "had rejected all United Nations proposals" to bring about a cessation of hostilities in Korea, the wording of Paragraph 2 was changed to read that the Chinese government "had not accepted United Nations proposals." In the case of Paragraph 8, respecting a committee to consider additional measures to be employed to meet the aggression in Korea, an important addition was made. The effect of this change was to defer consideration by the Assembly of further measures in the event of the Good Offices Committee's reporting progress. Thus the essential principle was maintained that the United Nations would continue its efforts to arrange for a peaceful settlement and that there could be no question of the United Nations proceeding to further measures until it had been apparent that those efforts had failed. It was the earnest hope of the Labour government that Peking

[50] Sir Gladwyn Jebb, *Official Records of the United Nations General Assembly, Fifth Session, First Committee*, Four Hundred and Thirty-first Meeting, January 25, 1951, pp. 544–47.

would respond to any efforts which might be made by the Good Offices Committee to bring about a cease-fire and a negotiated settlement in the Far East. The United Nations had pointed the way and shown the will for peace. China had much to gain by co-operation and much to lose by withholding it.[51]

For the Labour government, the conflict in Korea changed the tempo of the international situation, signalizing the re-emergence of warlike aggression in the world. Hitherto there had been no overt attack, but here was military aggression against a state set up by the United Nations. Here was a direct challenge to world authority. The aggression by North Korea had shown that the authority of the United Nations was not backed by enough armed force to provide a firm guaranty against the possibility of war. If incidents like Korea were not to ignite a world-wide conflagration, the peace-loving nations must spend a larger proportion of their resources on building up their strength in arms. What had happened in Korea might in one form or another be repeated elsewhere, the Prime Minister warned: the fire that had been started in distant Korea might yet burn down British homes. The attack by Communist North Korea, condemned by the United Nations, had the approval of Soviet Russia and the support of another Communist power, China. From the Soviet point of view, it had an obvious utility in diverting forces to the East and in weakening the forces of the Western powers in other areas of more immediate interest to Russia. There were obvious danger spots in many parts of the world and, in these areas, Russian actions had shown clearly the peril to the democracies of insufficient forces. In the face of these dangers, Britain had joined with other democratic powers in building up, in Western Union and the Atlantic Pact, a system of collective security, not for aggression but for mutual defense. It was partly to enable Britain to make her contribution to this force that she was increasing her own armed strength. The Labour government believed that if the international situation was to improve, the democracies must demonstrate beyond any possibility of doubt that they had the will and the means to resist an attack on their way of life. They must have adequate strength so that if there was danger in some part of the world it would be known that they had forces available to meet it. "There is nothing provocative in this," the Prime Minister asserted, "any more than it is provocative to have a policeman on the beat."[52]

The Labour party, on the whole, had endorsed the government's

[51] Prime Minister Attlee, 482 *H.C.Deb.*, February 12, 1951, cols. 60–63.

[52] Broadcast speech to the nation, July 30, 1950, *The Times*, July 31, 1950, pp. 4–5; address at Forest Hill, London, January 26, 1951, *ibid.*, January 27, 1951, p. 6; 478 *H.C.Deb.*, September 14, 1950, col. 1257.

decision to increase its armaments in order that it might play its part in the defense of the free world. There was virtual agreement that the government had been right to uphold by armed force the principle of collective security under the United Nations in Korea and to contribute to the strengthening of Western defense by participation in the establishment of an integrated force under the Treaty of Atlantic Defense. The party was also agreed that the purpose of increased armaments was solely a defensive one—to deter aggression—and that peace could be preserved not by arms alone but also by removing the causes of international strife and tension.[53] The divergencies of view within the Labour movement on the problems of defense and rearmament were a matter of degree rather than of kind. While accepting the necessity for defense, there were those who felt that too large an armament program might destroy the economic and social achievements and aims of a socialist government, revive the militarism of the defeated Fascist states, and perpetuate an arms race between East and West, thus rendering inevitable a world-wide conflagration. These fears, expressed at the annual conferences of both the Trades Union Congress and the Labour party, were evidence of the hesitations and the qualifications with which the government's rearmament program was endorsed. Within the Labour movement there still existed the hope that the government would take the initiative

to strive to end the differences between the five great powers, to which end a Conference should be called immediately; to renew its efforts to create friendly relations with the U.S.S.R.; to support the outlawing of the atomic bomb and all other means of mass destruction, the international control of atomic energy, and the limitation of armaments, through the United Nations.[54]

Although the government's defense program was not openly challenged or pressed to a division in Parliament, a considerable group of back-bench Labour members submitted a series of critical motions reflecting in varying degrees uneasiness about certain aspects of the government's international policy. Two of the motions related to the

[53] The T.U.C. and Labour party conference approved their Executives' reports on the international situation: the former by 6,942,000–595,000, the latter without a division. Cf. Reports of the *Eighty-second Annual Conference of the* T.U.C., 1950, pp. 425, 576–84; and *Forty-ninth Annual Conference of the Labour Party*, 1950, pp. 25, 150.

[54] Resolution, "Foreign Policy and War Danger," moved by Harold Davies, rejected by 4,861,000–881,000. *Report of the Forty-ninth Annual Conference of the Labour Party*, 1950, pp. 141–50. Also cf. resolution on "Atomic Weapons," moved by Walter Padley and rejected, 5,601,000–1,972,000. *Report of the Eighty-second Annual Conference of the T.U.C.*, 1950, pp. 411–31.

rearmament of Western Germany: one, standing in the names of R. H. S. Crossman, Ian Mikardo, and seven other members, urged reconsideration of the proposal to rearm Germany; the other, standing solely in the name of Eric Fletcher, welcomed "the statement made on behalf of the Government that no irrevocable steps have been taken for the rearmament of Western Germany which this House would deplore." The government had been publicly informed by four of the sponsors of the first motion, in addition to Barbara Castle and Michael Foot, that they would "do nothing to weaken the Government's hands." The two additional motions, relating to the wider issues of foreign policy, both had passages referring to the "arms race." One, which stood in the names of twelve members, including Emrys Hughes and Sydney Silverman, called for "a new initiative" in formulating a policy which would secure peace between the Eastern and Western nations, halt the arms race, and lead to the establishment of a new world order. The other motion, supported by Leslie Hale, Seymour Cocks, and several other Labour M.P.'s, expressed the earnest desire

that the Government should continue to secure the peace of the world, and in particular to spare no effort to prevent a widening of the conflict in Asia; should maintain their policy of preserving democracy with a view to resisting the resurgence of totalitarianism in Western Germany and, following their initiative at the Colombo Conference, should make a forthright reaffirmation of their desire in consultation with the Great Powers to lead in a policy of world co-operation for the development of those vast areas, whose inhabitants suffer from poverty, malnutrition and disease, so that the resources of the world now being so tragically expended in an arms race may be devoted, without discrimination of race, colour or religion and political creed, to the raising of the standard of living of all mankind.[55]

It was the view of these critics that if the government continued at the rate of its proposed armaments program, it would encourage a "speeding-up of the so-called defence programme on the other side." Eventually, in a year or two, all that it would have achieved by its rearmament efforts would be a lower standard of living; and by creating a lower standard of living it would create the very conditions which would result in communism. As leading spokesman for the latter view, Aneurin Bevan declared that he could no longer remain a member of the government when it became clear to him that the defense program could not be achieved "without irreparable damage to the economy of Great Britain and the world." Bevan maintained that as a result of the "anarchy of American competitive capitalism," as evidenced in the

[55] *The Times*, February 12, 1951, p. 6. Also signing the motion were Acland, Craddock, Houghton, Hynd, McLeavy, Moeran, O'Brien, and Thomas.

stockpiling by the United States, raw materials, machine tools, and components were not forthcoming in sufficient quantity even for the earlier defense program. Consequently, the figures for arms expenditure in the Chancellor of the Exechequer's budget were based upon assumptions already invalidated; the £4,700 million arms program was already dead. In his opinion, these figures ought to be revised to conform with the principle that "the defence programme must always be consistent with the maintenance of the standard of living of the British people and the maintenance of the social services." Mr. Bevan agreed that the British people should do what was necessary to defend themselves—not only with their arms but with their spiritual resources. At the same time, however, he warned that,

if in attempting to meet the military effect of those totalitarian machines, the economies of the Western world are disrupted and the standard of living is lowered or industrial disturbances are created, then Soviet Communism establishes a whole series of Trojan horses in every nation of the Western economy.[56]

The government shared the "grave anxiety" of its critics regarding the existence of "international tension, fear and suspicion in the world today." Nevertheless, the Prime Minister insisted that they had to face "the grim facts of the situation." During the last five years they had seen continued obstruction and lack of co-operation on the part of the U.S.S.R. and her satellites. The purposes of those states had been not to promote peace but to cause trouble everywhere in the world. They maintained immense armaments, they carried on a hostile and subversive propaganda against all noncommunist states and against a communist state such as Yugoslavia when it did not take its orders exactly from the Kremlin. That was the reason why Britain and the other Western powers had found it necessary to build up their armaments. There was a great deal of "sham peace propaganda," Mr. Attlee said, which represented this rearmament as if all nations had been disarmed and then suddenly one or two started rearming. The real fact was that the Western powers were faced by the immense armaments of the Soviet Union and the Soviet bloc. The Russians had not disarmed after the last war; they had been increasing their armaments and they had been arming their satellites. In the government's opinion, it was the existence of those forces and the fact that those forces were controlled by a government which carried out consistently a certain policy that caused the grave anxiety and international tension

[56] 487 *H.C.Deb.*, April 23, 1951, cols. 35–43. For the views of Bevan and his supporters cf. *One Way Only* and *Going Our Way* (London: Tribune Publications, 1951).

throughout the world. Today those anxieties centered particularly on three major problems: the problem of the Far East, the problem of Europe, and the problem of the Middle East.

In Europe, there had been considerable progress since the West had experienced the lesson of Korea. There was the signing of the Treaty of Atlantic Defense, the appointment of General Eisenhower, and the establishment of the integrated force under his command. In the decisions of the Atlantic Council there was one to include in that integrated force a contribution from Germany. The first steps were being taken to build up the integrated force, and exploratory discussions with the German federal government with regard to a German contribution were proceeding. There were, however, a great many things that would first have to be settled. One of the most difficult questions facing the Western powers was how to integrate any German force into the forces of the Atlantic Treaty nations. One proposal was for a European army. As originally put forward, there were features of that plan which the British government could not accept. There was the linking of it with a political superstructure, a minister of defense for Europe, and even an assembly. Nor was Britain entirely agreed that this was a really possible plan, unless it were worked out within the framework of the North Atlantic Treaty organization. As to the concern expressed regarding the revival of German militarism, the government reiterated the view that German rearmament was "only one part and not the predominant part of the defence plans for the whole of Europe." Since 1945 the German power to wage war had been far more drastically destroyed than after the first World War. The purpose of the Allies in ensuring the removal of the menace of German militarization had been achieved. After the demilitarization there was a way open for the removal of the tension which heavy armaments had caused in Europe for so many generations, provided all other nations were prepared to play their part. Unfortunately, that had not happened. While Great Britain and the Western powers demobilized their forces at the end of the war, Soviet Russia did not. By the existence of these immense forces she had been able to surround herself with a ring of satellites, dominated by communist governments obedient to the will of Moscow. In those satellites, strong forces were being built up; into this circle of satellite states the Soviet government had sought in every way to include Eastern Germany. Like other countries in that orbit she had been organized on the Soviet pattern. Cliques of Communists were in control and a force of so-called police had been created which was being trained and equipped as a military force. Therefore, any examination of the problem of German rearmament must start at the place where it was actually happening—in the Soviet zone of Germany; just as any discussion of the danger to the world of armaments must consider those in existence rather than to consider rearmament which was still only in the planning stage. It was the existence of those arms which had caused the West to rearm. The major question facing the world at present was not the demilitarization of Germany but whether the communist states could be brought to reduce their armed forces to reasonable proportions and abandon their imperialist policies.

It was in this context that the Labour government approached the question of the rearmament of Western Germany. If the Western powers could get a real and genuine settlement with Soviet Russia, the matter of German rearmament would become less important and fall into its natural place. But if they could not get this agreement, they would have to consider the defense of the West and that included the defense of Western Germany. If the West Germans were not to be allowed to defend themselves, then an obligation rested upon the occupying powers to defend them and that had been accepted. What did that mean for Britain and the other Atlantic powers? Were they to provide all the men and materials to defend Germany? Or, alternatively, were the occupying powers to withdraw, leaving an unarmed Western Germany as the neighbor of an Eastern Germany with her para-military organization, the armed satellites, and the Soviet Union? Neither of these propositions, in the Labour government's opinion, was a practical one. The only other course was to allow Germany to make her contribution to the integrated forces for the defense of Western Europe. This could be done only with the full agreement and co-operation of the German people. Britain had accepted the need for a contribution from Germany, but the time, the method, and the conditions would require a great deal of working out. There was, first of all, the provision of arms. Obviously, the rearmament of the countries of the Atlantic Treaty must precede that of Germany, and the building up of forces in the democratic states must precede the creation of German forces. Secondly, the arrangements must be such that German units were integrated in the defense forces in a way which would preclude the emergence again of a German military menace. Finally, there must be agreement with the Germans themselves. German democracy must make sure that the armed forces would be its servants and not its masters. The Labour government agreed that there was always the danger of an emergence again of the same kind of forces that made Germany a menace, but it did not think that it was possible to get rid of that menace by allowing Germany to remain as a vacuum. Nor was it possible to take the line that it wished to see Germany back in the comity of nations and yet suggest that somehow or other she should be occupied and protected by other powers. In due course, occupation would end and the German people would become entirely responsible for their own country. If that was to be, sometime or other Germany would have to be on terms of complete equality and she would have to take her share in the defense of democracy. To those who had protested against "rearmament in the abstract" without considering what was the real position of armaments in the world today, the Prime Minister directed the question, "Are you prepared to go and defend Germany while they do nothing?" The only answer, in his opinion, was that "there should be democratic forces democratically controlled in Germany."[57]

The Labour government took the view that it was impossible to discuss the question of German rearmament in isolation, insisting that the problem must be considered in the wider context of how the tensions existing in the world could be reduced. The government had been forced to build up its contributions to the defense of the West "owing to the continued aggressiveness of the Soviet Union." Those forces were entirely for defense. The Labour government had no aggressive designs on anybody and it sought to settle its problems always by peaceful means. It was this resolve that defined its attitude toward the proposed four-power meetings. While anxious to bring about the meetings, the government was seeking to ensure that the agenda corresponded with the realities of the world situation. To rush into a matter like this with an ill-considered agenda or an agenda which restricted the essential matters for discussion would result only in failure. Nor did the government accept the suggestion frequently put forward by the Opposition that all these difficulties could be smoothed out by a meeting of three or four men. It did not believe in "these dramatic meetings, miraculously changing the whole situation." All four powers had their own points of view which had to be considered. The government was, therefore, taking counsel with the other Western powers, considering the various items that might be raised in the agenda and making careful preparation for the proposed meetings. The Labour government was most reluctant, as were other nations of the West, to increase its armaments; it did not want these burdens on its own people. Consequently, in welcoming any opportunity to discuss these matters, it was quite certain that the desire of the people all over the world, not excluding those behind the Iron Curtain, was "for relief from this burden and for getting on with the real job of

[57] 484 *H.C.Deb.*, February 12, 1951, cols. 66–67.

creating increased prosperity and happiness, instead of devoting this mass of treasure and work to armaments." The Labour government would do its utmost to seek a meeting and to secure agreement. As Prime Minister Attlee expressed this determination: "We have to find some way by which the free world and the totalitarian world are able to live together."[58]

It was evident to the Labour government that present events in the Far East and in Europe offered a warning in terms of other problems and other areas. The moral was plain to draw. There were no free countries behind the Iron Curtain and on this side of it there was no safety in weakness or in isolation. If free countries wished to remain free, they must not only develop their own internal health and strength but concert with other free countries for their safety. In particular, there was the problem of the Middle East, traditionally the scene of international disagreement and rivalry. The defense, as well as the stability and prosperity, of this area had been an essential part of Labour's foreign policy. In order again to make its own position clear, the Labour government, on May 19, even before the aggression in Korea, had reaffirmed with the United States its continued concern for the independence, integrity, and security of Greece, Turkey, and Persia. As the Foreign Secretary explained, "We are convinced that the strengthening of the North Atlantic Treaty will be conducive to that end." His government was determined to continue its policy of direct support to these and to other countries who were striving through military and economic efforts to safeguard their independence and territorial integrity. The Labour government had also derived considerable satisfaction from the conclusion of the Tripartite Declaration, with France and the United States, of common intent to insist on the preservation of peace and stability in the Middle East. "Turning their backs on any old-fashioned ideas of sphere of influence," the three governments took the opportunity of proclaiming "their unalterable opposition to the use of force or threat of force between any of the States in that area." In return for assurances given by the Middle Eastern states that they would not undertake any act of aggression against any other state, the three governments declared that if they should find that any of these states was preparing to violate frontiers or armistice lines, they would, "consistently with their obligations as Members of the United Nations, immediately take action, both within and outside the United Nations, to prevent such violation." This joint statement was proof, in the Labour govern-

[58] *Ibid.*, col. 70. Cf. Elaine Windrich, "British Labour and the Defense of the West," *World Affairs Interpreter*, XXIII (April 1952), 72–82.

ment's opinion, that the three powers had "abjured any idea of selfish national rivalry or sphere of influence in the Middle East." On the contrary, with a common approach to these issues, they were animated by one and the same desire—the promotion of peace and stability in the area. They hoped for a strengthening of their friendly relations with all the countries concerned, whose independence, integrity, and prosperity they desired to see maintained and developed. The Labour government was watching with sympathy the practical development of plans and reforms under discussion in Persia, Iraq, and other Middle Eastern countries. In addition, it welcomed the support of the Middle Eastern countries in the United Nations for the General Assembly resolution, "United Action for Peace," providing for action to be taken by members of the United Nations in the event of a threat to peace or an aggression, should the Security Council be prevented by the veto from taking action. "Within this framework," the Foreign Secretary declared, "many obstinate problems might well be settled. That was the spirit in which they would continue to work."[59]

Although the spirit of international collaboration in the Middle East had been most heartening and had given the Labour government "solid grounds for hope for the future," the pattern of co-operation was not complete. There was a piece still to be fitted in : that piece was Egypt, a territory representing a center of communications of tremendous importance not only to Britain but to the rest of the world as well. It had been the desire of the Labour government "to settle outstanding differences with Egypt in the spirit of the long tradition of friendship between the two countries on a basis of equality and with full respect for the independence and sovereignty of Egypt." The two governments had in fact been in contact for many months on defense matters, with the object of removing misunderstandings and difficulties which had arisen with regard to the provisions of the 1936 treaty. In these discussions, no difference in principle had arisen over the defense of the Middle East in time of war. Both for this reason and in view of its obligations under the treaty, the Labour government had continued to give assistance to the Egyptian government in the training and equipment of its forces. For the government to deny such assistance to Egypt, as proposed by the Opposition, would be contrary to treaty obligations. The difficulties which had not yet been resolved did not concern action in the event of war but the question of defense measures in time of peace. The Egyptian government had stated that it would insist on the evacuation of British troops from the Canal Zone and on the unification of the Nile Valley under the

[59] 481 H.C.Deb., November 29, 1950, cols. 1167–68. Also cf. Lord Henderson, 168 H.L.Deb., July 26, 1950, cols. 759–62.

Egyptian crown. The Labour government was eager to solve this problem in good faith and co-operation; that had always been its policy. It was not pursuing a policy of occupation in the old sense but one of mutual defense. Just as in the Atlantic Pact, it was here also striving for a solution which would be a contribution to the peace of the world. The principle of common-defense measures in time of peace had been accepted by all the Western powers as fully compatible with national independence and sovereignty, and other countries in the Middle East were co-operating in this way. What was at stake in this matter concerned not merely the United Kingdom and Egypt, but the safety and independence of other countries as well. The Labour government had, therefore, no intention of taking any steps or agreeing to any measures which would leave the Middle East defenseless or would needlessly prejudice the safety of free and friendly countries in that area. As to the Sudan, the government, while fully recognizing the vital importance of the Nile waters to Egypt, reaffirmed its pledge that the Sudanese should in due course freely decide their own future. "It would be a tragedy," Mr. Bevin said, "if the clock were to be set back and the progress of the Sudanese people, which in many ways, both in economic and other respects, is a model to others, should be halted." In spite of the difficulties, the Foreign Secretary did not despair of being able to reconcile differences with Egypt on a basis of full respect for Egyptian independence and sovereignty. The Labour government, for its part, would adhere to the 1936 treaty until and unless it could be replaced by mutual agreement, but it did not admit that the treaty could be amended or abrogated by unilateral action. Mr. Bevin assured the Egyptian government that in any future discussion it would be met in the friendliest possible spirit and with the feeling that both countries had a duty to perform, not only to themselves but to the rest of the free world.[60]

The Labour government's task was to persuade the Egyptians to face the "inescapable fact" that they could not stand aside in any major conflict and to convince them of the dangers to them and to the entire Middle East of neglecting defensive preparations in time of peace. In undertaking this task, the new Foreign Secretary, Herbert Morrison, asserted that he was desirous of carrying on the "unflagging efforts" of his predecessor Ernest Bevin, to place Anglo-Egyptian relations on a footing which would both preserve the best elements in the close relationship which had long linked the two countries and, at the same time, to take account of the realities of the dangerous situa-

[60] 481 H.C.Deb., November 20, 1950, cols. 36–38. For background of negotiations cf. Papers Regarding the Negotiations for a Revision of the Anglo-Egyptian Treaty of 1936, British State Papers, Cmd. 7179 (1947).

tion which faced the civilized world today. Morrison, like Bevin, believed that one of the cornerstones on which stability and security in the Middle East must rest was friendship and co-operation with Egypt in the various fields of common interest. The Labour government, well aware of the difficulties which faced the Egyptian government and knowing that the stand taken by Egypt had its roots deep in the past, had tried to approach their common problems with patience and understanding of these difficulties. Unfortunately, its patience and understanding had not always been reciprocated, and it was still faced with "uncompromising insistence on demands which bore no relation to present-day realities." The problem of the presence of British troops in Egypt was not now a purely Anglo-Egyptian problem, Morrison reiterated. Britain was a power bearing responsibility in the Middle East on behalf of the Commonwealth and the Western Allies as a whole. Egypt was in some respects the key to the Middle East: "situated as she is on the bridge between two Continents and upon a vital link in the sea communications between the Eastern and Western hemispheres, she is an objective of first importance for any aggressive Power in the Eastern Mediterranean and the Levant." The Labour government felt that the destinies and civilization of the two countries were bound up together and that it was unrealistic for Egypt to pretend that she could avoid danger by refusing to allow Britain to share in the defensive organization of the area. Moreover, Egypt could no more stand alone in the defense of her own country than Britain could in the defense of her territory. The government was confident that should war be forced upon the free nations, the Egyptians would, as in the past, join with them in resisting the aggressor. But the vital difference between the two governments was disagreement over the measures required to prepare to meet such an emergency. The Labour government felt that, without extensive preparations in time of peace, the cause would be lost before the struggle began. In common with its North Atlantic and Commonwealth allies, it had assumed a great burden in time of peace in order to make the world safe for those countries with whom it shared a common heritage and civilization. It invited Egypt's participation as an equal in this common effort to make the world safe; it wanted to plan their relationship on an entirely new basis. If Egypt rejected that invitation, the government could not allow that rejection to prejudice the fulfillment of its international responsibilities. But it would not give up hope of persuading the Egyptian government to offer the spontaneous co-operation which would make their task immeasurably easier.[61]

[61] Foreign Secretary Morrison, 491 *H.C.Deb.*, July 30, 1951, cols. 973–74.

In spite of the Labour government's efforts for a settlement, the Egyptian government decreed the abrogation of the Anglo-Egyptian Treaty of 1936 and the Condominium Agreement of 1899 regarding the Sudan. Refusing to recognize the legality of the unilateral denunciation, the Labour government took immediate action. First, it assured the Sudanese people that there was no question of a constitutional bargain with Egypt over their heads by reaffirming the fundamental principles of its policy in regard to the Sudan, namely, that it would agree to no change in the status of the Sudan without consultation with the Sudanese and that it would maintain the right of the Sudanese freely to choose their ultimate status. Secondly, in a note to Cairo relating to the riots and demonstrations, it reminded the Egyptian government of its responsibility in the event of the loss of British life or damage to property. In addition, encouraged by the firm support given by the United States, France, and Turkey to its stand against the Egyptian moves, the government decided to go ahead with its planned approach to Egypt on the basis of the four-power Middle East proposals. These proposals, while taking account of Egypt's sensibilities, would enable the 1936 treaty to be superseded by multilateral arrangements for the provision of adequate defenses for the Middle East and particularly for Egypt. At the same time, however, the Labour government made it clear that it would not submit to the unilateral denunciation of a treaty which was vitally important to the whole defense of the Middle East and the free world. This could not be done, the Foreign Secretary insisted.

We are there, we have the right to be there, and we shall stand absolutely firm in exercising our undoubted rights until some new agreed arrangement comes along to be substituted for it.[62]

The Labour government regretted that the Egyptian government had seen fit to introduce legislation designed to abrogate the treaties between the two countries, particularly in view of the fact that, as the Egyptians well knew, proposals were about to be made to them in connection with the organization of Middle Eastern security, which would have had a direct bearing on the Anglo-Egyptian position. Nevertheless, as indicated in the Foreign Secretary's statement of October 9, the action taken by the Egyptians would not affect the Labour government's decision to put forward the new offer. The four-power defense proposals, as presented to the Egyptian government, envisaged a new Allied Middle East Command which Egypt would be invited to join as an equal partner. In the event of full Egyptian co-

[62] Address at Staines, October 12, 1951, *The Times*, October 13, 1951, p. 6; government statement of October 9, 1951, *ibid.*, October 10, 1951, p. 4.

operation, Britain would agree to the supersession of the Anglo-Egyptian Treaty of 1936. The present British base in the Suez Canal Zone would be formally handed over to the Egyptian government on the understanding that it would become an Allied base with full Egyptian participation. Since the Labour government did not agree that the defense of the Middle East and the Sudan question were in any way connected, it presented a separate memorandum containing proposals for the future of the Sudan. In the memorandum, the government called for "an international commission to reside in the Sudan watching over constitutional developments of that country and tendering advice to the Condomini; a joint Anglo-Egyptian statement of common principles with regard to the Sudan; an international guarantee of the Nile Waters agreement; establishment of a Nile Waters development authority to develop the Nile possibly with assistance from the International Bank and an agreed date to be fixed for attainment of self-government by the Sudanese as a first step on the way to the choice by the Sudanese of their final status." The British proposals, the Labour government insisted, represented great care on its part to understand and to meet the Egyptian point of view, and also they appeared to be the only way to provide an adequate safeguard for Egyptian interests in the Sudan. In view of the wide differences in culture, race, religion, and political development existing among the Sudanese, the process of attaining self-government would require the co-operation of Egypt with Great Britain in the Sudan.[63]

The four-power proposals for the defense of the Middle East met with a flat rejection: the Egyptian government refused even to consider the new initiative and, instead, proceeded to obtain parliamentary enactment of the decrees abrogating the Anglo-Egyptian treaties. For the Labour government it was necessary to decide, in consultation with its allies, what the next step was to be. As far as it was concerned, it had "no desire to control in any way the policy of the Egyptian Government"; it regarded Egypt and treated her as a fully free and independent nation. At the same time, however, it was "most intimately concerned with the strategic needs of the area and in particular, with the defence of the vital Suez Canal area against any potential aggressor." Its latest proposals to the Egyptians made it perfectly clear that this was the sole consideration behind its policy. It had offered the Egyptians full and free participation in a defense organization which involved no more interference with Egyptian sovereignty than the North Atlantic Treaty interfered with its own. Either the Egyptians could share responsibility for the defense of this vital area with all

[63] *The Times*, October 15, 1951, p. 6.

the rights and obligations which such acceptance would entail or they could show themselves to be a people devoid of any sense of international responsibility, whose government fomented international disputes in order to divert popular attention from much-needed reforms at home. It seemed to the Labour government that, unhappily, they were moving in the latter direction. The Egyptians could not have their cake and eat it too, the Foreign Secretary warned; for themselves they loudly demanded independence and freedom from foreign occupation, but for the Sudanese they said "independence," but only under the Egyptian crown. Anyone who had followed the foreign policy of Great Britain in the last six years, Morrison asserted, could attest that charges of "British imperialism" were least of all applicable to the Labour government.[64]

Although it had welcomed the emergence of national consciousness and national aspirations in the Middle East, knowing them to be "potentially good influences" and indeed "essential to the maturity of a nation," the Labour government felt that there was "every difference between patriotism and xenophobia." As Britain and the West had learned, the interests of a nation could not be served by "unbridled nationalism." Those who espoused it sooner or later destroyed themselves and their followers. In addition to nationalism, the other major force shaping policies and events in the Middle East was "the urge for social and material benefit." Much of the frustration existing in the Middle East was due to the failure to satisfy this urge. The best ideals of the West—the ideals of social justice and conquest of poverty, disease, and illiterary—had deeply stirred the peoples of the Middle East, particularly since the second World War. In many parts of the area society was still organized on feudal lines, with glaring extremes between rich and poor—between a small minority of extremely wealthy individuals who had profited from the economic impact of the West and the great mass of poverty-stricken peasants. Little had been done so far to remove these anomalies. Taken as a whole, the Middle East was poor; it had vast regions that were deserts incapable of developing on an economic basis. Nevertheless, it did have great resources, particularly in oil, which required development. Since the end of the war, the Middle East governments had shown an increasing realization of the need for economic and social development. During these past five years a number of over-all development plans had been prepared, and a number of individual schemes had been surveyed. All these measures, however, represented only the first step in tackling the immense problems of poverty, disease, and illiteracy in the area. In

[64] Address at Greenford and Acton, October 15, 1951, *ibid.*, October 16, 1951, p. 6.

most cases, the plans were still mainly at the paper stage. Further progress in the area as a whole now depended largely on two main factors: first, on the willingness of the Middle Eastern governments to improve their administration and, secondly, on the provision from outside sources of the necessary capital and technical skill which were not available in the area. With regard to the second factor, the Labour government had so far made the major contribution. This policy had been carried out in a number of ways, both directly by the government and indirectly by British oil companies and other firms. In addition to direct forms of economic aid—including contributions to the Arab refugee problem and loans to Jordan and Iraq—the government had, despite the strain on its own balance of payments, permitted a number of Middle Eastern countries to draw extensively on their sterling balances which were blocked during the war. A series of sterling re-lease agreements with Egypt, Iraq, Jordan, and Israel, beginning in 1947, had enabled those countries to cover their financial requirements, including large purchases of capital goods. The British government had made every conceivable effort to supply the capital goods required to equip the new industries which had developed in the Middle East since the war and for the many new development projects. But perhaps the most significant factor in the postwar economy of the Middle East had been the development of its oil resources through the efforts of British, as well as American, oil companies. Oil had become the most important industry and source of revenue for a number of Middle Eastern countries and it had made a major contribution toward the financing of projects designed to raise productivity and living stand-ards in the area. In addition to the revenues, the oil industry had brought to the region substantial economic and social benefits, such as transport facilities, water supplies, and health, education, and welfare services. Revenues from oil had vastly increased and concession agree-ments were being modified to take account of changes in circumstances which had occurred. It was the earnest hope of the Labour govern-ment that the future development of the Middle Eastern oil industry would be toward even closer partnership between the countries possess-ing the oil and the foreign companies contributing the capital, technical skill, and marketing facilities, so that they might "jointly and in full harmony develop the natural resources of the area to meet the world's requirements." The Foreign Secretary could "imagine no greater contribution to the solution of the Middle East problems than the wise and effective ulitisation of these oil revenues for purposes of social reform and raising the living standards of the people, not only in the oil producing countries, but throughout the whole area." Morrison was sure that the British would be "ready to contribute towards this objective by any means within their power."[65]

Unfortunately, in the Labour government's view, Persia, like Egypt, afforded an excellent example of the difficulties which excessive national consciousness and national aspirations, unless allied with statesmanship, could bring in their train. The concession which the Anglo-Iranian Oil Company had been operating in southern Persia since 1933 had, in the past, provided an opportunity for British technical skill and commercial knowledge to come to the aid of the Persians in the development of the natural resources of the country and at the same time to secure an increase in the revenues of the Persian state. During the years since the present concession was negotiated, the A.I.O.C. had not only brought very considerable prosperity to the oil fields but had provided a steadily increasing revenue to the Persian state which, if properly handled, could have brought a great increase of prosperity to the country as a whole. Indeed, when the Persian government, in 1949, evolved a seven-year plan of economic development based upon a report prepared by an American firm of consultants and estimated to cost £210 million, which was to have been entirely financed out of its share of the oil revenues, it looked as though "a new era for the Persian masses was in sight." When the Persians asked for a greater share in the profits of oil, the A.I.O.C., with the approval of the British government, negotiated with the Persians the Supplemental Oil Agreement of 1949. Under this agreement, which was retroactive in character, Persian revenues would have received some £38 million for the years 1948–50, over and above £38,670,000 which would have been obtained under the 1933 concession. The Supplemental Oil Agreement was signed by the Persian minister of finance in July 1949 and was submitted to the Majlis for ratification. Dissident elements in that parliament succeeded in preventing its ratification for over eighteen months, and in the meanwhile a vocal minority on the Majlis Oil Commission, after rejecting the Supplemental Oil Agreement, began to exert increasing pressure for nationalization. The British government made it clear to General Razmara, who was then the Persian prime minister, that the company's concession could not legally be terminated by an act of nationalization; nevertheless, the company voluntarily informed him, on February 10, that it would be ready to negotiate an entirely new agreement based on an equal sharing of profits. It was almost immediately after this that General Razmara was assassinated and that an extreme right-wing group of deputies, the so-called "National Front" under the leadership of Dr.

[65] 491 *H.C.Deb.*, July 30, 1951, cols. 960–70.

Mossadegh, pressed a demand for the complete nationalization of the oil industry. Both the Majlis and the Senate were induced to pass a resolution accepting the principle of nationalization and giving the oil commission a period of two months in which to work out the means of putting it into effect. The proposals produced by the oil commission, subsequently endorsed by the Majlis and the Senate, provided for the assumption of control by the Persian government over all the A.I.O.C. assets and operations in Persia, the revenues from which would be regarded as belonging to Persia. The effect of these measures involved a complete change in the company's position as provided for in the existing concession agreement which was valid until 1993. This change would be made unilaterally, although the concession agreement itself provided that it should not be altered, even by legislative action, otherwise than by agreement with the company. The Persian government, under Prime Minister Hussein Ala, resigned immediately after these proposals had been made known, even before they had been voted upon by the Majlis, and a new government under the National Front leader, Dr. Mossadegh, was formed.

From the very outset of the Persian crisis the Labour government had indicated its readiness to meet the legitimate aspirations of the Persian people. Sympathizing with the natural desire of the Persians to control the mineral wealth of their own soil, the government had agreed to accept the principle of nationalization. Even before the resignation of Prime Minister Ala, it had attempted, with the full agreement of the A.I.O.C., to reach an understanding with him on the lines along which a satisfactory arrangement between the Persian government and the company could be worked out. In general terms, these proposals, based on the principle of association between the government and the company, provided for the transfer of the company's operations in Persia to a new British company, on the board of which the Persian government would be represented; for a progressive increase in the already large proportion of Persians employed by the company throughout its operations and for an equal sharing of the profits of these operations between the Persian government and the new company. It was not possible for these suggestions to be pursued, however, before the oil commission's new proposals were issued and Prime Minister Ala's cabinet resigned. While the Labour government was still most anxious to settle this matter by negotiation, it could not negotiate under duress. Nor could it agree that the company's whole position in Persia should be radically altered by unilateral action when the agreement into which the Persian government freely entered with the company itself provided against such action. All that the Labour government asked was that agreements freely entered into under international auspices should not be broken unilaterally without discussion or negotiation. It was ready to sit down with the Persians and work out a solution in a reasonable atmosphere. In view of its longstanding ties of friendship and its mutual interests, political as well as economic, with the Persian people, it was convinced that such a solution could be found.[66]

The Labour government felt that the essential point in the Persian dispute was not the right of a sovereign state by its legislation to nationalize commercial enterprises carried on within its borders or the measure of compensation it should pay for doing so. The real issue was that if the Persian government had grievances against the A.I.O.C., the remedy was to seek arbitration as provided by Articles 22 and 26 of the 1933 concession agreement. Since that remedy had been "rendered illusory" by the Persian government's repeated rejection of the company's offers "to discuss and seek to solve by agreement with the Imperial Government all outstanding questions," the British government, separately from the company, decided to bring the oil dispute before the International Court of Justice. At The Hague, the government asked the Court to declare that the Persian government was "under duty" to submit the dispute to arbitration as provided in the 1933 agreement and to accept and carry out any award issued as a result of such arbitration. Alternatively, the Court was asked to declare that the enforcement of the Oil Nationalization Act of May 1, 1951, effecting a unilateral alteration of the agreement's terms "would be an act contrary to international law," that by denying the exclusive legal remedy in Article 22, Persia would be committing "a denial of justice contrary to international law," that the 1933 agreement could not be legally altered except by negotiations with the company or under conditions provided by Article 26, and that Persia should give "full satisfaction and indemnity for all acts against the Company contrary to international law."[67] Although the conflict had been referred to the International Court for arbitration, the Labour government was "still anxious to see this dispute settled by negotiation." Its offer to send a special mission, if that would help, was still valid. Moreover, while it could not accept the right of the Persian government to repudiate contracts, it was prepared to consider a settlement which would involve some form of nationalization, provided the solution were satisfactory in other respects. The difficulty had been, and still was, that the Persian government had hitherto not seen fit to respond in any way to the

[66] Foreign Secretary Morrison, 487 H.C.Deb., May 1, 1951, cols. 1008–14.
[67] Text of British case, The Times, May 28, 1951, p. 3.

repeated suggestions of negotiation but on the contrary had indicated merely the intention to proceed unilaterally. The Labour government, however, refusing to accept such a procedure, earnestly hoped that "wiser counsels, taking full account of the dangerous potentialities of the present situation," would prevail in Teheran and that negotiations could be initiated "in an atmosphere of reason and goodwill."[68]

In accordance with its acceptance of the principle of nationalization and its readiness to negotiate a settlement on the basis of that principle, the Labour government supported the decision of the A.I.O.C. to send a mission to Teheran to discuss Persian plans for the nationalization of the oil industry. Unfortunately, without awaiting the results of the discussions with the company representatives in Teheran, the Iranian board which was to take over the company issued a proclamation that all the staff of the company were now employees of the Persian government and informed Mr. Drake, the company general manager, that in accordance with Article 2 of the nationalization law the entire proceeds from the sale of oil since March 20 now belonged to the Iranian nation. The company was to hand over immediately seventy-five percent of these proceeds to the Iranian government and the remaining twenty-five percent would be deposited in a bank against any future claims of the "former Company." When the company's delegation met the Persian representatives, it made proposals which were designed not only to meet the Persian government's present and urgent need for funds but also to indicate an arrangement which would maintain the efficiency of the industry and be consistent with the principle of nationalization. In its *aide memoire*, the company proposed that to solve the question of payments during negotiations, a sum of £10 million would be advanced to Iran immediately, against future concessional payments, and a further sum of £3 million would be paid monthly from July. In order to meet the terms of the nationalization law, it suggested that all the oil properties in Iran be vested in a Persian national oil company, and in consideration of such vesting the national oil company should grant the use of those assets to a new company to be established by the A.I.O.C. The new company would have a number of Persian directors on its board and would operate on behalf of the Persian national oil company. At the same time, the distribution of oil products within Persia itself would be transferred to an entirely Persian-owned and operated company on favorable terms, as regards the transfer of existing assets, to ensure that Iranian oil

[68] Foreign Secretary Morrison, 488 *H.C.Deb.*, May 29, 1951, cols. 40–43, repeated offers of negotiation made in British Notes of May 2 and May 19, 1951. Cf. *The Times,* May 21, 1951, p. 3.

could still be used with profit both to Iran and the company through the world-wide organization of the company and yet be under the actual ownership of Iran. The company's offer, the Labour government was convinced, would be regarded by "all fair-minded opinion as eminently reasonable." As the Foreign Secretary explained:

Money for present needs is there, acceptance of the principle of nationalisation is there, and an obvious foundation for fruitful partnership is there.

Unhappily, however, the Persian delegates required only half an hour in which to arrive at a contrary opinion, declaring that the company's proposals conflicted with the new nationalization law and that as they had no authority to deviate from the letter of the nationalization law, they considered the discussions closed. In view of this decision, the British government had no alternative but to recall the company's delegation. Meanwhile, it proposed to follow up its application to the Court at The Hague by a further application for an indication of provisional measures to preserve the rights of the United Kingdom, pending a decision on the merits of the case.[69]

The Labour government was attacked by the Opposition parties for its policy—or, as they put it, lack of policy—in the Persian oil crisis. Condemning the government's lack of "foresight, preparation, firmness and care" in allowing the Iranian dispute to reach its present pitch, Anthony Eden warned that any stoppage in the flow of oil from Iran would have grave strategic implications for the whole free world. The evacuation of the British from Iran, he said, would be a surrender to force. Simultaneously, the president of the Liberal party, Philip Fothergill, convinced that it was high time that Britain made a show of "physical and moral resolution" in an area for which she had special responsibility, demanded that the government take "effective military precautions" as a prelude to a "vigourous diplomatic offensive." The Opposition was undoubtedly aware that if Britain were to send troops into southern Persia, Soviet Russia, under the 1921 treaty with Iran, would have the right to occupy northern Persia. Nevertheless, Tory spokesman Duncan Sandys was "perfectly prepared to say," in words echoed by his colleague Colonel O. E. Crosthwaite-Eyre, that if the only alternative was to "scuttle" British interests in Persia, with all the grave consequences which that would have both now and in the future, then he certainly thought that the government "should not hesitate to use troops or any other appropriate measures" that might be necessary in order to discharge its responsibilities to its own people and

[69] Foreign Secretary Morrison, 488 *H.C.Deb.*, June 14, 1951, cols. 2516–17; 489 *H.C.Deb.*, June 19, 1951, cols. 240–42; June 20, 1951, cols. 519–26.

to the rest of the free world. The Labour party, on the other hand, did not agree that the choice of policy in Iran was between "diplomatic catastrophe and weakness and gunboat psychology." If the government sent in troops to protect the oil wells, then it would be committing an act of aggression against a friendly power. It had no right to send its troops into somebody else's country, against the wishes of the government of that country, because it had a factory there and was not satisfied with the nationalization terms. It could not do in the twentieth century what was not uncommonly done in the nineteenth century; it could not colonize countries which had reached the stage of self-government. The government certainly did not wish evacuation to take place. It "remained ready and willing to discuss all outstanding points fully and frankly." At the same time, however, it warned the Persians that they were responsible under international law for ensuring the protection of any British subjects in Iran and that should they prove incapable of discharging that task, the British would be compelled to assume it themselves, using such means as were necessary. There was "a world of difference," in Labour's opinion, between occupying a province of Persia, which meant running the oil wells under British military government, and sending in troops to rescue British citizens who were in danger of their lives.[70]

The Labour government's determination to reopen discussions with the Persians was finally realized through the efforts of President Truman's special representative to Iran, Averell Harriman, who succeeded in obtaining from the Persian government a formula for resuming negotiations. While still anxious for a settlement of the oil dispute, the British government insisted that two prior conditions were necessary if the negotiations were to stand any chance of succeeding. Earlier negotiations had broken down because the Persians had insisted that they should take place solely on the basis of the text of the Oil Nationalization Law of May 1. This law, which attempted to provide for the practical implementation of the principle of nationalization, had been hastily drafted without the necessary reflection or consultation with qualified technicians and was, in the British government's opinion, not only entirely unworkable in practice but represented a clear breach of the Persian government's contractual obligations. The British had accepted the "principle of nationalization" and were quite willing to conduct negotiations on the basis of that principle, but they could not accept the position that negotiations should take place on the basis of the rigid text of a single Persian law. The second

[70] For the government's defense cf. Foreign Secretary Herbert Morrison and R. H. S. Crossman, 489 *H.C.Deb.*, June 21, 1951, cols. 772–74, 824–33.

prerequisite was that the existing tense atmosphere in the oil fields should be relieved. There was strong popular feeling in Great Britain about the administrative interference and provocation carried out by Persian authorities against British personnel in the oil fields, and it was clearly impossible for negotiations to succeed if these conditions persisted.

With assurances from the Persian government that a basis for negotiation existed, the Labour government made one final attempt to reach an agreement by sending to Iran a new British mission headed by the Lord Privy Seal, Richard Stokes. The eight-point proposals put forward by the Stokes mission fully accepted nationalization of the oil industry in Iran on the basis of the nationalization law of March 20 and offered a practical method, on commercial terms, for continuing co-operation between Britain and Iran. Under these proposals, the A.I.O.C. as such would cease to operate in Iran and the whole of its assets would be transferred to the National Iranian Oil Company under compensation arrangements. The N.I.O.C. would sell oil under a long-term contract to a British purchasing organization outside Iran, which would use the world-wide facilities of the A.I.O.C. to sell the oil in world markets. The N.I.O.C. would also be able to sell oil to other customers, subject to the terms of the long-term contract. The purchasing organization would pay commercial prices for the oil bought, subject to a discount which would have the effect of sharing the profits fifty-fifty between the N.I.O.C. and the purchasing organization. To ensure that the oil would be delivered under the contract, the purchasing organization would agree with the N.I.O.C. on the establishment of a nonprofit agency inside Iran to be responsible for running the technical side of the industry. This would have a number of Persian directors, and the British technical staff in Iran would work for this agency, subject to suitable arrangements to be made.[71]

In the course of the discussions between the Stokes mission and the Persian government, it became increasingly clear that the latter had no intention of negotiating on the basis agreed by Mr. Harriman with both governments. Instead, the Persian government was, in effect, insisting upon the full implementation of the nine-point nationalization law of May 1. Furthermore, the Persian government took no steps to mitigate the campaign of interference with the company's personnel in southern Persia. In a final effort to devise acceptable working conditions for British technicians in the oil industry, Mr. Stokes put forward as a minimum requirement the appointment of a British general manager who would have full responsibility for directing

[71] Text of proposals, *The Times*, August 14, 1951, p. 6; August 16, 1951, p. 4.

operations, though under the authority of the N.I.O.C. It was when this proposal was rejected and when the Persian government refused to agree to any arrangement which would have allowed the British staff to work under proper management and in acceptable working conditions that the Stokes mission was recalled to London. While deeply regretting the Persian government's departure from the basis of the negotiations established by Mr. Harriman, the Labour government remained prepared at any time to reopen the discussions on the basis of the Harriman formula, whenever any disposition was shown on the Persian side to consider the questions in dispute in a spirit of reason and good will. Meanwhile, it would take its stand on the interim decision of the International Court, indicating that neither the Iranian nor British governments should take any measures of a kind designed to hinder the operations of the oil company's management as it was constituted before May 1, 1951, pending a final decision by the Court on the case before it. A nucleus of British technicians would remain at Abadan ready to start the oil flowing again should it be possible to reach agreement in the future.[72]

The Persian government's announcement that the remaining British staff of the A.I.O.C. would be given one week to leave the oil fields at Abadan put an end to the Labour government's policy of maintaining operations in Iran while seeking a basis for renewed negotiations. Although the expulsion order had created a situation which might well have justified the use of force in order to preserve the British rights and interests involved, the Labour government was reluctant to take any action which might have the effect of weakening the authority of the United Nations, on whose principles its policy was based. It decided that the right course in the present circumstances was to bring the situation urgently before the Security Council, which was the appropriate body to deal with matters likely to endanger the maintenance of international peace and security and which had been notified of the provisional measures indicated by the International Court. In the Labour government's opinion, it was intolerable that one party to a matter laid before the International Court should be allowed to flout the Court's findings and to impose unilaterally its own will in regard to this matter. If Iran, an original signatory of the Charter, were allowed to continue on the path which she was now following, a grave step would be taken toward international anarchy. The rule of law as opposed to the rule of force could obviously prevail only if all concerned conformed to the decisions of the International Court—

[72] For breakdown of negotiations cf. *The Times*, August 23, 1951, p. 6; and Persian "counterproposals," *ibid.*, September 6, 1951, p. 4; September 7, 1951, p. 4.

the principal judicial organ of the United Nations. Thus, in issuing an arbitrary order expelling three hundred fifty members of the British staff, the Iranian government was "acting in a manner entirely contrary to the elementary principles of international usage" and by so doing, it was "creating a highly inflammatory situation" which might well be a threat to international peace and security. Concerned with the dangers inherent in this situation, the British government submitted to the Security Council a draft resolution calling upon the government of Iran "to act in all respects in conformity with the provisional measures indicated by the Court and in particular to permit the continued residence at Abadan of the staff affected by the recent expulsion orders." In view of the last precipitate steps of the Iranian government, it was essential for the Security Council to pass this draft resolution before the expulsion order of September 25 came into effect. The British delegate therefore asked the Council "to indicate to the Iranian Government that it should not proceed in this arbitrary manner and that its latest arbitrary action should be rescinded before the ultimatum expires."[73]

Failing to obtain immediate intervention by the Security Council, the Labour government was faced wtih the alternative of awaiting the expiration of the Persian expulsion order or withdrawing the remaining British technicians from Abadan. In taking the latter course, it noted that such action in no way lessened the urgency of its proposals calling upon Persia to rescind the ultimatum and to abide by the provisional injunctions of the International Court. However, in the absence of firm American support and with no clear assurance of seven affirmative votes, the government was obliged to shift much of the emphasis of its proposals from the interim findings of the Court to a resumption of negotiations. The revised proposals, while giving full expression to the insistence of the United States on "a resumption of negotiations at the earliest possible moment," secured the British position, though far less forcefully than in the first text, by providing that further efforts to resolve the differences between the parties should be in accordance with the principles of the provisional measures indicated by the International Court, unless mutually agreeable arrangements were made "consistent with the purposes and principles of the United Nations Charter." In addition, the resolution called for "the avoidance of any action which would have the effect of further aggravating the situation or prejudicing the rights, claims or positions of the parties concerned." In presenting this proposal to

[73] Sir Gladwyn Jebb, *Official Records of the Security Council, Sixth Year*, Five Hundred and Fifty-ninth Meeting, October 1, 1951, pp. 11–13.

the Security Council, the British delegate, Sir Gladwyn Jebb, earnestly appealed to the Iranian government "to forget old imagined wrongs and to join in a constructive approach to the solution of this important problem."[74]

With the Security Council's decision to defer further consideration of the British appeal pending a final pronouncement by the International Court of Justice on its own competence in the matter, the Labour government ruefully bowed to the evident fact that the United Nations would not intervene effectively in the Persian oil dispute. The British delegate, "with the greatest reluctance," accepted the joint amendments by India and Yugoslavia which, by omitting any direct reference to the interim findings of the International Court, reduced the British proposals merely to a suggestion that negotiations between the parties should be resumed. Even this emasculated draft, however, was rejected by Dr. Mossadegh as "unjustifiable interference by the Security Council in the sovereign affairs of Persia." In addition, a last-minute change of front by Yugoslavia, which now could tolerate no reference to the Court's interim findings even in the preamble of the revised British resolution, made it evident that the requisite seven votes were no longer available. Rather than give the Persians a moral victory by pressing his proposals to a vote, the British delegate supported a French motion to adjourn the oil dispute. For the Labour government, some satisfaction could be derived from the fact that the Security Council, although reluctant to take a strong position on the issue, had clearly committed itself to the final judgment of the Court of The Hague on the question of competence, and to that extent, the Persian government was still subject to the Court's provisional indications, whatever its obstinacy in rejecting them as a violation of Persian sovereignty.

Before the Security Council adjourned, the British delegate did not let the occasion pass without expressing a feeling of "restlessness, not to say indignation," over the clear imputations that his government was at fault in asking the Council to uphold the provisional indications of the Court, that the case had been brought prematurely, or that there was no evidence of a denial of justice. He found it hard to understand all these criticisms and the lack of support for the British in bringing the case to the Council. The British government, throughout, had taken the greatest care to act as a loyal member of the United Nations and to follow scrupulously the proceedings enjoined by the Charter for the settlement of disputes. It had observed all the methods indicated by Article 33, but its efforts to negotiate a settlement had

[74] *Official Records of the Security Council, Sixth Year*, Five Hundred and Sixtieth Meeting, October 15, 1951, pp. 1–3.

been rendered fruitless by the Persian government's negative attitude, and its recourse to the International Court had been without avail as Persia had frustrated any judgment that the Court might give by flouting its interim findings. In spite of this, a cabinet mission had been dispatched to Teheran and advantage had been taken of President Truman's generous action in sending Mr. Harriman as a conciliator. There could be no doubt that there had been a denial of justice. What other course had been open to the British government than to seek the Council's support in reaching a just settlement? Since the Council had now declined to act effectively, the British delegate could not help thinking that this would create a serious precedent for the future. This tendency, he declared, would be to diminish the Council, the Court, and the United Nations itself. "If States were thus denied redress, they would be increasingly reluctant to bring their disputes to the United Nations: if the rule of law were rejected, a step would have been taken towards the rule of anarchy." The Council as a whole, Sir Gladwyn Jebb observed, seemed to ignore these dangers, but it would be a pity if a member came to them asking for simple justice only to have it refused. Had the British government's modified proposals received seven votes, he said, it would have been under some moral obligation to resume negotiations. Even now, the British Government would not refuse to discuss the matter further if Persia showed some change of attitude. The trouble was that Dr. Mossadegh, far from making genuine counterproposals, resorted to a mechanical repetition of ultimatums, and no government or company could accept his views on questions of compensation and the sale of oil to Britain. How could the Persian government conceivably pay compensation, or even discuss such questions, if it had not the revenues with which to pay or the oil to sell? There was nothing in these various offers that the British government had made, and was still willing to make, that was inconsistent with full and complete nationalization. The British delegate continued to hope that the Persian prime minister would still accept the will and determination of the Labour government to reach a settlement satisfactory to both parties.[75]

The Labour government's foreign policy, and particularly its policy in the Middle East, became one of the most important issues in the General Election of October 1951. On the whole, the Opposition parties agreed with the government's support for the United Nations, its fulfillment of British obligations in Korea, its rearmament program, and its participation in the North Atlantic Treaty to strengthen the defense of the West against armed aggression. On questions of

[75] *Ibid.*, Five Hundred and Sixty-fifth Meeting, October 19, 1951, pp. 6–9.

Middle Eastern policy, however, there was a vast difference of outlook and approach between the two competing groups. The events in the Middle East which occurred during the period of the election campaign—the worsening of the oil dispute with Persia and British evacuation, under pressure, of the great oil refinery at Abadan; Egypt's sudden abrogation of the 1936 treaty and her attempt to oust British forces and authority from the Suez Canal zone and the Sudan—were pointed to by the Opposition parties as examples of the government's "inexpert handling of foreign affairs" and of its failure to resort to "strong action." The "logic of Conservative arguments" and "their real complaint," according to Labour, was that the government "did not resort to force and become involved in all the incalculable risks of war." Behind the issues of Egypt and Iran, the Labour party maintained, was "one great question : Are you going to have peace or war ?" Its answer was that in a dangerous world the statesmanship of Mr. Attlee and the policies of the Labour party were more likely to help in preserving the peace and avoiding war than were the statesmanship of Mr. Churchill and the policies of Conservatism. The Tories were "the nineteenth century party"; they still thought "in terms of Victorian imperialism and colonial exploitation"; their reaction in a crisis was "to threaten force." Judging by the "semi-hysteria of the Tory back benchers about Persia, the attitude of Tory newspapers, the line Mr. Churchill took about India, the Imperialist background and thinking of so many Conservatives and their frequent strong-arm talk," the Labour party was convinced that peace was "safer under a Labour Government than it would be under the Tories."[76]

The Labour party—"proud of its record, sure in its policies"—confidently appealed to the electorate to renew its mandate. Labour's first aim was "to save the peace of the world." It had "striven hard since 1945 to bring all the nations together in world-wide co-operation through the United Nations." It had had "grievous disappointments, particularly with the Soviet Union," but it would persevere. It did not for one moment accept the view that a third world war was inevitable. The Labour government armed to save the peace. It decided without hesitation that "Britain must play her full part in the strengthening of collective defence. Britain must be strong: so must the Commonwealth." But peace could not be preserved by arms alone. Peace depended equally on bringing freedom from poverty to lands

---

[76] Cf. Foreign Secretary Morrison, address at South Lewisham, October 11, 1951, *The Times,* October 12, 1951, pp. 4, 7; electoral broadcast, October 17, 1951, *ibid.,* October 18, 1951, p. 2; address at Battersea, October 24, 1951, *ibid.,* October 25, 1951, p. 2; Prime Minister Attlee, electoral broadcast, October 20, 1951, *ibid.,* October 22, 1951, p. 2.

where hunger and disease were the lot of the masses. The British Labour government had taken the lead in economic assistance to these lands. As its own armed strength grew, more attention would be given to the underdeveloped regions of the world. "Only a Labour Government would do this"; the Tory outlook was "an obstacle to that world-wide co-operation which alone makes peace secure." It was this that made the election "so critical, not only for the people of Britain but for the whole world. If the Election were to result in a Tory victory there would be no major power in the councils of the Western nations represented by Labour." Surely now, even more than ever before, it was "vital to the fate of civilisation that the voice of Labour should be heard wherever and whenever the issues of war and peace are discussed between the spokesman of the great powers."[77]

Although the Labour party succeeded in obtaining a larger popular vote than its Conservative opponents, it failed to capture a majority of the seats in the House of Commons. The key to the whole Conservative victory was the Liberal vote. As a party, the Liberals virtually disappeared; but the Liberal voters did not. In the absence of a candidate of their own party, those Liberals who went to the polls endorsed a candidate of the Conservative party.[78] As Mr. Attlee admitted:

There was no reason to dispute that the Labour Party's loss of seats was due to the fact that when it came to the point more Liberals voted for Conservatives than for Labour candidates.

However, Labour could derive some satisfaction from the fact that it had increased its aggregate vote and that its foreign, as well as its domestic, policy had been endorsed by an even greater proportion of the electorate than in the General Elections of 1945 and 1950. This, Mr. Attlee concluded, was "an extraordinary achievement."[79]

[77] Labour Party, *Election Manifesto* (Scarborough, September 30, 1951), p. 1.
[78] Labour received 13,911,582 votes and 295 seats, as compared with 13,721,346 Conservative votes and 321 seats. The Liberals contested only 109 seats, received 722,679 votes, and won 6 seats.

[79] *The Times*, October 27, 1951, p. 6.

14

CONTINUITY

Opposed to the traditional view of continuity in foreign policy, the Labour party has, nevertheless, maintained a continuity in the principles and aims of its own foreign policy. From *Labour and the New Social Order* in 1918 to *Labour and the New Society* in 1950, those aims have been to achieve peace, security, independence, and prosperity. Labour has consistently opposed the balance of power, secret diplomacy, alliances and ententes, militarism, and imperialism. It has upheld the doctrines of international co-operation, open diplomacy, self-determination of nations, arbitration, collective security, and the rule of law in international relations. While in the Opposition, the Labour party has advocated these propositions; while in office, it has, whenever possible, applied them in practice. Differences of opinion within the movement have not had an appreciable effect upon the continuity of adherence to these principles. Those who have attempted to substitute idealogies of pacifism or class war have been in a distinct minority, and their views have not altered the official party policy of support for collective security and international co-operation.

Although such aims as peace, security, independence, and prosperity are not necessarily or distinctively "socialist," they may be determined by socialist beliefs and principles. By establishing socialism on a firm basis at home, by encouraging socialism abroad, and by aiming at the extension of international planning and co-operation, the Labour party has attempted to apply the fundamental principles of socialism to international affairs. However, it is the application of these principles that proves most difficult, for no government has in foreign affairs, as it has in domestic affairs, the power immediately to apply its principles. This limitation is, therefore, primarily responsible for any discrepancy between the theoretical basis and the practical application of a government's foreign policy. In spite of this limitation, the Labour government did not deviate, in any fundamental way, from its traditional foreign-policy objectives. In applying socialist principles to international affairs, the Labour government concentrated its attention upon building a successful socialist experiment at home in order that Britain might appear as a counterattraction to both American capitalism and Soviet communism. Co-operation with other socialist governments was one of the chief objectives

258

of the Labour government, and on many occasions, it expressed a desire to see all countries embrace the principles of democratic socialism. Nevertheless, this predilection did not drive the Labour government to force the principles of socialism upon unwilling subjects or to refrain from associating with nonsocialist governments in the effort to achieve international collaboration. Support of the United Nations, of regional arrangements to strengthen that organization, and of instruments to further international agreement in the economic, social, and cultural fields were all part of the Labour government's international policy. In these endeavors, Labour did not depart from the major premises of its foreign policy as set down by party spokesmen after the first World War. The fact that these policies often received the support of the Tory Opposition did not necessarily deprive them of their socialist content. Although there were certain issues, such as Franco Spain, to which the Labour government was unable to apply socialist principles, in such instances, the conditions which normally limit any government's determination of foreign policy—the inheritance of previous commitments and the necessity of concurrence from other foreign powers—go a long way toward explaining the policies adopted by the Labour government. Nevertheless, it must be realized that only if the long-range goal of a world "co-operative socialist commonwealth" were achieved, would it be possible for the British Labour party to apply, in all instances, a truly socialist foreign policy.

INDEX

Abadan, 252–53, 256
Abyssinian war, 127–38, 150, 176
Acland, Richard, 232 n.
Adams, Richard, 201 n.
Adamson, Jennie, 133 n.
Admiralty, 58
Africa, 193
Ala, Hussein, 246
Alexander, A. V., 26, 89 n., 91 n.
Allen, Arthur, 201 n.
Allied Powers, 16, 18, 21, 24, 50, 52, 74
Amery, L. S., 90 n.
Anderson, W. C., 4 n., 9 n., 14
Angell, Norman, 56 n.
Anglo-American–Russian co-operation, 166, 170, 172, 186 ff.
Anglo-Egyptian Treaty, 238 ff.
Anglo-French naval compromise, 61–62, 67, 69 n., 70, 74
Anglo-German Naval Treaty, 126–27, 149
Anglo-Iranian Oil Company, 245 ff.
Anglo-Italian Agreement, 141–45
Anglo-Soviet Pact, 193
Anglo-Soviet Trade Agreements, 23, 42–47
Anglo-Spanish Monetary Agreement, 184–85
Arab refugees, 244
Arbitration, 7 ff., 12, 17 f., 25, 29, 32, 38–41, 46, 53, 63–68, 69, 79–86, 98, 119 f., 165 ff., 258; and British Memorandum, 64–66, 83; and Convention on Financial Assistance, 83–85; and Convention to Improve Means of Preventing War, 83–84; and Covenant revision, 81–82; and General Act, 66–67, 85–87; and Geneva Protocol, 39–41; and Locarno Pacts, 50–53, 63; and Mutual Assistance Draft Treaty, 36–38; and Optional Clause, 63 f., 79–81; and Pact of Paris, 54–55
Arbitration and Security Committee, 62, 64–66, 83 f.
Arcos Limited, 71
Armaments, 3 f., 8 f., 17 f., 25, 53, 68 f., 78, 87–95, 98 ff., 119, 119 f., 122, 131, 165 ff., 221, 230 ff., 258; and Anglo-American naval negotiations, 69 f., 87–91; and Anglo-French naval compromise, 61–62 n., 69 n.; and Anglo-Ger-

man Naval Treaty, 126–27, 149; and British Draft Convention, 58, 108–9, 122; and British Memorandum, 111; and British White Paper, 111; and Draft Disarmament Convention, 94–95, 100; and Franco-Italian naval conversations, 89, 92 f.; and Geneva Convention on Traffic in Arms, 57; and Geneva Disarmament Conference, 104–10, 114, 116, 122; and Geneva Naval Conference, 60 ff., 87, 90, 94; and Geneva Protocol, 39–40, 46; and League Preparatory Commission, 56 ff., 66, 68, 70, 84, 87, 91 ff.; and Locarno Pacts, 52, 56; and London Naval Conference, 89 ff., 100; and Mutual Assistance Draft Treaty, 36–38; and Pact of Paris, 54–56; and Washington Naval Conference, 60, 87; and Western defense, 230 ff., 255
Armistice, 18 f., 21–22, 24
Arnold-Forster, W., 64 n.
Asia, 193, 216, 221, 226; Southeast, 195, 197
Asquith, Herbert, 44, 44 n.
Atlantic Charter, 166, 170
Atomic bomb, 224–25, 231, 231 n.
Attlee, Clement, 4 n., 25 f., 99 n., 104 n., 107 n., 109, 111 n., 114, 120 f., 124 f., 125 n., 126 n., 127 n., 132, 132 n., 133 n., 140 n., 141 n., 142, 145 ff., 148 n., 152 n., 154 f., 155 n., 157 n., 162, 164, 187–88, 190 f., 198 n., 204–5, 212–15, 217 n., 218, 224–26, 230, 233–37, 256 f.
Australia, 180 f.
Austria, 10, 138, 151–52, 160, 188

Bacon, Alice, 224 n.
Balance of power, 6, 8 f., 12 f., 98, 120, 258
Baldwin, Stanley, 29 ff., 48, 56, 67, 134, 134 n., 140 n.
Balfour Note, 75
Baltic States, 152
Belgium, 11 f., 51, 152, 173, 193
Benelux, 185
Bevan, Aneurin, 232–33 n.
Bevin, Ernest, 77 n., 120, 132 n., 172, 174, 177 ff., 182–83, 186–87, 190–91, 193, 218–19, 222–23, 226 n., 237–39, 240

261

United Action for Peace, 238; UN-
RRA of, 195; and Western Union,
186 ff.
United Socialist States of Europe, 172,
191, 208–11
United States: Anglo-American co-
operation, 119, 166, 170, 172, 186 ff.;
Anglo-American naval negotiations,
69 f., 87–91, 96; and Chinese Communist government, 218 ff.; and Dawes
plan, 33–34; and debts (inter-Allied),
113 f.; and Egypt, 241–42; and Franco
Spain, 176 ff., 185; and Geneva Disarmament Conference, 107, 109, 113 f.;
and Geneva Naval Conference, 60–61,
67, 87; and Iran, 245, 250–53; and Korea, 212 ff.; and London Naval Conference, 89–91; and London (World)
Economic Conference, 116; and Manchuria, 102 f.; and Middle East, 237 ff.;
and NATO, 192 f.; and Preparatory
Commission, 87; and Western defense, 230 ff.; and Western Union,
186 ff., 200; and World War II, 163

Versailles Peace, 21–22, 23, 25 ff., 29,
32, 34, 93, 95, 111, 126, 149
Vigilantes, 123 n.

Wallhead, R.C., 43 n.

Walling, William, 12 n.
War Aims Memorandum, 17–19, 24
War and Peace, 117–21 n.
War resistance, 5–6, 10–11, 13–15, 99–
100, 117–19
Washington Naval Conference, 60, 87,
89, 127
Wedgwood, Colonel Josiah, 21 n., 26
Werth, Alexander, 147 n.
Western Union, 186, 188 ff., 198 ff., 230 ff.
Wheeler-Bennett, John, 60 n.
Wilkinson, Ellen, 73 n., 139 n.
Wilson, Woodrow, 18 f.
Winterton, Earl, 135
Woolf, Leonard, 168
World federation, 8, 16 f., 120
World Federation of Trade Unions, 183
World Trade Union Conference, 170
World War I, 10–19
World War II, 161–72
Wyatt, Woodrow, 224 n.

Yalta, 170 f.
Young, Owen D., 74; plan, 74–77, 113
Younger, Kenneth, 220, 226–27 n.
Yugoslavia, 173, 233, 254

Zilliacus, K., 175 n.
Zinoviev letter, 46